NO LESS A WOMAN

Ten Women Shatter the Myths About Breast Cancer

Deborah Hobler Kahane, M.S.W.

A FIRESIDE BOOK

Published by Simon & Schuster

New York   London   Toronto   Sydney   Tokyo   Singapore

FIRESIDE
Simon & Schuster Building
Rockefeller Center
1230 Avenue of the Americas
New York, New York 10020

First Fireside Edition 1993

FIRESIDE and colophon are registered
trademarks of Simon & Schuster Inc.

Designed by Richard Oriolo
Manufactured in the United States of America

1   3   5   7   9   10   8   6   4   2

Library of Congress Cataloging-in-Publication Data

Kahane, Deborah Hobler.
No less a woman: ten women shatter the myths about breast cancer/
by Deborah Hobler Kahane. —
     p.   cm.
Includes bibliographical references (p.   ).
     1. Breast—Cancer—Psychological aspects.   2. Breast—Cancer—Case
studies.   I. Title.
RC280.B8K34   1990
362.1'9699449—dc20   89-28212
                                                      CIP

ISBN 0-671-86899-3

This book is dedicated to

Barbara Rosenblum
(1944–1988)

who through her courage, grace, and determination
taught so many of us about hope and
living on the edge.

Acknowledgments

If it weren't for Dr. Hewlett Lee and Dr. Gordon Ray of the Palo Alto Medical Clinic in northern California, I might never have written this book. Because of their outstanding and caring medical treatment, I was able to join the growing ranks of cancer survivors. I admire them tremendously because they believed there were new and effective ways of treating breast cancer, and were willing to offer these new treatment options to their patients. I am deeply grateful to them both for their care.

Jean Baptiste Massieu once wrote, "Gratitude is the memory of the heart." My heart is filled with the memories of the ten wonderful women who trusted me enough to openly and lovingly share their personal experiences for this book. I can only say that I am enormously grateful to each one of them, many of whom have become my friends. Their stories were a constant inspiration; every time I reread them, I cried and was reminded why it was so important to keep writing. They were my teachers too. It is through them that I faced my worst fears about having breast cancer again, and realized I had ten role models to emulate if a recurrence does occur. Each one of them will hold a special place in my heart forever. I thank them, too, on behalf of all the women who will benefit from their stories.

This book was conceived more than six years ago and many people have helped me through the different stages of conceptualizing, writing, and editing. Originally, I was very fortunate to have Barbara Lazarus, Ph.D., as a coauthor. For the first year we worked together, developing questionnaires and trying to create the best format for the book. Unfortunately our bicoastal lives made it difficult to continue working together. I am most grateful to Barbara for her investment in and commitment to the book in its early stages.

Through the writing stage, I am forever indebted to a number of close friends—my personal support group—Nancy Saks, Ann Wang, Vicky Wells, and Pat Wyatt, who not only patiently listened to me for hours on end but also gave me wise counsel, kind feedback, editorial criticism, and the emotional support that kept me going for more than four years. I couldn't have more wonderfully loving friends. My sincere thanks go to numerous other friends and family members who reviewed parts or all of the book at different stages—Randy Hobler, Susan Walker Kowen, Anne

Bucknam, Sally Shaw, Rosemary Miller James (who died of cancer in May 1989), and Nancy Bruning. I also want to acknowledge Treya Killam Wilber, who died of breast cancer in January 1989, for her review of and perceptive comments about the manuscript.

I would also like to recognize my cancer support group at the Stanford University Medical Center, led by Isabel Walker, M.S.W., and American Cancer Society staff members Mardi Robers, M.S.W., May Sung, M.P.H., Terry Schroeder, and Becky Moore Flati (from the California Division, Area III Office, and the Northeast Los Angeles County Unit) for their enthusiastic support of my efforts.

The astute editorial skills of Cecilia Fox, who worked with me for many months during the final stages of writing, are much appreciated. In the most gentle of ways, she helped me improve and polish the manuscript, as well as sharpen my focus.

Thank God for connections. I am forever indebted to Steve Wechsler who introduced me to Marilyn Abraham, editor-in-chief of Prentice Hall Press, who bought my manuscript. I thank her for believing in the book and understanding how important it is to get this information out to the public.

Gail Winston, my editor at Prentice Hall Press, has provided me with encouragement and sound guidance over the past year. She has been a constant source of creative ideas. This book is better because of her good editorial instincts.

To Mrs. Anne Shepard, my Princeton Day School English teacher, who thought I was a lost cause on paper and would never learn how to organize my thoughts in recognizable written form—I say never give up hope on your students. Your teaching skills were not deficient, nor forgotten.

Special strokes for Moses and Obie for their companionship during the long hours in front of the computer.

Spending more than four years working in front of a computer has meant that I haven't seen much of or paid too much attention to my friends or family. Thank you all for your love and patience. I hope this book makes you proud of me.

This book truly could not have been written without the love and extraordinary support of my husband, Bill. From the beginning, I can only describe Bill's behavior with the "E" words—enthusiastic, encouraging, emotionally supportive, and editorially challenging. His belief in me, my book, and my ability to write it never wavered, especially at those times when I was most insecure, frustrated, and about to give up. I deeply appreciate his being on my team and providing me with great coaching. Because of his support, I think I did my personal best. There is no way I can thank him for everything he has done for me to make this book possible. I thank him for loving me so well.

Contents

Part One

COMING OUT OF THE DARK AGES

I have met brave women who are exploring the outer edge of human possibility with no history to guide them, and with a courage to make themselves vulnerable that I find moving beyond words.

—Gloria Steinem
The First Ms. Reader, 1972

1

Going Public

In 1974, Betty Ford, the wife of the president of the United States, publicly announced that she had breast cancer and had undergone a radical mastectomy. Mrs. Ford's open discussion about her illness significantly affected American women and changed the course of public education about a disease that previously had been unmentionable.

Since then, many famous women, including former First Lady Nancy Reagan, actresses Ann Jillian, Jill Ireland, and Jill Eikenberry, and writer Gloria Steinem, have gone "public" with their breast cancer. They have become powerful role models for the 185,000 American women who are diagnosed with this life-threatening disease each year. Through their example, they have demonstrated that breast cancer patients can and do adjust successfully and feel good about their lives. They also represent a new generation of breast cancer patients who can employ highly accurate methods of detecting this disease in its earliest stages, choose from a variety of treatments, frequently save their breasts, and, most important, can live long, satisfying, productive lives.

I, too, am one of the new generation of breast cancer patients. And because of it, in a strange and wonderful way, I had a positive breast cancer experience. Had I been diagnosed just a few years earlier, I know my situation would have been radically different, medically and psychologically, and much more difficult.

GOOD NEWS, BAD NEWS

I was thirty-one years old in 1980 when I learned I had an early stage breast cancer. Only a year before, I had left my job at the American Cancer Society (ACS), where I had worked on a National Cancer Institute community cancer project that involved developing breast cancer programs for health professionals. I could not believe my luck. Had I not worked for ACS, I never would have thought that *I* could get breast cancer—particularly as a young woman—nor would I have been practicing breast self-examination, which is how I discovered my lump. And not only was I well educated about the disease but I was informed about new treatment options. I knew that because my cancer was at an early stage I was a candidate for a lumpectomy and radiation and would probably not have to lose my breast. I was also fortunate to have been diagnosed at a progressive medical institution—the Palo Alto Medical Clinic in northern California—that offered treatment options to breast cancer patients at a time when it was still considered unusual to conserve a woman's breast, much less to let her choose her own treatment. I was offered, and chose to have, a lumpectomy, radiation treatments, and a radiation implant. Although I had breast cancer, according to my doctors, there was a very good chance that I might live as long as my ninety-five-year-old grandmother, and with my own two breasts.

In addition to being well educated about breast cancer, I worked with breast cancer patients prior to my diagnosis, both as a social worker and as a health educator. I had found that most of these women, regardless of the kind of surgery and treatment they had undergone, had come through the crisis of breast cancer and were living remarkably normal, full lives. They were still married, or dating, and were sexually active, and they were working or raising children. They felt good about themselves. Of course, there are women who do not fare as well, but it seems to me that they are the exception, not the rule.

After my diagnosis, although I was scared about having a life-threatening disease, I knew from working with these women that I would get through it all. So much of the cancer experience is filled with fear of the unknown, and I was lucky to have these role models who helped me fear less and know more. Being informed both factually and emotionally about breast cancer made me feel more in control of my life and certainly less anxious.

What upset me was that I knew many breast cancer patients did not have the same kind of opportunities that I did. Many were not offered treatment options, did not participate in their own care, and were offered no social support or resources. It seemed horribly unfair that they should have to suffer any more than necessary when there was no reason for it. I was also aware that most women still lacked basic information about the disease. During my treatment, I made a commitment to educate as many women as I could—not just breast cancer patients—about the importance of being informed about the disease, its early detection, and its treatment.

Over the next few years, I made hundreds of presentations to women in churches, corporations, community agencies, colleges, and schools. The questions remained the same, over and over again. "Did I feel less a woman?" "Didn't I feel less attractive?" "Wasn't it true that men left women who had breast cancer?" I didn't understand why the myths still persisted, but it was obvious that they were still very much alive. I realized that there was a tremendous need for psychosocial and sexual information. It was clear to me that women needed to hear the intimate, personal experiences of breast cancer patients in order to dispel the myths. They needed to know that breasts are not necessarily central to man-woman or woman-woman relationships and that breasts do not define total womanliness or femininity.

Moreover, I was greatly disturbed that the less-of-a-woman perception was affecting how women cared for their breasts. Long-held myths about the social and sexual characteristics of the woman with breast cancer have done nothing but frighten women. In response to this fear, many women stick their heads in the sand and deny to themselves that they need to take care of their breasts and be responsible for their bodies. A serious social and medical problem arises, because if women do not take an active role in their breast care, there will be no early detection of breast cancer; successful treatment becomes all the more difficult. Only by becoming knowledgeable can much of the fear about breast cancer be relieved, thereby enabling women to take responsibility for their breast health.

A ROAD MAP

I wrote this book to help both men and women become better educated about breast cancer and its impact on the lives of women. In Part One, I provide an overview of both the historical and cultural perspectives on breast cancer, as well as the medical options presently available in its treatment. This information provides you with the necessary background to better understand the women's stories that make up Part Two.

In Part Two, ten women who have had breast cancer describe what happened to their perceptions of themselves when they were confronted with the diagnosis and treatment of this disease. Each woman answers the questions that all women have about breast cancer: What will treatment be like? What kind of woman will I be and what will my life be like? How will having this disease affect my self-esteem, my body image, my sexuality, my femininity, and my relationships? Will I feel less of a woman?

In Part Three, I review and assess the impact of breast cancer on women's self-esteem. As both a social worker and breast cancer patient, I feel comfortable drawing some conclusions about how these women were able to navigate successfully through the different phases of the breast cancer experience.

Breast cancer is a broad topic about which volumes can be written, and this book in no way addresses all of the medical, social, and psychological issues involved. What I have chosen to do is focus on some of the major issues raised by this disease through interviews with ten ordinary, yet remarkable, women who speak about the profound impact of breast cancer on their lives. I found them through referrals by oncologists, social workers, and friends. Each woman was chosen because in her own way she adjusted successfully to breast cancer and was willing to share her experience and the intimate details of her personal life.

It is never easy to talk about the intimate details of one's personal life, but the women profiled in this book have shared their stories because they wanted to help women with breast cancer feel less alone. They have also told their stories because they wanted all women to know that a woman's self-esteem and her femininity are not necessarily compromised by cancer. Because of the nature of the interviews, most of the women chose to remain anonymous and their names, as well as those of their doctors, and some circumstances of their lives have been changed to protect their privacy. However, the book accurately presents their stories.

I conducted and taped all the interviews in person, and each interview lasted from three to six hours. After transcribing the interviews, I then edited the stories. I had asked each woman to discuss four areas of her life with a particular emphasis on her body image, social and intimate relationships, sexuality, and femininity. She was asked to describe (1) her family background and childhood, (2) her life as an adult prior to breast cancer, (3) what happened to her during her diagnosis and treatment, and (4) how she felt about herself and her life after treatment. Each woman also discussed what she had learned from the experience and what advice she might give to other women about breast cancer.

I included the women's personal history prior to breast cancer, because in order to understand how a woman responds to this disease, it's important to know who she was before she was diagnosed. Recent research studies have shown that a woman's perceptions of herself, her self-esteem, and her adjustment to cancer are influenced strongly by her personal background. In large measure, the state of her emotional and physical health before her diagnosis—how she felt about her body and breasts, her sexuality and relationships, and what coping skills she utilized in the past—determine how she will change and who she will become.

The women's stories reflect the diversity and wide range of experiences and feelings that breast cancer patients may have. They have undergone biopsies, lumpectomies and radiation, radical, modified, and simple mastectomies, chemotherapy, and hormone therapy. Some have had breast reconstruction and some have had recurrences.

At the time of the interviews, two women were still undergoing treatment. Some were diagnosed more than nineteen years ago, and others within the last four years. They represent a variety of religious, educational, and socioeconomic backgrounds, but most are now middle-class working women: They are teachers, writers, hairdressers, photographers, nurses, homemakers, and community organizers. They are single, married, or divorced; some are homosexual, others are heterosexual. More than half are mothers. Their ages range from twenty-seven to seventy-four years old.

The stories are arranged chronologically by age at diagnosis, which seemed a logical way to order the stories for a number of reasons. First, age and life stage are key variables in how a woman responds to breast cancer. Second, there have been many books that have provided an excellent in-depth snapshot of one woman's breast cancer experience at one particular time of her life. (See appendixes for further information on books.) *No Less a Woman* offers a presentation of multiple snapshots of the breast cancer experiences of women of all ages. Though each woman is very different, their stories also can be read as the experience of "Woman," seen in her youth, middle age, and older years, who at different life stages confronts the same issue from different perspectives. Third, once a woman has been diagnosed with breast cancer, she lives with it for the rest of her life. Cancer is not a onetime event but an ongoing process of growth and change in which one learns to live with cancer and an uncertain future. Cancer patient and author Dr. Fitzhugh Mullan calls this process "the seasons of survival."[1] Whether a woman lives one year or thirty years after breast cancer, her life continues to be influenced by the disease, albeit more acutely at the beginning and more subtly as time passes. Finally, when a person is diagnosed with a life-threatening disease, her concept of time is radically altered. Suddenly, every minute counts and each day is a lifetime.

Though having breast cancer is a traumatic experience, the crisis provided each of these women with an opportunity for growth and the development of a broader definition of femininity. By living through and with breast cancer, these women found new strengths and new meaning not only in their femaleness but in their humanness. Cancer placed their self-worth in a new perspective; it redefined and enlarged on what being a woman meant to them: to be caring, nurturing, assertive and strong, and committed to making each day of life count.

It is my hope that more women, armed with this knowledge, will be moved to take the best possible care of their breasts and their bodies with less fear and more courage.

2

Coming Out of the Dark Ages

Prior to 1974, most women were uninformed about breast cancer, what its signs, symptoms, and risk factors were, and how to detect it early. There were very few public education programs about the disease and even less written on the topic. This lack of public information, coupled with a general fear of cancer and the radical treatment of the disease, often had disastrous consequences. Though a woman might discover a breast problem, she often delayed seeing a doctor, and by the time she made an appointment, the cancer was often in its later stages. Her chances for long-term survival were curtailed and many women died because these cancers were not found early enough.

In fact, at the time, it was very difficult to diagnose early stage breast cancers because safe and highly accurate methods of early detection did not exist. Although mammograms were available, there was concern that their high radiation levels could possibly cause future breast cancers. As long as this risk remained, wide-scale breast cancer mammography screening projects could not be conducted. Breast self-examination, only developed in the early 1950s, was neither widely taught by physicians nor even practiced regularly by those women who had been trained. A yearly clinical breast examination by a physician was the most frequently utilized detection method, but many women didn't visit their doctors regularly. Most breast cancers were detected accidentally by women themselves in between yearly visits to the doctor. There wasn't much good news about breast cancer.

Most women didn't want to talk or hear about breast cancer—it was a dreaded disease that suggested fear, mutilation, shame, and death. In those days, being a breast cancer patient—any cancer patient—was very much like being an AIDS patient today. People avoided cancer patients because they were thought to be infectious: They were often treated as if they were lepers, being placed in isolation wards in hospitals. Once a woman was diagnosed, she not only lived with the stigma and shame of having cancer, but she also had to undergo an operation that removed her entire breast, underlying chest muscles, and underarm lymph nodes, all of which often left her with a sunken chest wall, arm edema, and limited arm movement.

She had no choice in this matter: The radical mastectomy was the only treatment for breast cancer at the time. (It sometimes was followed by cobalt treatments.) The surgery was usually done in a one-step procedure: A biopsy would be performed and if cancer was found the breast was removed immediately. Any delay was considered life-threatening. As she was wheeled into an operating room, a woman would not know if she would wake up with or without a breast. More than likely, she would have to use a prosthesis for the rest of her life, because breast reconstruction was in its most rudimentary stages and its cosmetic results were not good. Even if she wanted reconstructive surgery, insurance companies would not pay for the operation because they considered it an "elective" procedure. The general attitude about women who had lost their breasts was that they should be glad they were alive: What meaning could a breast have in comparison to a life? There was tremendous attention paid to the medical care of breast cancer patients and little attention paid to the emotional quality of their lives.

Clearly, having breast cancer before the mid-1970s was a traumatic and devastating experience for a woman. She had to live with the stigma of having breast cancer, the possible loss of her life, the removal of her breast, the disfigurement of her body, and perhaps rejection by friends and sometimes even by family. All the more difficult was the fact that it was not acceptable to discuss her disease openly.

Over time, as with all things that are feared, unknown, and not discussed, a stereotype of the breast cancer patient developed: She was deformed, less sexually attractive, less feminine, and therefore had less worth as an individual. Because of this stereotype, she would be rejected by future suitors or abandoned by her partner, and somehow was "less a woman." This stereotype evolved from our culture's linking of a woman's identity to her attractiveness and worth, and of her femininity to her breasts and body. A woman's value also has been defined in relation to men: How could a woman who is considered "damaged goods" ever attract a man?

Given this stereotype and the seriousness of the disease, it is not surprising that women feared breast cancer more than any other disease.

Because of all these factors, it is also not surprising that having breast cancer was a very lonely experience. Though many breast cancer patients survived and learned to adjust to the changes they experienced, they did it very much alone. Many women were too ashamed to talk about their feelings, fears, and experiences. If they did reach out for help, there were few avenues of support. There were no YWCA Encore programs, Y-Me hot lines, breast cancer resource or advisory centers, or support groups in existence. Nor could a woman go to a bookstore or library to find information: There were almost no books written on this topic available to the public.

Not until 1974, when First Lady Betty Ford informed the public that she had breast cancer and had been treated with a radical mastectomy, did breast cancer finally come out of the closet. As a result of her disclosure, women were able for the first time to see a positive role model of a woman with breast cancer—a woman who was alive and looked well and continued to function in society. Women finally began to find out that there was productive life after breast cancer. Coincidentally, First Lady Betty Ford's announcement occurred during a time of great social and technological change in this country. The women's movement, the consumer rights health movement, and major breakthroughs in medical technology began to have a significant impact on the field of breast cancer.

THE WOMEN'S MOVEMENT

The women's movement played a major role in changing the traditional breast cancer patient-doctor relationship. Feminists, who asserted that it was a woman's right to control her body and make informed decisions about her medical care, worked to legalize birth control and abortion. As women began to "own" their bodies, they started to look at other areas of women's medical care. Books were published, such as *Our Bodies, Our Selves: A Book by and for Women*, Second Edition (Simon & Schuster, 1979), that questioned the way the medical profession and society treated women.

It was natural that the treatment of the breast cancer patient would be discussed. Weren't there alternatives to radical mastectomies? Did a woman have to lose her breast? Shouldn't she have a say in her medical care? Whereas women traditionally did not question the doctor, now they began to demand participation in their treatment decisions and to ask for alternatives to the radical mastectomy. Rose Kushner, who struggled with these questions herself as a breast cancer patient, wrote the pioneering book on issues and options in breast cancer treatment, *Why Me?* (Warner Books), in 1975. It was the first book to provide the kind of information women needed to make informed choices about their breast cancer treatment. Since then, hundreds of publications have been written on this topic.

THE CONSUMER MOVEMENT

After years of pressure from the medical community, the U.S. Congress made fighting cancer a national priority and major funding was approved for research and public education. Since breast cancer was the number one cancer killer of American women, the National Cancer Institute (NCI) and the American Cancer Society (ACS) ran large-scale public education campaigns that taught women about the disease and the importance of early detection. The National Cancer Care Foundation began holding yearly National Breast Cancer Awareness Week to raise public consciousness about the disease. This new public awareness also has resulted recently in extensive media coverage of breast cancer: Continuously there are articles in women's magazines, and radio and TV shows discuss the disease and the importance of early detection.

Health professionals are taking an interest in the psychological well-being of breast cancer patients. In response to the expressed needs of patients, breast resource and advisory centers, telephone hot lines, and support groups have been developed throughout the country. Many of these resources have been started by breast cancer patients themselves. Hospital and medical clinic breast centers offering comprehensive diagnostic and treatment services to women have appeared in all major cities.

The consumer rights movement, which advocated a person's right to accurate information and freedom of choice in medical care, was responsible for the development of national coalitions and associations that became involved in the medical, social, and legal issues of breast cancer. Both individual women and these consumer rights groups have been responsible for the passage of laws requiring physicians to inform breast cancer patients about all of their treatment options. Other new laws have been passed requiring insurance companies to pay for reconstructive surgery and both screening and diagnostic mammographies.

*   *   *

MEDICAL ADVANCES

New advances in medical technology have made it possible to offer women safe, reasonably accurate, low-dose mammograms that are able to detect tiny, nonpalpable breast cancers in their earliest stages. If a woman's breast cancer is found early, she has the best chance of cure and long-term survival. It is now recommended by the ACS that all women over the age of fifty have mammograms every year, and it has been estimated that if this recommendation were followed there would be one-third fewer women who would die from breast cancer each year. In addition, women should have one baseline mammogram between the ages of thirty-five and forty, and women between the ages of forty and fifty should have a mammogram every other year. Armed with this knowledge, the ACS is offering low-cost mammography screening programs to women.

Another effective method of early detection that should be performed once a month is breast self-examination (BSE), in which a woman becomes familiar with the look and feel of her breasts. New training programs in BSE have been developed by such companies as Mammacare and by the American Cancer Society, and are now offered by hospitals, doctors' offices, and medical clinics. Because they are now more aware of early detection methods and the signs and symptoms of breast cancer, more women are coming into their doctors' offices with earlier stage breast cancers than in previous generations.

Alternative surgical treatments for early stage breast cancer, such as lumpectomy and radiation that involve less extensive surgery, are now an option, as studies have shown there is no difference in survival for mastectomy patients versus those treated with lumpectomy and radiation. With early detection, women can now save their lives *and* their breasts, and nine out of ten women treated for early stage breast cancer are alive and well at least five years after their diagnosis. Radical mastectomies now account for fewer than 3 percent of all breast surgeries, and have been replaced by the modified radical (removal of breast tissue only and underarm lymph nodes)—a far less disfiguring surgery—to treat later stage breast cancers.

Physicians are now encouraged to use a two-step procedure (biopsy and diagnosis first, treatment choice second) in diagnosing and treating the woman with breast cancer. Women no longer have to undergo anesthesia wondering if they will have a breast or not when they awake. They will not endanger their lives if they want to take time to become educated about breast cancer and their own diagnosis, and then decide, in conjunction with their doctor, the kind of treatment they wish to have. Seeking a second opinion on a diagnosis, previously considered to be heresy, is now commonplace and recommended by most physicians. Insurance companies, too, reimburse patients for second-opinion consultations.

Chemotherapy and antiestrogen drugs have become standard protocol in treating women with not only more advanced cancers but some early stage cancers as well, and have been shown to prolong survival. New treatments continue to be developed, such as autologous bone marrow transplants, which are now being used to treat advanced stage breast cancers with encouraging results. Reconstructive surgical techniques now produce good cosmesis, and most women are now candidates for having a mastectomy and immediate reconstruction in the same operation, if they so choose. Most insurance companies, persuaded that breast reconstruction can be an essential part of a woman's rehabilitation, cover expenses for the operation.

THE ROAD AHEAD

There is no doubt that in the past fifteen years there has been major progress in the field of breast cancer. However, there are still some things that haven't changed. First, breast cancer is still a very serious disease, and next to lung cancer, it kills more women than any other cancer. It strikes younger women with deadly force, killing more women between the ages of forty and forty-five than any other disease. There have been no overall changes in the death rate from breast cancer in the past thirty years, but the incidence of breast cancer in American women is rising: In 1978, one out of fourteen American women got the disease; in 1992, one out of eight American women will get the disease.

Second, though they may be candidates for newer treatments such as lumpectomy and radiation or reconstructive surgery, many breast cancer patients are not being offered these choices, in spite of new laws and studies supporting these new medical interventions. Nor are the psychological services that have been shown to be crucial to breast cancer recovery included as a standard part of medical team treatment.

Third, though most American women are now aware of breast cancer and the methods of early detection, according to a recent survey poll, less than 15 percent of all women have had mammograms, less than 24 percent practice breast self-examination regularly, and 53 percent do not have regular checkups.[1] Why? Though at least six times as many women will die from heart disease than from breast cancer each year in this country, it is still breast cancer that they fear more than any other disease. According to a study by the National Cancer Institute, women tend to overestimate their personal risk of developing breast cancer—perhaps because three out of four women know someone with the disease.[2] Getting a diagnosis of cancer is still a traumatic experience, and a woman's inaction in using early detection methods is partly a result of normal fears about a life-threatening disease. Also, the loss of a breast and death are still the first thoughts that come to a woman's mind when she hears the words *breast cancer*.

But the inaction also stems from the continued belief in the less-of-a-woman stereotype. Over the past fifteen years our society's views of women have not radically changed. We still live in a culture that places heavy emphasis on a woman's appearance and her relationship to men. These values and attitudes are reflected in advertisements, the media, films, and magazines. For example, a national talk-show host recently asked on his program on breast cancer, "Is it true that if you lose a breast, you lose a man?"

What women need to know today is that many breast cancer patients can and do successfully adjust to the disease: They survive and feel good about themselves as women. I believe that the best way to convey this information and destroy the myths is to provide in-depth stories about women with breast cancer with whom other women can identify. The following ten stories are not tales of women's sufferings but rather of women's victories. Though at times they may have felt depressed, devastated, or unattractive, the ten women in this book ultimately emerged with their self-esteem intact. These are success stories of women with breast cancer who dispel the myths. They prove that it takes more of a woman, not less, to complete the journey of breast cancer successfully.

Part Two

SELF–EXAMINATION: IN THEIR OWN VOICES

A self is made, not given. It is a creative and active process of attending a life that must be heard, shaped, seen, said aloud into the world, finally enacted and woven into the lives of others. Then a life attended is not an act of narcissism or disregard for others; on the contrary, it is searching through the treasures and debris of ordinary existence for the clear points of intensity that do not erode, do not separate us, that are most intensely our own, yet other people's too. The best lives and stories are made up of minute particulars that somehow are also universal and of use to others as well as oneself.

—Barbara Meyerhoff
October 6, 1982

3

Sarah

"I decided that if I got through this cancer experience, I was going to be one hell of a lady."

In 1981, Sarah was twenty-seven years old when she was diagnosed with a stage two breast cancer, with lymph node involvement. Sarah describes what it is like for a young single woman to have breast cancer and face the possibility of never attaining her goals and realizing her dreams. Following almost a year of treatments, including a lumpectomy, a lymph node operation, eight weeks of radiation, and seven months of chemotherapy, Sarah often wondered if she would be able to pursue a career, date, marry, or have children. Unable to find other young cancer patients with whom she could share experiences, Sarah felt a great sense of isolation from her peers and plunged into a deep depression. Still in the throes of young adulthood, yet confronted with her mortality, she struggled with her identity as both a breast cancer survivor and a young woman. During radiation and chemotherapy, Sarah decided that the only way to end her depression was to make something of her life. As a result of this commitment, she learned who she was and determined what direction her life would take.

I was born in 1954 in New York Hospital in Manhattan and raised in an intensely artistic environment. My father, born in England, who emigrated after World War II to New York, was a professor of art history, and my mother, American-born, who died when I was twenty-five, was an actress. Growing up, I understood that I would be educated in all things artistic and cultural. Of course, living in New York City was the perfect classroom for me—so from a very young age, I was taken to what now seems like millions of museums, galleries, and theaters. After I finished high school, I didn't feel ready to go to college, so my parents suggested I go live in England for a year and a half where I could, they said characteristically, get more exposure to the arts! I lived with family friends, who were in the theater in London, and had a wonderful year exploring everything from Shakespeare to pubs.

In addition to my parents, I had an older sister and brother. They were seven and eleven years older than I was, so I was really raised as an only child. My parents believed I was special and different. I thought I was too! Being an only and kind of strange child, I was somewhat of a loner. I seemed to keep my own counsel and not be like other kids my age. I was a thinker, very serious, and contemplative—I guess I could best be described as an inward-directed kid who had an active fantasy life. I remember wanting to do something dramatic in my life that would have special purpose and meaning.

I had a very feminine upbringing and a wonderful role model in my mother. An affectionate woman who was very comfortable with herself, she really enjoyed being a woman, a mother, and an actress. She was dramatic, outspoken, and intelligent. I was very close to her. She loved dressing well and wore clothes that accentuated the shape of her body. I thought she was a sexy woman and I noticed that other people thought so too. Because of her, I have always had a concept of a woman's sensuality and the way a woman carries herself. I knew my mother had something special because all of the boys I went out with told me how attractive she was. How painful that was to hear when I was in my teens.

My mother dressed me in feminine but not frilly clothes as a child. The one thing my mother used to *make* me wear that I hated was undershirts. They were so ugly and it didn't help that I was the only girl in school who wore them. I did not want to be different. So when I started developing breasts I was thrilled about the possibility of wearing a bra. No more undershirts! I almost couldn't wait for breasts! Training bras were fashionable when I was growing up and it did not matter whether you had anything to fill up the bra. It was just *very* important to have a training bra because everyone else had one. No shame—it was an absolute necessity.

The first bra I owned was in sixth grade. I'd wear light, white blouses that barely camouflaged my new white bra so the world would know I was wearing what everyone else was wearing.

Interested in this new development, the boys in my class had to check out each girl's bra status. The boys employed this routine whereby they either snapped the back of our bras or would just stare at our backs through our white blouses, of course. This was our introduction to everyone's newfound interest in bodies.

Growing up, I was self-conscious about my body. I was never a slender child but rather I was a bit chunky. I was not pleased when I realized that I was never going to look like the American dream. Of course, having a good-looking mother did not help me at all. I was so embarrassed when I was thirteen and fourteen that I wouldn't go to swimming parties if I had to wear a bathing suit. I didn't thin out until later.

During my teenage years, in spite of the fact that all my friends fooled around sexually, I did not. When I graduated, I think I was one of the few virgins left in high school. My parents were actually pretty strict with me, and I was pretty naive. Besides, there weren't many chances for fooling around in high school as I didn't date much. I was still pretty much a loner and stayed close to a few girlfriends. My major involvement in high school was a theater group. I wasn't the cheerleading type. During this time, I had what I thought were two conflicting goals in life: to get married and have babies, or to be an activist.

When I graduated from high school in 1972, I went through a serious rebellion and starting doing what everyone else had done in high school. Since I was in London at the time, I didn't worry too much about what my family would think. I believe I was aggressive enough to make up for all my lost time! I had a very active social life and started dating a number of men but had no serious relationships. In retrospect I seemed to attract a lot of boys who were good-looking but who were more interested in a good time than in a relationship! But I learned to feel good about myself as a sexual being. The men I went out with gave me lots of positive reinforcement.

During my year and a half in England, I thought a lot about what I wanted to do careerwise when I returned to the States. I knew I wanted to work with people. College still did not interest me at the time, so my parents and I talked about how I could best use my skills. I, of course, had a strong background in the arts, and coincidentally, my dad heard about a program for handicapped kids that needed an art therapist. So a few months after my return to New York, after completing a special training program, I took the job as an art therapy counselor. I really enjoyed working with the kids. I loved them, and learned so much about myself in the process. I stayed there for about five years.

I didn't have a serious relationship with a man until I was twenty-four. I met Mitch, a thirty-five-year-old attorney, through friends. He was a very gentle and sensitive man. I remember feeling that I wanted to settle down, get married, and have a baby. I really lost my desire to be with anyone else. But this became a very touchy issue for my parents who did not like him. As it turned out, Mitch got a job opportunity he couldn't turn down in Chicago. He asked me to go with him, but I guess I wasn't ready because I said I wanted to remain in New York. So, the relationship ended. I just sensed there wouldn't be a future for us. But it was the first time I knew what a grounded relationship was like. Because of my relationship with him, I learned that sex was important for me only if it was complemented with stability, nurturing, and authenticity. I no longer wanted to fool around.

About this time in 1979, my mother was diagnosed as having an inoperable brain tumor. She died five months later. It was so tragic. I felt particularly guilty that she never saw me settled and balanced. When she died, reality hit me. My life as I had known it was gone. I missed her terribly.

I was definitely in a state of transition, grieving, feeling confused, and questioning everything. Suddenly, I felt that I was a twenty-five-year-old going nowhere. My relationship with Mitch was over and I wasn't dating anyone else. I was sad about that. I remember thinking, by the time someone gets me I am going to be a has-been. I thought I was over my prime. Little did I know what was on the horizon. I also didn't feel like being an art therapist anymore and many of my plans seemed frivolous. I realized I was not very satisfied with my life. There were many unresolved emotions associated with my mother's death. I don't believe it is a coincidence that those emotions were locked in my heart and my breasts are over my heart. That's one of my theories about how I got breast cancer.

As usual, I seemed to be moving in the opposite direction from my peers, who were all getting married and having children and settling down. I, on the other hand, was searching for something that I could do to give meaning to my life and my mother's death. What could I do that was important to society? I really wanted to accomplish something in my life. I thought about becoming a social worker. It was too much to do too soon. It was too emotional; I was too emotional and strung out. I decided to take time out. Since I'd been putting off college, I thought maybe this was the time to start taking some courses and to begin to focus on some specific career. I enrolled at CCNY and started my freshman year, as a twenty-five-year-old, also working part-time as a waitress.

I'd been in school for about a year and a half when I found a lump in my left breast. I went to the doctor immediately. A mammogram was done and a needle biopsy was performed and everything was negative. I was told

I was too young to have cancer and there was nothing wrong with me. After all that, I decided not to take the lump seriously.

A few months later, during the fall of 1981, I was taking courses, still working part-time and socializing with friends a lot. I really had worn myself out and started losing weight. I wasn't feeling too well either, and as my weight dropped, the "nothing" lump in my breast was noticeably larger and harder than when I first felt it. I went for another checkup to a different doctor. He told me, "You'd better go to a surgeon and get that taken care of." It had been three months since my first checkup.

I made an appointment with a surgeon who told me the best thing to do was to remove the lump, which was about an inch big, in his office. A "simple five-minute procedure," he said, turned into a half-hour procedure. I didn't like the waiting and the uncertainty was killing me. The surgeon finally said, "I'm closing you up now. Let's meet in my office when you're dressed." He began to tell me about the pathology report—they had done a frozen section—and that, unfortunately, it looked like cancer. Further surgery would be required to determine exactly what was going on. I thought he must be mistaken and asked him, "Are you saying that *I* have cancer?" He said, "Yes."

The diagnosis was confirmed four days later. It appeared to be a stage one cancer, but they couldn't be certain until other tests were done. I was angry because they could have diagnosed it sooner. I had been there three months earlier, but because young women "don't get breast cancer," I had lost precious time. My first thought was that my mother had died from cancer. I speculated, "Okay, will what happened to my mother happen to me? I am in big trouble." I felt very, very threatened. I thought about my grandfather who had died of cancer too. I remember thinking, "I'm too young for this. I'm only twenty-seven years old."

The further surgery required was an axillary dissection in which the doctors would remove lymph nodes from under my arm. Other tests such as bone scans would also be performed to determine the extent of my disease.

I was scheduled for my operation four days after my diagnosis. Even though no one mentioned mastectomy to me, I knew that depending on the results of all the tests, I might have to prepare for one. I bought loose clothes for my hospital stay. I purchased a few other things with the idea that I might lose a breast and I would need clothes that could be slipped off easily. Wednesday night at the hospital, as I was getting ready for bed, I looked at myself in front of the bathroom mirror and thought maybe I should begin saying good-bye to my breast. I remember feeling, "Gee, I am glad I had what I had." I instinctively did this; nobody told to have a good-bye ceremony. I will never forget that night at the hospital. As it turned out, the removal of my breast was not necessary. I was so pleased about being able to keep my breast.

All my life my mother had encouraged me to keep a daily diary, and prior to breast cancer, I had kept a journal of my feelings, particularly when I was going through tough times. I wanted to keep a diary of my experience while I was in the hospital so I wrote what I could each night because I often couldn't sleep anyway. This was a great tool to let me hear myself and what the doctors were saying at a later time when I wasn't so emotional. With my diary, I felt as if I was keeping my own patient chart.

The doctors told me one of my lymph nodes was cancerous, which now meant I had decisions to make about my treatment, and they recommended both radiation and chemotherapy. At first, I was totally confused about what to do. I mean, what were the long-term implications for me—a young person—having all these treatments? If I didn't die from breast cancer, would I die at fifty from the unknown side effects of the radiation or get a second cancer from chemotherapy? Then later, after I had read some more information and was able to start thinking more clearly, I decided to go with their treatment plan: two months of radiation and seven months of chemotherapy.

My journal became an integral part of dealing with my illness because I didn't have anyone really close to me, like my mother, to act as a sounding board or an ally. It was hard to talk to my father and brother, and my sister was flipped out completely because she thought she was next. I needed someone to talk to, and with my writing, I created someone to listen to me—myself.

Surprisingly, even the hospital staff was not communicative to me. Not one social worker came to see me nor one Reach to Recovery volunteer. I was completed untouched. Part of the problem might have been that when I was diagnosed, in 1981, it was less common to hear of young women with breast cancer. There was no routine way to deal with a young woman with this disease. The nursing staff almost treated me as though I was not there. I guess because I was a contemporary of some of them, they were scared and didn't know what to say to me. I've learned that when people don't know what to say, they don't say anything.

When I was discharged from the hospital, I wrote a note to the nurses. It was a very warm letter stating that for their own growth in the future they ought to speak to their patients! I knew, on the one hand, that they are trained to be clinical and professional, which may result in little warmth for and human contact with the patient. On the other hand, as a patient I didn't understand at all. I needed more attention. Although I found the experience to be dehumanizing, I hoped my letter expressing my displeasure might prompt medical professionals to treat patients with more care.

Because I was feeling isolated and lonely, I asked around to see if there were other people with cancer that I could talk to. I had no role models and no one to compare my experience to. I was concerned about whether or not I would ever marry and have children and what would happen in my work.

My oncologist suggested I go to a cancer support group, but I couldn't find one that fit my needs.

In addition to my sense of isolation, part of my need to talk was that I suddenly had a very low tolerance level of healthy people's concerns. I was thinking life and death, and they were worried about boyfriends, cosmetic surgery, or the plumber. Once I was out to lunch with a friend, who was smoking, drinking wine, and eating a plain salad with lemon juice as a dressing, who talked to me about her weight and how she looked. I found it very hard to relate to her—I mean here I was, someone who had taken pretty good care of her body and *I* had breast cancer, and there she was, abusing her body, taking it for granted, and she was fine. It seemed so unfair. At that time, I began to exclude some of these people from my life because it was so hard to chitchat, and I seemed so angry about things that bothered no one else.

I found, too, that people were just ignorant about dealing with cancer patients and their concerns. A girlfriend would call up and ask me, "How are you feeling?" I'd say, "Oh fine, fine, thank you," when I was feeling awful. I was very hostile. People would say, "Oh, you're so strong," and yet there were moments when I was afraid to go to sleep at night because I did not know if I would wake up in the morning. My way of handling all of this was to withdraw from the social mainstream during that time. A few close friends stuck by me, and they would come over sometimes after chemo to visit and could understand how I was feeling. What I really needed was people who relieved me of the job of making *them* feel better, and who were able to listen to both my bad and good feelings. You know, on the other hand, I had such a strong need to feel as if I was normal and like everyone else. I didn't want to be treated differently, but I did.

What I would have liked at that time was to have a boyfriend. I wanted companionship and warmth more than anything else. I certainly was not feeling sexual; I wasn't in the mood for that at all. Then I got depressed thinking about what man was going to get close to me? I wasn't certain how I was looking or how long I was going to be around.

It's funny but when you least expect something to happen, it happens. After I started chemotherapy, I did have a very significant relationship with an artist I had known through my family. I hadn't seen him in years but ran into him when I was with a friend at a Broadway show. He had heard about what happened to me and wanted to talk. This was a very therapeutic relationship for me. Shawn was a loving, forthright and honest man who nurtured me. It helped that we had had a friendship before. It was a healing time for me to have someone who was so caring. I wasn't fearful of being rejected because he was so sensitive, and his mother had died of cancer too. There was less mystery for him about cancer. He held me a lot. The touching was the kind of sensual experience that I needed. Shawn wasn't afraid to touch my treated breast either, which made me more accepting of my breast. A few months later, he ended up moving out of New York and we broke up. But we have remained in close contact and I am forever grateful for his gift of time and love when I really needed it.

Soon after my lymph node operation, I started eight weeks of radiation. I thought that radiation therapy was more devastating than the lumpectomy. During the time I was undergoing radiation treatment, I felt as if I was exposing my breast all the time to technicians, doctors, and oncologists. I didn't like having to lie on that table every day. It was a constant reminder that I had cancer. One of my first treatments was very upsetting. During treatment, you have to hold your arm back in a certain position and I couldn't reach where I was supposed to because my arm was sore from surgery. The radiation tech said, "Oh, you haven't been doing your arm exercises," and proceeded to push my arm back with great force. It was very painful and I felt so battered. During times like that I felt sorry for myself.

Sometimes dealing with health professionals was so frustrating. One day, when I was undergoing some evaluations for radiation treatments, the radiation oncologist came in and was examining my breast. He said, "I don't understand why you didn't have a mastectomy—we really don't know the long-term effects of radiation on young women." I almost burst into tears, wondering if I had made the right decision or not, and angry at him for being so insensitive. Then I thought, "Oh, it doesn't matter any more." You just don't have the energy to fight at those times.

After that session, I had purple indelible marks drawn on my chest to outline the area where I would be radiated. I also had small pinpoint tattoos placed on my breasts, to indicate the outside boundaries of my radiation. I felt as if someone could have played chess on my chest what with all the lines and crosses. For the next eight weeks, my bras, slips, and T-shirts were always purple, and because the purple lines were drawn up to my neck, people would often stare at me. One woman in a store thought I was part of an Indian tribe. You get tired of explaining stuff.

In spite of all the human problems, my breast looked pretty good after radiation treatment. Because I am fair-skinned, my breast did burn. It looked like a sunburn with swelling. I couldn't wear polyester during this time, because it doesn't breathe well, so I looked for all-cotton clothing. It was a challenge. For starters, cotton bras were rarely made at the time. Then when I did find one, it was tough getting into the bra because of the breast swelling and tenderness. Some days I just went without one. It was not an easy time. It was also uncomfortable and hot because it was summer. I also couldn't really take showers because all the marks would be washed off, so I bathed from the waist down, and washed the top of my body with a washcloth. Believe me, I did not feel like the essence of femininity during this time.

One thing I did do to make me and my breasts feel better during treatment was go to a Chinese herbalist, who developed a skin lotion for me that my radiation oncologist said was okay to use. After each treatment, I would gently massage my breast with the lotion. It was a protective thing to do for my breast and me. If I was going to keep my breast, I wanted to treat it carefully.

Within a month after finishing radiation, I started chemotherapy for seven months. I had Cytoxan, 5-FU, and methotrexate. I had very severe reactions with lots of nausea and vomiting. By the time I got home, I would experience this bad taste in my mouth and then vomit all night long. It was emotionally and physically exhausting and I often felt as if I was going to feel that way forever. Lying there in bed, I'd think I was crazy to have *chosen* to do the treatments. I thought a lot about quitting and wondered what kinds of risks I would be taking if I stopped. I didn't stop; I was too scared of the alternative.

Though my friends would give me rides to and from chemo treatments, I usually stayed by myself at night. I just didn't feel comfortable asking my friends and family to watch me get sick. I didn't think it was their role. So I really went through the worst of times alone.

During chemo, unlike many other breast cancer patients, I had regular periods. I also didn't lose much hair. I did have some thinning and would find hair on my pillow and in the tub. A fellow cancer patient suggested I use a satin pillowcase to make my head feel good because it reduced friction. It did help and felt wonderfully soft too. Right before treatment started, I decided if I was going to lose my hair that I might as well get ahead of chemo by cutting it short and then it wouldn't look too shocking. So I cut my hair like an English punk crew cut. Luckily it was very fashionable. I also decided if I went bald, I was *not* going to wear a wig. I was going to go with the baldness and use scarves.

Even though I felt horrible, I knew I was only going to feel that way for a short period of time. But there were still times I was so depressed no one could get me out of the house. I remember one weekend some friends took me to Rockaway, Long Island, to cheer me up. I felt so isolated and strange and I cried all the way through the weekend. I kept thinking maybe it would be the last time I would see the ocean or be with my friends and what was the point of continuing?

That was really when I hit bottom; then gradually, my depression lifted. One morning, despite missing my mother and having cancer, I decided I wanted to get back to living. I figured there were two ways of looking at

my situation—either the glass was half empty or half full, and half full
sounded better. I decided that to get through I needed to ask myself,
"How am I going to take this situation and deal with it creatively?" I
decided that if I got through this cancer experience, I was going to be one
hell of a lady. I would have much to offer others and was trying to figure
out what I could do. I wanted to do something for other young breast
cancer patients like me. My friends all thought I was going to stand up and
condemn the medical establishment. But they misunderstood me.

It had been during chemo treatments that I started thinking about
actively working with other cancer patients. As a young patient, I had been
sorely in need of help and resources and knew how important it was to
share feelings and know you are not so alone. So, I started working with
local community cancer agencies and then hospitals, volunteering for support groups and counseling. I even was able to use my art therapy skills
very effectively. Because I was dealing with breast cancer patients in such a
positive way, there was little time to think only about myself.

My work with cancer patients helped me particularly when I finished
chemo treatments five years ago. Going off chemo is very scary. I had come
to rely on chemo and I saw myself as indestructible because I had this
intense chemical in my system. Without it, you feel you're not fighting the
disease and are no longer protected. Being with other people who had been
through this helped me know I would get through too. As each day passed,
and I got stronger and life got easier, I began to forget. It took some
months for the chemo to leave my system but then I began to feel like
myself again. I realized it was over and it was history. I could go on living.

Being involved with other breast cancer patients helped me realize where
I had been and where I was going. I viewed my work as a forward step in
applying meaning to my experience. It was my way of coping and confronting breast cancer. I wanted to continue in the cancer field, so I decided to
go back to college to pursue an undergraduate degree in social work and
then eventually get a master's degree. This will enable me to teach and
counsel cancer patients much more effectively.

Since I have had breast cancer, it is clear that I have changed. For
starters, I value my body more now. I treat it more carefully and don't take
it for granted. I also think I look better than before and like the way I
look. Though I know I don't have a killer body, I have no doubt about my
good looks. Over the years, I have developed a dress style that covers up
my bad parts and plays up my good parts. Though I am still not comfortable in a bathing suit, it's never been my style to be revealing, so it doesn't
bother me so much. Well, I never had a summer body anyway. Since I am
covered up most of the time, there have been no external signs that I have
been through anything.

The way my body looks is different in that there are breast scars, and some skin changes from radiation. During radiation, my breast was also quite swollen, and with the biopsy scar and all, my poor breast looked like a battlefield for a while. I never thought it would look normal again. After radiation, my nipple was not at all reactive but now the feeling is back. I have also had some edema in my breast, which subsided. Every once in a while my body still acts up, like having edema in my arm or hand, or my breast will hurt if I am under a lot of stress. This makes me sad but having these body changes occur is a good reminder for me to keep grounded.

I have never had a problem attracting men since I had breast cancer. I knew after I finished treatment that there would be a cross section of men who would not be interested in me. I have heard that some men want to be involved only with women who are healthy, because they don't want to mate with someone who may produce children who get cancer. My experience is that some men are drawn to a woman who has been through a life-threatening situation. So I guess it can turn men on as well as off. I have dated some wonderful, good men. Oh sure, once in a while there are jerks, but on the whole, my fear of rejection has not materialized.

One problem I do have in dating is that if I like someone and decide I want to go out with him, I may not want to tell him on the first date that I have had breast cancer. But one of the first questions that a man will ask is, "What do you do for a living?" I say, though I am in school, some of my time is spent working in the community with cancer patients. The follow-up question is usually, "Well, how did you get into that?" I probably wouldn't choose to tell someone why until we've spent some time together, but sometimes there is no choice. By virtue of my cancer-related work, everyone knows everything about me pretty early on and that is sometimes hard for me.

I do have an advantage, however. I find out right away if a guy is worth pursuing. If breast cancer gets in his way, I don't need him to begin with. To get me into bed is a long process! It will not happen one-two-three. I am not interested in somebody who just wants to sleep with me and say good-bye in the morning. So actually, dating is a much easier task for me because the undesirables have been skimmed from the top already!

I do feel now that I have to accept the reality that I may not marry and have children. A *Newsweek* article I once read talked about the chances of a woman over thirty-five marrying being slim. It could be very bleak for someone like me, especially with my medical history. I am not giving up on having a wonderful relationship, but I was not raised or prepared to consider the alternatives. It was never once suggested to me that I would not marry and have children. My sister is married with three kids; my brother has one child. I was advised to wait five years after my treatments before I had children. The way I am going, it is going to be an easy wait. There is no one knocking at my door saying, "I want you to have my baby."

Because I am so committed to this work, I sometimes think it might be hard for a man to break into my world. That is not to say that if the right man approached me right now I wouldn't go for it! But I am well prepared to live my life alone. I don't blame the situation on breast cancer.

Personally I really think I am one hell of a find and feel sorry for the bright man who hasn't figured it out! There are some friends I work with who have told me I am hard to fix up because I have become too honest. I have learned that there is nothing to lose by being honest. I just think that now I am in charge of my life and a lot of men are threatened by that. The women with breast cancer who think "I can't have a man" are focusing on the wrong issue. The men aren't the problem; it's the women. Men don't look at you and know. It is a woman's own self-perception and how much she buys into looks determining her value.

But I understand why the problem exists. I do not like the fact that women's worth in this culture is measured by their attractiveness. You see it portrayed in the women's and fashion magazines all the time. I feel sad because that is not where it's at for me. I wonder what happens to the Playboy bunny who gets breast cancer? How does she feel? I take this personally because it sets us all back.

Women are so conditioned with everyone else's values that they get insecure and think they may not be worth anything once they've had breast cancer. It is overwhelming to think about adapting to a new definition of oneself. How are women supposed to think about the positives, given our culture? It is very difficult because our culture does not prepare people for *not* being perfect. Everybody in the media, films, and TV looks so good that imperfections aren't acceptable. We don't think in terms of the quality and creativity in people's lives. Although you know, given all that, I do believe that ultimately breast cancer patients end up adjusting pretty well and most women who don't have breast cancer aren't aware of that fact.

For me, femininity is a feeling that resides somewhere very deep inside in women, and unfortunately society and advertising have taken that very pure state of femininity and made it into something else. We have become so overwhelmed with qualities that are superficially feminine that I think we've forgotten what *our* femininity is. What does it mean to be *more* or *less* female? Who's the judge of that? Having breast cancer actually enhanced the essence of my femininity, because I confronted some very basic questions on who I was as a woman. I had to work hard as a woman to get back to my pure state.

My sense of myself was strengthened because I had to rely more on my inner strengths than on the "goods" to make it. Now I groom my insides as well as my outsides. I am a whole package. There is something that I know about life now that I didn't know before, which makes me feel womanly and more worldly. I have that much more to give in a relationship and to others.

I didn't worry about my femaleness through the experience of breast cancer because I always knew that my femininity did not rest in my breasts. Yes, it would have been nice to be unaltered and not have scars, but had that not happened to me, I wouldn't be doing what I am doing now. At least this way I have been given the opportunity and the gift to do something important with my life. Breast cancer has shaped my future and is continuing to shape it in a very positive fashion.

4

Valerie

"Cancer doesn't necessarily change your life and cancer doesn't make you a different person and cancer doesn't solve your problems, but it gives you an experience so intense, so frightening, and so energy-creating, that it's almost like being launched from a pad. You *must, must* change."

In late 1983, Valerie, a thirty-year-old divorcee, was told she had a stage one breast cancer. Treated with a lumpectomy and axillary dissection, she also underwent six weeks of radiation and a radiation implant. Her treatments ended in the early spring of 1984. Able to keep her breast and undergo treatments that had a minimal effect on her appearance, Valerie was able to function and look well soon after her treatment ended. However, still faced with the emotional impact of being a person with a life-threatening disease, she sought help from cancer support groups. She discovered that the broad-based support of others with similar experiences played a significant role in her ability to cope with her disease and get on with her life. Still dealing with unresolved issues of dependency with both her family and boyfriends, Valerie felt that breast cancer made her confront everything she had been trying to avoid in her life. As a result of having breast cancer, Valerie emerged as a responsible adult woman, who, for the first time, was willing to take risks and be independent.

As a little girl I remember being in awe of my mother's clothes. Because she was a successful model, Mom had a closet filled with the most incredible clothing, from sequined and feathered costumes to beautiful satin shoes and frilly underwear. Though not a conventionally feminine woman, she always had a girlish streak about her, and though she wasn't pretty in a traditional sense, she had a wonderful face full of character. She was at times fun to be with. But unlike a lot of little girls, I did not want to be like my mother. She was an alcoholic. I remember many long nights of her drinking, playing music, and crying. She didn't stop drinking until just a few years ago. So I really grew up in an alcoholic family. In some ways, Mom never grew up to be an adult. Mothering her was very much a role of mine. On a day-to-day basis I took care of her, but when it mattered the most, and today it's still true, she was there for me. She reminded me more of an animal mother than a human mother. For example, when I was a child, if someone bumped into me by mistake on a street, she'd turn viciously on the person and say, "Get your hands off of her!" She harbored a deeply felt mother instinct, kind of like a Mack truck.

I was born in Chicago in 1953 to two people who had a pretty crazy relationship. They didn't communicate very well with one another, and my brother and I played the role of go-betweens in their communications with one another. It seemed the older we got, the more we became their negotiators. This was hard for us and it was a real burden.

My father was a conservative man who worked in the advertising business. He was also very concerned with appearances and aesthetics, believing that things and people that looked good had value in and of themselves. He believed that girls should wear dresses and be quiet and good. His only daughter had to look good too, and from an early age, this gave me problems. I think I made an unconscious decision early on to pretend and behave as if anything to do with appearances didn't matter to me. So basically I did everything guaranteed to make my father crazy. I was always overweight and there was constant family pressure on me to lose weight. I also chewed the inside of my mouth and my fingernails.

Although both my parents would say in one breath, "What a pretty girl you are," in another they'd say, "So how can you destroy yourself?" It didn't help that my father would say things like, "No man will ever be able to make love to you as long as you bite your fingernails." That's how I went through adolescence. The only man in the whole world that I knew spoke for manhood in general and assured me that I was not going to be acceptable. When other girls were discovering makeup and putting on stockings, I was walking around looking like a slob, on purpose. So as a young teenager I felt like hell a lot of the time.

Luckily, I had two very strong influential women in my life who loved me unconditionally. There was Margie, a nanny of sorts who lived in our home and helped raise me and was very much my second mother and still is. My childless Aunt Peggy and I spent most weekends together and summers too. Both of these women provided me with a lot of unconditional and intense love, support, and nurturing, which resulted in making me basically feel okay. They provided me with an anchor to hold on to.

It was my Aunt Peggy who took me to buy my first bra. Today I would *never* buy a girl a bra with breasts as small as mine were. But in 1966, that is what you did. After I got my first bra, I remember wearing this blue V-neck sweater. I felt like Jayne Mansfield, naked and huge and thrusting out into the world. The whole world knew I had giant breasts, right? I remember actually feeling my breasts growing. That feeling lasted for at least a year before it felt reasonably normal to have these "things" attached to me. To my surprise, they stopped growing and weren't as huge as I thought. They were just average-size breasts.

I was tortured by sexual matters in fairly standard ways in spite of my mother's telling me about the facts of life ad nauseam. She was very open about it. The conversation I remember best was when she talked about how incredibly glorious, uplifting, loving, and fantastic lovemaking was. Angels descending from heaven and trumpets blowing—I was overwhelmed—I thought one must obviously make love solely for the purpose of making children because who could survive it otherwise? My mother is a very romantic and wonderful woman who thought she was giving me the most beautiful possible image of sex and love, but it threw me for years! Where were the angels? I didn't hear angels. What was wrong with me?

Even my father talked to me about sex. When I was about twelve, we were on the beach and I saw an octopus on the sand and said, "Look at those testicles!" He looked at my mother and said, "I thought you took care of this!" I mean she didn't talk to me about tentacles—she talked to me about angels. Anyway, Dad freaked out and marched me up the beach to a quiet area and gave me a long talk about the facts of life. Then he told me he was going to quiz me in six months on all these words.

As a teenager, I acted seventy years old. I was an inner-directed, shy child and took everything very seriously. Though I was very bright, I didn't excel at school and basically squeaked by. Since I was overweight, I was very self-conscious. I spent all my school years getting out of gym. As an escape mechanism, I read a great deal and talked to a couple of very good friends who were just like me. The three of us would have intense, soul-searching conversations.

My parents were concerned about me. I was so acutely shy that sometimes I wouldn't even answer the telephone because I felt incapable of dealing with whoever it might be. I couldn't go into a store and make a purchase on my own. We're talking about a kid who walked to school alone in the streets of Chicago every day, yet there were these sort of quirky things that I couldn't handle. My parents accurately perceived me as someone who played it safe to a fault. They were always pushing me, saying, "Take a risk already!" I think that's when they decided to send me away for high school. My father said, "We have to get this kid out of the house."

In 1968, when I was fifteen, I went to a coed boarding school in the East for two years. Three days after I arrived, it was clear it was going to be the happiest time of my life. It felt like home to me. Three weeks after I arrived I met a boy at my school whom I married six years later. We were the "high school couple" and Peter was my very first serious relationship. I even lost weight for the first time in my life. Though I hadn't been sexually active before, being with Peter was enough to get me started. After we graduated we separated for two years while he attended college in the East and I went to a midwestern university. Being apart for two years was very hard and crazy for us, so I transferred to the University of Pennsylvania to be with him in 1972.

We got married our last year of college and lived in Philadelphia until 1978. I wanted to write and began working for a public relations firm and Peter began a career in journalism. Then Peter decided to attend graduate school in journalism in Chicago, and we lived there for two years until we separated in 1980. We broke up because we had become very much who we were going to become; we had stopped growing. We were very middle-aged and all of twenty-seven years old. He was someone who always saw the doom and despair in life and I, on the other hand, was successful and optimistic. He couldn't deal with all my happiness. My role in our relationship had been to try to get him to talk about his feelings—and sometimes he talked. When I decided to give up that role, he just didn't talk at all. Soon after he fell in love with another lady. I too became involved with someone else. It was a devastating time for both of us because we'd grown up together.

I had never been grown-up without him and didn't know who I was without him. After we separated, I became severely depressed and gained a lot of weight. Once we stopped living together, he wanted the divorce so he could get married again. Following the divorce, I realized there was nothing in Chicago to hold me there—few friends, no activities, work was nothing exciting—so I decided to move back to Philadelphia. Soon after I moved there, I started dating a recently divorced man named Brian.

I was practically programmed into having cancer. My whole life I had heard from my family, "Be careful, there's cancer in the family—cancer,

cancer, cancer—you have to go to doctors and be checked." I seem to have followed the classic Dr. Simonton schedule of events leading to cancer—he believes stress has a strong relationship to cancer—having had a really stressful time precisely the year before I was diagnosed. Nineteen eighty-two was easily the worst year of my life. I probably scored eight thousand points on the anxiety scale. I had gotten divorced, left my job, moved, was unemployed, and the new man in my life had an affair with another woman soon after my arrival in Philadelphia. At that time, I just couldn't say to Brian, "Well, I'll go my way, you go yours." I stayed in the relationship. A year later, the affair was history and things were fine again.

Then I couldn't find a job and felt so much pressure to get work that sometimes I became immobilized. It was also the only year in my life that I didn't make one penny. Not one! I was financially dependent on my parents, which is really unpleasant in your thirties.

The final *coup de grâce* was I wasn't taking care of myself and was eating the most insane diet of my life, and believe me, I have been on some weird ones. I lived on broiled chicken, Brie cheese, Früsen Gladje ice cream, white wine, marijuana, black coffee, and cigarettes. Occasionally I would have a salad. I was overweight and felt gross.

I realize now that I was then a very angry person with a tremendous amount of suppressed rage, which never got expressed. When you don't yell at somebody you're mad at, you end up yelling at yourself. And that's what I did—scream at myself. It was a sick time for me.

During this time, though I didn't regularly examine my breasts, I discovered a lump in my left breast. I'd already had a two-year history of lumpy breasts before each period. The first time I felt them I completely freaked out and had gone to my gynecologist. He had said, "All you have is lumpy breasts. If they're still there five to six days after your period, call me again." The lumps went away, but each month for a year or two that happened. Then one day, one of them didn't go away and I thought, "Oh yeah, big deal, so next month it won't be there." By then I was so used to them I didn't think too much about it.

I was visiting my parents in Chicago at that time and mentioned the new lump to my mother, who insisted I go to her gynecologist. I did. Dr. Warner felt my breast lump and said, "I think it's benign; I know it's benign. But I can't have you walking around with a lump in your breast." From what I know now, his attitude sets him apart from most gynecologists who "watch" lumps for a long time. I had a mammogram and an ultrasound test. The results were negative. Up until this point, I really hadn't worried about this, although I did have a dream right before I came to Chicago in which a voice said to me, "You're dying." I woke up and thought, "What the hell is this?" and dismissed it. I remember touching my breast then. That was the first and last moment of concern I had. I was thirty years old, for God's sake, I wouldn't have breast cancer. But Dr. Warner insisted the lump had to come out. I asked him, "Do I have to have it out in a month or next week?" "In the next two weeks" was his reply. This surprised me because I wasn't really thinking seriously. Since I didn't know any doctors in Philadelphia, had no money, and no health insurance—which had lapsed for the first time in my adult life— I decided to have the surgery while I was at home in Chicago. "Oh Christ, what a pain," I thought. "I've never had surgery before. Illness, what is this?" My family kept telling me I was fine and there wouldn't be anything wrong.

I went to a surgeon, Dr. Jackson, who had been recommended by Dr. Warner, who turned out to be the old-fashioned, grandfatherly type of doctor. He informed me that biopsies were now done under local anesthetic. He said also if he were concerned it was a cancerous lump, he probably would put me under a general anesthetic. I responded by saying I would never go under without having a reasonably clear picture of the outcome, that is, whether I was going to have a breast when I awoke or not. Dr. Jackson got angry. "Oh, I know that's the latest women's talk and that's such a mistake. Because you have to put them under again after they talked to their friends and you have to take the breast off anyway; it just gives women time to get crazy." Let me tell you that doctor may have been a fine surgeon but he was coming from another decade. At the time, I was completely unpoliticized about breast cancer and didn't know enough to get angry with him.

I said, "Fine, we'll do a local." Boy, was that a mistake. Surgery under a local is the most unpleasant thing. He removed the breast lump from my left breast. After he finished, Dr. Jackson left the room for a few minutes and came back, looking stunned. "I don't know what to say, but it's malignant." I *was* stunned.

I remember thinking, "Well, I'll just live in a small place somewhere and write; at least I can still write because I'm right-handed and my left side has been operated on." I wasn't worried about dying. I was much more worried about being mutilated. I was devastated. "Now we're talking mastectomy," Dr. Jackson said, "and further tests." He went on to describe the mastectomy operation and a little black curtain came from either side of my head and I fell back on the table. I just passed out! I came to a few seconds later and he was still talking! I told him, "Listen, I'll tell you what—I don't want to talk to you today. I don't want to talk to anybody. I want to go home and be left alone. I'll see you tomorrow, so shut up." He wrote out a prescription for Valium for me. Some painkiller for the news I received. Now I had to go home and tell everybody I had cancer, which was easily as devastating to me as the news.

My mother was incredible—she went into her Mack truck character. She called an oncologist she knew and put me on the line. I was still in shock and not dealing with reality. The doctor said, "Did the surgeon seem to have a bias about treatment?" "No, no bias at all," I said. "He just wants to remove parts of my body!" The oncologist suggested I come see him that afternoon, but I felt if anyone touched my body again that day, I would end up screaming. We agreed to meet the next day.

That twenty-four-hour waiting period was the worst. I assumed I was going to lose my breast. I pictured myself living a life alone because I thought I would be a completely sexless being. I didn't think that other people could deal with it—*I* couldn't deal with not having a breast. I wasn't going to ask anyone else to deal with me either. I suddenly felt so different from everyone else. My biggest concern was that I would become isolated because nobody else my age had breast cancer. Who was I going to talk to? I was too young for this disease! I didn't know anyone who had breast cancer.

During that twenty-four-hour period, I called Brian with the news and he asked me to come live with him. My first reaction was absolutely not—what a stupid reason to go live with somebody, because I have some disease. Ridiculous. My second reaction was that I was going to need somebody to love and take care of me, and I should stop being so conservative, safe, and boring. Brian was a wonderful man, besides the fact he fooled around with other women. I agreed to live with him. I didn't realize until later that he assumed I would be losing a breast when he invited me to live with him. The next day I knew I wasn't losing a breast. But it made a huge difference to me that he wanted me with one or two breasts.

The oncologist, Dr. Simon, was and is a wonderful man and he saved my life. After reviewing the pathology report, he said, "You are as cancer-free as I am." What an idea! I thought I was riddled with cancer and he says, "It's all over. The cancer has been removed and everything we do from here is designed to keep it from coming back. You are not having a mastectomy. You will need radiation and since you're going home to Philadelphia, I can recommend a terrific radiation oncologist that I know there. You need someone good because many doctors are still learning how to provide these treatments and the one thing you don't need is a deformed breast." Dr. Simon called the oncologist and arranged for my radiation treatments in Philadelphia.

I stayed in Chicago an additional week to undergo the lymph node surgery. He had explained the operation to me as primitive because the surgeon would have to cut me open and do permanent damage just to see if the cancer had spread anywhere. There was no option on this operation. It was *real* surgery and painful. I couldn't move my arm much at all and had to do these silly exercises for weeks to regain my arm mobility. I understood very little about what was going on.

I was amazed at how ignorant I was about breast cancer. I didn't even know there was something other than a mastectomy to treat the disease. Right after I was diagnosed, I went out and got every book on breast cancer and read volumes and couldn't get over what I didn't know. I understood it moment to moment but I wasn't thinking—I just reacted. I felt as if there was a constant, incredible upheaval of my inner self, as if volcanoes were erupting inside of me. On the other hand, Dr. Simon made me feel that everything was going to be all right. Because I felt I was in capable hands and I trusted him, that made me feel less worried and more safe. I think it's crucial you feel that way about your doctor or you'll be worrying about yourself *and* the quality of your medical treatment.

After recuperating from the lymph node operation, I went back to Philly to live with Brian. He convinced me that this was a time for me to rest and that he would support me while I got well. So I didn't work while I had treatment, nor for about seven months after that.

I met with a team of radiation oncologists who were very careful about telling me about the consequences of radiation therapy. Because I was thirty, they couldn't say what was going to happen to me in twenty years. Obviously, if I were seventy years old, the long-term radiation effects wouldn't be as much of a concern. If there was a recurrence in my breast, they couldn't radiate me again and I'd have to have a mastectomy. Interestingly, I was told very little about what radiation did or how it might affect my breast. At one point, my radiation oncologist was discussing my follow-up treatment and said, "After treatment is finished, we'll have to do a mammogram each year." I looked at him and said, "I don't know if I want *that* much radiation." He laughed at me, "Are you kidding? After all the rads you're getting?"

Before I could start actual radiation, I had to go through a couple of hours of what they call simulation. It's a procedure in which they find the exact location of your removed tumor through the use of computers so they know where to radiate you. I had purple lines drawn on my chest to outline the boundaries of this area. That was certainly a reminder of my status as a cancer patient. It was like having a scarlet "A" painted on you. The lines were later replaced with small tattoos.

Then for six weeks, except for the weekends, I went to the hospital every morning for radiation treatment. Having treatment was the event of my day. I would walk to the hospital and back home. It wasn't a thrill. In order to get to the radiation department, I had to pass many patients in the hallways who were in obvious pain and I'd think, "Thank God, that's not me." The hospital was a place in celebration of surgery where I felt cancer translated into a very ugly picture. So I made a point of looking well, wearing makeup and doing my best to walk into the waiting room and have everyone think, "What's she doing here, this wonderfully healthy person?" I wanted to be different from everyone. I learned, of course, that I was not different at all. I was not as sick as some, but not different.

No matter when I got to the waiting room, it was always jammed. There was an average of a two-hour wait to get treated every day. So I sat and waited with lots of other cancer patients. It was like any group. There were some who looked beaten and totally defeated, others just frightened. You could see the results of cancer surgery, from missing necks and parts of faces, to scars on arms and legs. This was hard for me to look at and deal with. This was my first real exposure to cancer patients. That I ever went to a cancer support group after that was amazing. One lady with lung cancer was our camp counselor and made everybody talk and get positive. We were not allowed to be depressed when she was there.

Though I didn't become friends with anyone, we all shared common experiences. For example, one thing that happened frequently was when the radiation machine broke down. You can imagine how you'd feel if you were the one who'd already been waiting two hours for treatment? *Auggggh*! You could bet on waiting another two and you couldn't leave! You had to have the damn treatment. The tension and pressure was pretty bad but all you could do was laugh, which is what we did.

I saw lots of kids with cancer, too, and it was hard for me to feel special or different. I thought having cancer was sad for me but a lot sadder for them. Once I passed a crib gurney that had an infant inside who had the most incredible, irresistible face and a huge, huge tumor on the side of his face. The look in his eyes was so devastating that I went into the elevator and burst into tears. That was what radiation was like. Frequently I'd see this sadness. It was not so much the treatment as the environment I found myself in that was difficult. Here we all were gathered to be tortured and see awful things.

What was strange was to be in that environment and then start walking home. No one would know I was a breast cancer patient. Only minutes before, technicians were hiding behind two tons of steel while I was being blasted and then nothing. What would people on the street think if I wore a sign saying, "I am having radiation therapy"? It made me start looking at people differently, because they may look normal but they may not be.

Contrary to how others felt, I couldn't believe that the radiation machine was scary, that the poisonous rays are destroying your body slowly. No, it seemed to be a very benign treatment. I'd lie under this incredible Star Wars piece of machinery and nothing happened. I couldn't feel a thing. I don't know what I thought would happen, but the way people talked, it sounded so awful. Even now when I hear other patients speak about their radiation experience, I feel they had a different treatment than I did. My attitude was different, too, in that I tried not to fight the idea of treatment; rather I accepted the fact that this was going to make me well. Actually, I worried more about the machine falling on me. I used to pray, "Dear God, cancer won't get me, but this machine will!"

Every day while I waited for treatment, there was also an older, depressed patient who sat in the waiting room with her husband. I never saw them talk to one another or to anyone else. She had the same chest markings I had. On the very last day of my treatment, I glanced at this woman. I had a sense that she had been waiting for me to look at her for a long time. From an angle that only I could see, she suddenly stood up with a totally passive look on her face, opened her hospital gown, and flashed me. I saw that she had no breasts, just a concave chest. It was a devastating sight. Then she closed up and sat down as if it never happened. It was like out of a movie. I believe she did that to me on purpose. Her nonverbal message was, "You're next!" Here I was, out of a sense of insecurity and need, projecting an attitude of youth and health, and thinking this cancer's not going to affect me much, *and* I still have my breast. She showed me clearly that she was angry at me and the world: "How can you look so well and have cancer?" She had a right to be angry but it was horrible for me.

I never had the feeling, as many cancer patients do, that the end of treatment was a bad time because it signaled the beginning of fears of recurrence. I couldn't wait to be finished and couldn't wait not to go back to that waiting room. Actually my treatment wasn't totally over until I finished an in-hospital radiation implant procedure, but at least I was alone in my room and didn't have to face angry women.

It wasn't until radiation started that I had time to really think about what had happened to me. Up until then my attitude had been, "Thank you for saving my breast. I love you, isn't this wonderful?" By the middle of my treatment, I was dealing with dying. But then I was sitting in a room full of people, some of whom *were* dying, and I realized just what was going on and why I was going through this treatment.

That feeling lasted a long time. It became a very introspective and quiet time for me. During and after radiation treatment, I had fear and anxiety attacks and it took me a while to identify what was happening. Looking at a TV program, I'd suddenly start crying. Then I had conscious fears in which I just knew the cancer was coming back. That kind of tension and fear were very acute during radiation and immediately after. Then I did intensive reading and talked with people to try to find ways to cope with these fears.

One of the problems I had in dealing with my feelings was our culture's obsession with being positive. You have to think positive to get well! Because of this I cut off the bad feelings that I had, by telling myself, "You cannot allow fear, Valerie, you can't focus on death, you must focus on life, life! Be high on life." One day I stopped doing that and let my worst fears play out in my head. Then I couldn't get over how good I felt! I spent too many months avoiding dealing with these fears. One of the most important concepts I learned, from a wonderful book I read, was if you keep having the same emotion over and over again, you probably should let it come through. Come on, we're talking about a life-threatening illness; I have every reason to be fearful and depressed! I don't think it's a matter of being positive; rather it's a question of being open. When the real trouble starts in your life, getting better seems to be a question of, if you are frightened, be frightened, and if you're angry, be angry, and if you're hurt, be hurt. I don't think anger and bad feelings make you sick; I think unexpressed feelings make you sick.

My radiation experience was therefore about learning to cope with all the ramifications of the breast cancer experience. The radiation treatment and the physical side of cancer were a piece of cake for me, but dealing with the emotions, that was the hardest part.

Radiation caused minimal physical changes to my breast. I had a mild sunburn for a short period of time. My skin was sore and tender but I didn't have blistering skin. I remember the hardest thing was not being able to sleep on my side. Having to sleep on my back was awful! After treatment, my breast did not change size or shape. If anything, the treated breast became uplifted and firmer. When my breast was radiated, all the breast hair disappeared. "Good," I thought. "I never liked them." But over time some of those hairs have grown back and now I say, "Hello there, my breast is okay." I like those hairs. It's me. Everyone, including me, is pleased with the cosmetic results. Doctors seeing me for the first time always pick the wrong breast as the one treated. Radiation worked for me.

My support during this time was pretty good. My family and friends were so wonderful to me! My oldest and best friend was in Philadelphia and she went to radiation with me for the first two weeks. It was great, but I finally convinced her I was okay and that she didn't have to come with me. Why should we both get depressed? When there's a disaster in my family, all the garbage washes away and what's left is probably the most intense love and support. They were all there for me. My parents paid for all my operations and radiation treatments—to the tune of $25,000. I felt such guilt for having been a burden and such gratitude for being so lucky. I allowed myself to go with those feelings, as best I could. My sense of indebtedness is still great. It's hard to be a young adult dependent on your folks when you're trying to be independent.

I also decided to join a cancer support group, because I was struggling with feeling different in terms of the outside world. One of my biggest concerns was that I, as a younger cancer patient, was feeling isolated in the community because nobody else my age was sick. The hardest thing for me was having to tell people I had cancer, then deal with *their* reactions. Some friends had funny reactions, and even parents and families deal differently with you than if you are older.

The group, which had about ten people of all ages, was very useful for me. In the first session someone said, "By the way, you know you *are* going to be all right." I thought, "Yeah, that's right, yeah!" Now I am not a joiner or an extrovert, nor was I particularly interested in hearing about the common denominator, but it was wonderful to talk, share, and be involved. People who end up in a group by definition are probably coping better or at least are searching for better ways of coping with cancer. They may be in bigger trouble, but they end up with skills that get them through.

When I moved back to Chicago a year later, I joined another cancer support group for younger people that meets weekly. I still go from time to time. I have found that I have to reexamine my reasons for being there because it can be very painful and draining. Some people in our groups die. But it keeps cancer in the forefront for me, instead of letting it recede, and I believe it's good for me. It helps keep in perspective what matters in life and what doesn't. Being with other cancer patients who have had much worse experiences than mine keeps me in line too. I sometimes have a sense that I almost slid through my experience.

One outgrowth of the group process for me was that I made myself available to other women with breast cancer. I still think the best thing you can do with this damn experience is turn around and show someone you're walking, talking, working, and living life with this threat. Another result was that I wrote a lot because I had huge chunks of free time. Though I made a living from writing before, I started to become the kind of writer I wanted to be. I wrote about myself and I wrote poems. I discovered the joy of writing; it became a passion instead of work.

Another area of great support came from living with Brian. He was wonderful. If there was any problem between us at all, it was this sense that we weren't going to make it over time but that didn't have to do with my cancer. Living with him at the time was the single-most wonderful gift he could have given me. He made it possible for me to have no sense of real world responsibility. I bought groceries, I cooked, I read, I wrote, I had a safe place to be, I had a home. Work, *who cared?* This was a time for healing and realizing that there are different ways of living. He gave me that opportunity.

I don't remember dealing with sexual issues at this time at all. Sex was a nonissue really because I was on a sexual sabbatical for a while. I was very much a sick person trying to get better. It wasn't life as usual. Brian and I held and hugged one another a lot, but there wasn't much intercourse. Brian was more concerned that I get better than he was about sex and so was I.

A year after I finished radiation, I suddenly wanted everything to change: where I lived, who I lived with, and who I worked for. Everything felt old and finished. I found that I had a low threshold for society's demands. I wanted to do what *I* wanted to do. It was no longer all right to live off Brian. I had to make my own way. I began to job hunt, interviewing with public relations firms. I didn't get any of the jobs, mainly because I really didn't want to work for public relations firms again. I knew I needed to do some serious thinking about my future, so I went to Chicago to visit my family before I made any decisions.

When I got to Chicago I called Mark, a friend of Brian's who lived there. I'd met him a couple of times and had to admit he was the sexiest man I'd ever seen. It seemed natural to call him. Surprisingly, he was attracted to me too and we hit it off. I remember thinking, "This is even before I lose weight!" Even weight and breast cancer don't get in the way of love, you see! By the time I got home, I realized I was falling in love and was going to leave Brian. It was hard to leave, to be the one who was hurting someone and the one who was ending the relationship. A few months later, I moved back to Chicago to be with Mark. I am still with him now. We're monogamous and about as married as you can get without the license.

When I first was told I had breast cancer, I thought I would lose my breast and be alone for the rest of my life. I automatically assumed that I would be unattractive and undesirable. It wasn't my femininity I was worried about because that wasn't an issue for me, but my sexuality *was* a concern. As it turned out, I didn't lose my breast, and because of that, even before I got involved with Mark, it really didn't occur to me that no one would be interested in me. I knew that my body looked fine, it looked fine! Having had breast cancer has never gotten in the way of a relationship or of getting comments on the street. I have always known my sexuality resides in my head. It's really me that determines what happens sexually and breast cancer didn't change that.

I honestly believe that having breast cancer has very little to do with a woman's ability to attract and keep men around. I knew a lovely woman who had a double mastectomy who later died. I was talking with her one day about my fears about mastectomy and sex, and she thought I was off the wall. She was single, dating, and sexually active. She didn't have a problem with her body image; she liked her body. Her attitude was the key factor in her sexual life. On the other hand, a forty-three-year-old friend of mine, who was happily married with two kids, got breast cancer, had a mastectomy, and found herself pushing her husband away. *She* felt she was deformed and ugly. Her husband was always there for her, loved her, and didn't care whether she had one breast or two. If you deal with breast cancer in this way, sex may be a more difficult part of your life. It's not necessarily that the men are the problem here.

The bottom line is, how you *are* is how people deal with you. If you walk around worried about being disfigured and ugly, whether you are minus a breast or not, take it from me, everyone deals with you as if you're ugly. It's true. It's also true that there have been a lot of loving, sexual romances that happened after people have had cancer or other life-threatening illnesses.

What has surprised me was that having breast cancer affected my sense of femininity. To me being feminine previously meant having no substance, being pink, wearing frills and painted nails. I never characterized myself as feminine before and was never overly concerned with the fact that I wasn't feminine. I was concerned with the fact that I sometimes felt unattractive, but it didn't matter that I wasn't feminine. Now in a funny way, that matters more. I've allowed much more femininity in my life. Femininity is not life or death but it's nice. I wear more dresses, jewelry, and makeup. I do my nails and am into buying clothes whereas I wasn't before.

But the important issues for me go much deeper than changes in my femininity and love life. If you lose an arm, the first thing you deal with is that you have lost an arm and you no longer have its use. You learn how to live without it. But then you must come to deal with much deeper questions about what it is like to walk around limbless and how people deal with you when you're handicapped. The woman with breast cancer faces an additional challenge in that she must get comfortable with the possibility that she may die from breast cancer. The fear of recurrence is strong and you must learn to live with that fear. One doctor I worked with said that breast cancer has become almost two illnesses: one found early and almost always treatable, and the other found too late and often fatal. I mean this illness kills women.

This is what cancer is about to me, living with possible recurrence. Cancer is not about two months of treatment and a couple of minor surgeries. I met three women recently who all had stage three breast cancers and had been treated with mastectomies and a year of chemo. When faced with histories like theirs, I think, "Thank you, whoever you are, whoever was in charge, thank you." I think the hardest thing for women like me who have found their cancers early and kept their breasts is to believe we are going to get away with all this. Am I *really* going to be okay?

Yes, it would be devastating to lose a breast, but much more devastating to me would be if I had a recurrence—what if it came back? I have already fought a good fight but I may have to fight it again. The fight isn't, am I too fat or ugly to have sex? Or do the scars matter? The fight is for living. I'd like to think now that as time goes on and I get healthier, both physically and mentally, that I will indeed be able to cope better if I have to have a mastectomy and face the possibility of dying.

I never thought of my breasts as great shakes nor had strong feelings about them, only that I got them to work in clothing. But I am still happy my breasts are with me. I don't think about them a whole lot but I like them. I talk to them and say hi and pat them and am so pleased I still have two. I noticed when Mark and I were first together that he didn't seem to be touching my treated breast a whole lot. I made some comment about this and he said, "You know it's funny, I don't want you to think that your breasts are so incredibly important to our lovemaking that if you lose one it's going to matter." I said, "Listen, that's sweet of you, but for now while they are still here, let's make the most of it." Right now, it helps me that I am with a man who doesn't care if I am minus a breast or not. He loves me and I know that clearly inside.

Talking about recurrences and dying brings up an issue I can't help but think about as a young cancer patient, and that is having children. I don't think it's generally recommended that breast cancer patients get pregnant, though I know some do. But the fact is by getting pregnant, I may be putting my life and health at great risk. So I probably won't have children. Before I got breast cancer, having children was a nonissue—I didn't want to have them. But surprisingly, I have softened in my attitudes about this over the past two years. I feel the biological imperative, which I never would have believed. Certain times of the month when kids walk by me, I reach out and pat them and can feel my face going into this silly smile and feel all goo-goo. I think, "What is this?" So even though I don't have a really strong drive to have children, there are obviously some unresolved feelings going on and I want to nurture others more now. One thing I know for sure, though, is that I am certainly not less of a woman for not having children.

Having cancer not only affected me emotionally and physically but intellectually as well. It politicized me. I was never sick before I got breast cancer, so I didn't care that much about how women were treated by the medical profession. But after some of my experiences, I care a great deal. I really think when it comes to treating women and women's diseases we're in trouble. Why did it take so long to come up with an alternative treatment to the disfiguring radical mastectomy? Why, when there are alternatives, are there still holdouts who perform unnecessary mastectomies? Many delayed diagnoses in breast cancer may be related to the fact that women's complaints about breast lumps are not taken seriously. I've read that 75 percent of hysterectomies are unnecessary and the way we deliver children is archaic. What kind of society is it that cuts out vital parts of women's bodies and makes them suffer unnecessarily?

I am not a feminist nor usually a politically involved person, but I have a strong feeling that many doctors are not coming from a healing and caring mode when it comes to treating women. Why? Male hostility, societal attitudes? I don't know exactly, except we need to confront these attitudes so that women can be treated with respect and dignity. This kind of experience makes you quite assertive about your body. I feel strongly that it's *my* body, and I will never ever consent to be treated with such a lack of respect.

Everyone seems to think that there is only one way to handle this disease and that is to fight and lick it. But everyone is different and uses his or her own unique strengths to muddle through. My strengths were a history of book learning, which was very important, and my writing. In order to cope with my diagnosis and treatment, I read. I read everything that was not nailed down on this topic. Not only about the medical aspects, about which I cared very little, but rather the emotional and nutritional ways of treating cancer. After narrowly escaping the first surgeon's recommended mastectomy, I thought, "Forget them, I want to find out what is going on *outside* of the mainstream." I even went to work for a while in a health food store to learn about macrobiotics and eating well.

I wrote a lot during treatment and I reached out for help with other people who had cancer. I also worried more about me for a change. I was always the one who said to someone, "What's your problem, tell me about it." I began therapy recently and, for the first time in my life, I look at and explore how *I* feel about something.

Learning who I am and what I want and don't want has all been a result of having cancer and not beating myself up over it. I used to translate my emotional responses into words and squash myself. Valerie never yelled; now she yells. I had a fear of being the hysterical woman who can't handle life and loses control. I've learned when I express my feelings that I can handle things much better. I survived one battle, didn't I? I am very proud of my breast and me, scars and all. I am proud of how I was during my whole experience. It makes me so much more sure of who I am now in other areas. I am much more open now to other people coming into my life and feel more balanced.

I am more sure of my work now. Presently I'm doing free-lance jobs and also write for myself, but something is inside me now *really* screaming at me, trying to get out. I feel my talent as a writer has been waiting to happen for thirty years and being sick has brought it out. It took me three years to get through this process but breast cancer pushed it and me. Having breast cancer made me confront what scared me about being a self-employed, full-time writer. What have I got to lose by trying? I am now determined to be a good writer and make a living from it.

I tend to think of catastrophic illness as a personal beeper tone that says something's wrong! something's wrong! Clearly, life couldn't have been so swell on all scores that I got this sick. I do believe that there is a matrix in which mind and body are connected. I don't know if you can be a totally happy being and do everything right for yourself and be thirty years old and get cancer. I know people who would knife me for saying that because it's not true for everybody. I don't think people make themselves sick either. People go through horrible things all the time and never get cancer, so it has to be a predisposition and other factors that go into this. I think I was predisposed to cancer because of my strong family history and that certain environmental factors—poor diet, lack of exercise all my life, and severe depression—may all have contributed to my illness.

I am not a different woman because of breast cancer. I am a changed and altered woman, but not different. I think you have to have lobotomies to become different. But this experience wakes you up. The physical side of having cancer was a piece of cake for me. It was dealing with the emotional side that was much harder. It forced me, and I know other women, to examine female issues that have been on the back burner for years. Breast cancer forces you to confront, emotionally, all the very basic elements of being a woman. Now, because of breast cancer, I have grown up as a woman.

Also, I learned that whatever you might have been covering up before you had breast cancer reveals itself after you have had this disease. Whatever is wrong in your life when you get sick floats right to the top and cannot be avoided anymore. Having cancer creates a situation in which there is suddenly a shining spotlight on your whole life and nothing can be hidden anymore. A year after a woman gets breast cancer, she may divorce, not because of cancer, but because she can't get away with not dealing with the problems anymore. You can't pretend. It's a hard time to pretend.

When I got cancer, I thought about my family's attitude about solving problems. "If only this problem would go away, wouldn't life be perfect?"

Yet when my mother stopped drinking, it didn't change anything except now she is sober. It hasn't made her a happier person. If anything, her problems are more clear. Cancer doesn't necessarily change your life and cancer doesn't make you a different person and cancer doesn't solve your problems, but it gives you an experience so intense, so frightening, so energy-creating, that it's almost like being launched from a pad. You *must, must* change.

I have seen people who do not pay attention to their illness and do not change and they often get sick again. It makes me nervous when people get cancer and then finish treatment and say, "Well, thank God, that's over! Now I can forget it." I just don't trust that. It's too big a deal to forget. Two years later, a recurrence occurs and *then* they start dealing with issues. You know how much energy and hard work it takes to deal with all that denial? Denial is like countersurvival.

Having breast cancer showed me that life is finite and can't be predicted. It could be cancer or it could be the truck coming around the bend, and so some effort has to be made to wake up and live a day, every day, as if it matters. So all the other stuff like my personal garbage may still be there until the day I die, but the grip isn't the same. It just isn't the same anymore. Because of that, all kinds of things become possible.

5

Susie

"Because of breast cancer, I am more self-confident and comfortable with myself. I care less about what others think and do what I want to do now. I used to be much more unselfish and would do for others at my own expense. Now I take care of me and have more to give to everybody else."

Susie, a happily married mother of two young children, was thirty-three years old when she was told she had stage one breast cancer. In June 1983, she underwent a lumpectomy and lymph node operation, and was treated with eight weeks of radiation. In the spring of 1984, less than a year later, she had a local recurrence in the same breast that resulted in her having a modified radical mastectomy and eight months of chemotherapy treatments. Her treatments ended in the spring of 1985. Treated for breast cancer twice, first with lumpectomy and radiation, and then with a mastectomy and chemotherapy, Susie's experiences highlight the dramatic differences these treatments can have on a woman's body image and sexuality. She felt great discomfort about being one-breasted and, in combination with the negative side effects of chemotherapy, this discomfort had an adverse effect on her sexuality and her intimate relations with her spouse. As a young mother, she experienced difficulties in trying to raise two children while taking care of herself during treatment. Susie overcame these obstacles and achieved a sense of well-being by setting and prioritizing her goals and then accomplishing them.

I was born in 1950 and grew up in a working-class neighborhood in New Haven. Although I only had one brother and one sister, I was part of a very large extended and close Italian Catholic family. My dad was a second-generation Italian-American construction worker. My mom was a third-generation Italian-American, who was a homemaker.

Although I had a lot of respect for my father and we were close, I was a little intimidated by him. He was still from the old world in some respects. I couldn't express my feelings about certain things to him. It wasn't until I got cancer and he had lung surgery that we were able to tell each other how we felt about each other and other issues.

My mother was a very pretty woman who was always a homemaker. Unlike my dad, who was affectionate, she wasn't a warm woman. We had rituals, like kissing before I'd go to bed, but that was about it. She was very strict and high-strung, and it seemed that many things I did annoyed her. I often thought she hated me. I don't think she realized how her behavior affected me, my brother, and sister. She had had a couple of nervous breakdowns and was fairly wrapped up in herself. There was a history of mental illness in my mother's family, ranging from my grandmother to all my aunts. They were often hospitalized for depression and having hallucinations. I used to wonder if this would happen to me. If I got upset, would I flip out too? So it wasn't easy growing up with my mom.

My mother never told me anything about having periods or becoming a woman. Luckily some of my girlfriends did. The first day I got my period, when I was eleven, I was standing in the bathroom with my legs apart, yelling, "Ma!" Having seen that first sign of blood freaked me out a little. Mom came in with a smirk on her face and said, "Well, now you are a lady. You have your friend." She offered no other details on what this all meant. She gave me a sanitary pad and belt and that was it. Thank goodness my friends had told me what it was like.

My breasts seemed to emerge full grown. I never needed a training bra, because all of a sudden, at age fourteen, I was developed. After that, I never grew anymore. I decided I had okay-looking, average-size breasts. Like all teenagers, I was self-conscious but was comfortable with my body and thought I was decent-looking. But I was very modest. I always hid in the locker room when I changed for gym. This started when I was in the eighth grade, when I was still wearing T-shirts when other girls my age were wearing bras. I didn't want to be different. On gym days, I would wear a slip under my gym outfit, so when I changed, no one could see my body! I wondered why I felt that way and thought maybe part of it was that my family was modest too. I never saw my mother's body that I remember.

I attended an all-girl Catholic school for twelve years and wore school uniforms the whole time. I am lucky I didn't end up a nun. I was the classic Catholic ideal girl, Miss Goody-two-shoes, who wore no makeup, had no sex, didn't smoke, was obedient, prayed, and studied.

I didn't really like school much and focused more on athletics. During my early teens, I was a bit roly-poly but I became very trim over the next few years because I was active and good in sports. I stayed naive and innocent and most of my friends did too. We never talked about boys and sex. I didn't start dating until I was sixteen, but thereafter I had steady boyfriends. I don't remember being aware of any sexual feelings, except at night in bed when I had orgasms and I never knew what they were until I was older. God forbid if a boy touched me! Until I met my husband I had been pretty much protected from any sexual activity.

Though my parents were supportive of anything I wanted to do, they had no aspirations for me in terms of my future. We never sat down and had a discussion on what I was going to do with my life. They didn't talk about my going to college. My father was interested only in my conduct and effort, values he felt to be most important in school. My trying was more important than getting an A.

There was no guidance or direction from the school either. So I had to form my own plans. During the late 1960s, girls still became either teachers or secretaries, then got married and had children. I knew I was good with my hands, so I thought I should become a secretary. So I did. I graduated from high school and lived at home while I attended a two-year executive secretarial program.

When I finished the program, I took a job at a big corporation in New Haven. I had just turned twenty and finally moved into my own apartment. I worked for this company for seven years.

I met my husband Rob through mutual friends at a party. I liked him immediately. He was in college at the time and about to enter the army reserves to get out of the draft. A few months later we met again, dated for three years, and got married in 1972. Rob was very sweet, loyal, gentle, and affectionate. I found him to be very nice-looking as well. He didn't flirt with other women. We were really devoted to each other.

We had been married for two years when Rob decided he wanted to go to graduate school in engineering. He was accepted at a school in San Diego and we thought, what the hell, we had no kids, we had never been to California, it would be a great experience. So we moved in 1975. Rob started school and I got a civilian job as a secretary on the naval base.

By that time, I had been on birth control pills for four years and my doctor told me I should take a break. As soon as I stopped, I got pregnant! Though we were financially not too well-off, we decided to go ahead and have the baby. I was covered by health insurance at work. I worked up until the last day before I delivered. Our daughter Becky was born by C-section in 1977.

Two months later, Rob graduated and got a good job in Seattle. While we were living there, three years later, we had our son, Mark. I breast-fed both the kids and enjoyed that experience.

After five years in Seattle, we decided we really missed living in warm and sunny San Diego, so we moved back to California in 1982. Because we couldn't afford to move all our belongings, we sold everything in Seattle. We really started from scratch in San Diego. We finally settled down; Rob started work for a good engineering firm and I got a part-time job working as a secretary.

Right before my diagnosis, I was a thirty-three-year-old, happily married woman with two healthy kids. I felt very attractive and desirable but wasn't a vain woman. I had a few gray hairs. Rob always told me I looked great or that he loved my eyes or my hair. We got along very well. He was always supportive and calm and had a very soothing effect on me particularly when I got angry. I felt very fortunate that he loved me, because I worried that given my family history and my type of personality—a tendency to be high strung—I would end up in my mother's shoes. At times I had a low boiling point. I could express my anger with my kids but I'd suppress it with Rob. I didn't want to hurt his feelings or be considered a nag. Of course, what would happen was I would let my angry feelings build up and then I'd explode and feel guilty!

Our sexual relationship was healthy. We hugged and touched a lot and were affectionate with one another. I was always a passive sexual partner but I enjoyed our lovemaking. My breasts were a very important part of our lovemaking. Most of my orgasms stemmed from breast stimulation. I was pleased that my breasts were in good shape even after breast-feeding. There were only a few times I really craved sex, like right before and after my period or after seeing a romantic movie. I wasn't as interested as Rob, who had a very high sex drive. I think I was brainwashed by the nuns to believe that good girls aren't supposed to excite boys. Rob always wanted more and I always didn't. We had many discussions on men's and women's sexual needs, and it seemed I'd always end up feeling guilty because I didn't want to make love as much as Rob.

As the kids were still young, I was content for the most part staying at home and raising them. Yet I wasn't entirely satisfied about me. I resented Rob because he had an interesting profession and I felt I couldn't talk to him as far as what happened in my day. I had nothing to contribute to a conversation. I was self-conscious about my intelligence and lack of schooling. Rob never said anything to make me feel this way; it was my insecurity. I wondered what I was going to do when Mark began kindergarten. I didn't want to be a secretary again. Given all that, I'd say I was in a state of transition when I got breast cancer. I was getting ready to do something different with my life.

Just before we moved back to California, I found a funny black-and-blue spot underneath my left breast but thought it was on my bone. During my annual physical I mentioned the spot to the nurse practitioner and asked, "Could I get that by wearing an underwire bra?" She said it was possible, examined me, and told me she didn't feel or see anything. I never thought about it again.

In the spring of 1983, less than eight months after my physical, I felt a lump in my left breast in the same place as my black-and-blue spot. It was about the size of a grape. It did not feel right to me. As soon as I found it, I started denying it. "Oh, it's probably nothing. It will go away." I convinced myself once that it wasn't there anymore. It took me three weeks to see a doctor, who told me to return when my period was over. The lump was still there. I was referred to a surgeon, Dr. Carlton.

Dr. Carlton aspirated the lump and nothing came out. He ordered a mammogram for me and scheduled the biopsy at the same time. I remember trying to sign my name to some papers but my hand shook. While I was struggling with this, Dr. Carlton discussed all the advantages of my situation. "You're only thirty-three with no family history. Don't worry." I tried to think optimistically. But I had to wait a week before the biopsy and *was* worried and afraid. I was all nerves. I couldn't eat and began losing weight. Rob kept telling me not to worry because we didn't know anything yet. I resented him because he wasn't worrying enough.

On a Friday afternoon, I had the biopsy under a local anesthetic in the doctor's office and then went home. I remember asking him, "Are you sure you got everything? Can you see anything?" Dr. Carlton said, "I can't be sure until I see the pathology report." Since he wouldn't commit himself, I knew right then there was something to worry about. He told me he'd call before noon on Wednesday with the biopsy results. By Wednesday, I was a mess. He called at ten minutes to twelve. When the phone rang my heart just totally dropped. Dr. Carlton asked me to come to his office but I couldn't wait to find out and asked him why. He hesitated and said, "I am sorry, it was malignant." I just didn't and couldn't believe it. He went on to say, "It was a small cancer and we got it all. There is a very good prognosis for you."

Rob came right home as soon as he heard. He cried and I cried. I kept saying, "What am I going to do?" I just thought the worst—death. All I could think of was who was going to take care of my kids? They were seven and three years old. I was also very concerned about whether or not the doctor got all the cancer out and what would happen if it came back. Why me? I searched for answers.

I thought maybe stress had caused it. I looked at the stressful times in my life. Maybe it was the move back to San Diego. I was under a lot of pressure at that time. Even after searching for answers to the "Why me?" question, I'd come up with no good reasons. Nothing that bad had ever happened to me. I had been a good person. But I quickly stopped thinking about the causes of my cancer, because I had to begin thinking about the kind of treatment I was going to have and how to arrange my life.

The next step for me was to have my underarm lymph nodes removed to see if the cancer had spread. If no spread had occurred, then I'd start radiation treatment. I had the lymph node operation and the nodes were clear. This was a good sign. It really was early stage breast cancer and my prognosis was excellent. I didn't need any more surgery or chemotherapy. I was so relieved.

With the encouragement of my friends, I decided to see a physician who specialized in cancer and nutrition before I started radiation treatments. Dr. Wyatt suggested I begin immediately on a macrobiotic diet, explaining to me that I would always have the cancer, but I could die of old age with it. That scared me a bit. The diet had to be for the rest of my life? He said, "You don't necessarily die from the cancer if your diet doesn't feed the cancer cells." I would believe anything at that point so I went on a strict macrobiotic diet for the next year. The diet was depressing because much of it was bland and tasteless. No one else in the family would eat the food so I had to cook two dinners every night. While I was on this diet, I wondered, "What would happen if this doesn't cure me?" Then little by little I got stronger and the diet made me feel energized. I never got tired. It was the best year of my life.

When I first heard I was going to have radiation, I worried most about who was going to be home for the kids when I went to treatment. Rob went to work early, and I couldn't rely on someone to show up every morning at 7 A.M. My mother offered to come stay with us and spent the next month with us. Though I felt relieved to have help, having my mom around was a mixed blessing. She was great with the housework and the kids but she was also a real worrywart. I could see that her being with me took a toll on her. She was too concerned about me. I had to keep reassuring her I was fine. "Mamma, I am *fine*; I am just a little tired from the radiation. That's all." She'd wait on me hand and foot as if I was an invalid. I often would hear her whispering to Mark not to go in my room and bother me. Poor thing, he heard that quite a bit and I knew that took a toll on him. He wanted my attention and wasn't getting much. He acted up quite a bit during that time. Becky, on the other hand, was pretty much able to take care of herself. So I didn't worry as much about her. The one neat thing that came out of radiation was that my mother and I grew much closer. Though we could get on each other's nerves, we were able to share with one another and talk about anything.

I had radiation treatments every morning at 7:30 for six weeks. By noon I would be really tired and would take a nap. But after resting I could go on the rest of the day. I had taken a few weeks off from work after the biopsy, but while I was having radiation, I went back part-time in the afternoon. It was good for my head to be occupied with something other than cancer twenty-four hours a day.

During treatment I was very thin. I had weighed about 115 pounds before the biopsy and dropped to 100 pounds during radiation. I am 5 feet, 2 inches. Everybody thought I was dying because I was so thin. But I was lean and trim, and didn't have an ounce of fat on my body. Also, once my breast healed, it wasn't deformed from the surgery and I had no burn from the radiation at all, though my breast was sore. For a while after treatment, I felt very protective of it and didn't want to be touched there for a time. My breasts were still important to me and I was glad I had both of them. I appreciated them more because I knew one of them might be gone some day. I didn't take them for granted anymore.

After my lumpectomy and radiation, Rob's and my relationship didn't change at all. He was as affectionate and supportive after breast cancer as he was before. I was so lucky. I count my blessings, because from the beginning of our relationship, he has never said anything unkind or degrading about me or my body. Our sex life was the same too. He never stayed away from me. Even during radiation, I was still sexually active.

The year following radiation I never felt better in my life, physically and mentally. I was so glad to be alive and had tremendous energy. I started exercising every day and joined a tennis league. I assumed because I felt so good that there couldn't possibly be anything wrong in me. Yet soon after my lumpectomy, I felt a hard lump near my lumpectomy incision. It concerned me and I kept asking the doctors about it. Four doctors, including an oncologist, a gynecologist, an internist, and a radiotherapist, all thought it was scar tissue that had built up from the lumpectomy. I figured these guys must know what they are talking about. If they were really concerned, they would have me in immediately for surgery, right?

I didn't worry about that lump until a year later. In the spring of 1984, I began having some nipple discharge from my left breast. At first, it was kind of orange in color. I convinced myself it was yellow because I didn't want to see red blood. I knew red was dangerous. Rob kept pushing me to go in and get my breast checked. I called the radiologist who insisted I see him right away. Then I called the surgeon who said, "Don't worry, if it's not bloody, there's no problem. It could be from hormonal changes." He put my mind at ease and I trusted him. I totally disregarded what the radiologist wanted to do. I didn't want another diagnosis. I blocked it out.

So I waited another month before I did anything. In the process, the discharge became redder and I'm sure that's when the cancer spread throughout my whole breast. I couldn't ignore it anymore. It was less than a year after my lumpectomy.

I took a girlfriend with me to the surgeon's office. Dr. Carlton performed a needle aspiration right then, taking sample cells from the discharge. I asked him if he could tell me quickly if there was anything suspicious. He got the frozen section and said they were definitely suspicious cells. I knew. There wasn't any doubt in my mind that there was a recurrence. I thought, "Oh man, not another heartbreak. Just what am I going to do? Am I destined to have this kill me?"

Over and over again I asked him, "Are you sure that you caught all of this the first time? Could this have been the remaining cells that kept multiplying?" He said, "Well, I thought I got all of it and even took a little more tissue than required to be on the safe side. But sometimes it's like pruning a tree; when you cut something off, sometimes you get new and faster growth."

"Oh Jesus," I thought, "what have they done to me? Is this their fault? If I had had another surgeon, would this have happened?" I was really mad at the doctor. I blamed him though I never confronted him. I called Rob from the doctor's office and told him, "It looks like it came back and I might have to have a mastectomy." I cried on the phone and Rob tried to calm me down but his voice was cracking too. We both felt in a daze.

Then we had to wait again for two days to get the official results from the biopsy. Waiting for test results is the worst. It was cancer, again. I had only one alternative: a mastectomy and chemotherapy. I really had no other alternatives the second time around. The doctors aren't going to take any more chances. After hearing the biopsy results, I talked about dying and Dr. Carlton talked about scheduling me for the mastectomy. It was a strange conversation. My operation was scheduled for a week later.

Besides being angry at the doctor, I was convinced that the radiation hadn't worked. Maybe my cancer was radio-resistant and the tumor had actually gotten bigger? The doctors told me no, this was not possible. The thing that upset me most was that my diet had failed. After a year of being on a strict macrobiotic diet, I felt so betrayed and disappointed. I knew in my brain there were no guarantees, but in my heart I believed I could control the cancer with the food. It had been my defense. I had been doing all the "right" things such as exercising and eating well. The doctors had been giving me glowing reports about my health all year.

But by the time of my operation, I was in a better place emotionally. I believed that everything was going to be all right after my breast was gone. The cancer wasn't going to get me after all; I wouldn't let it devour me. The night before I went in to the hospital, I looked at myself in a mirror and wondered how I was going to look with just one breast. I kept pushing my breast down and tried to imagine how flat it would be. I asked Rob, "What are you going to think of me with one breast?" He said, "Well, you are more to me than one left breast." I asked, "Yeah, but what about making love?" He just kept repeating the same thing to me: "There is no reason in my eyes why there will be any difference." That night I even got a good night's rest. The next morning I looked in the mirror, and seeing both my breasts thought, "This is the last time I am going to see both of them together."

By the time we got to the hospital, I wanted the whole thing over with. I didn't care what it took to get it out of me. I felt good about going in for the operation.

My whole recuperative period was incredible. First, I never had pain. Second, I was in high spirits because I went in feeling so healthy and was in good shape physically. I also thought, "Maybe this is *really* over this time." I first saw my scar with Dr. Carlton when he was removing my hemovac, this obnoxious drainage tube attached to my underarm. He asked me if I was ready to look. I wasn't so sure but he persisted, so I looked. It wasn't that bad. I was expecting a huge scar but instead it was very much like my C-section scar, a thin pencil line.

When I got home I asked Rob if he was scared about me dying. He said no, he wasn't frightened because he really believed I was going to be all right. Then I asked him if my chest looked bad. I was wondering how Rob was going to feel. I had all these bandages on, covered by a loose blouse. I thought I was uneven-looking; one side of me was flat. Could someone tell? He said, "You can't even tell." He was right because my other breast wasn't large enough for anyone to notice a difference. It was good to have someone with whom to test reality. I told Rob the scar wasn't that bad but he didn't ask to see it, ever. Later I asked him why and he said, "I didn't think you were comfortable showing it to me." His statement was accurate in that I didn't want anyone to see it. I was and still am very self-conscious.

After the lumpectomy and radiation, I was very comfortable with Rob in our bedroom, just sitting naked and talking together, as we had done before. It was no big thing. But after the mastectomy, I couldn't do that. I got dressed in the bathroom. Even now, two years later, when I am ready to go to bed, I have my nightgown hanging on the hook in the bathroom, undress there, and then get into bed. When Rob and I shower together, I sometimes turn my back to him so he can't see. But if I am close enough, face to face, I press myself up against him. I am embarrassed, really.

This was much more my problem than Rob's. He didn't give me any negative messages. He was still very attracted to me, always wanted sex, *still* always wants sex. It's funny—I can't remember the first time we had sex after the mastectomy, but it wasn't long after I got home. Rob told me, "I just won't touch you there if it's sensitive. But you're still fine down below! Remember it's all in your head and up to you. You're not handicapped in any way and I certainly don't look at you as being handicapped."

Having sex wasn't that comfortable, as I was protective of my remaining breast for a while after surgery and worried about the incision. Plus I had lost interest in sex. My own sexual pleasure didn't matter to me but I was always there to please Rob. We made the most of the one breast left! The first time after surgery that I had an orgasm, I felt renewed. "Oh my God, thank God, I can still be a woman and respond! I am a whole woman and can still function, have an orgasm, and even my nipple is sensitive enough that it got me there. But what if, God forbid, anything happens to this other breast?" Now I am so protective of my remaining breast that I am constantly examining it. I don't know if I would fall apart if I didn't have at least one. Where would my orgasms come from?

After the mastectomy, Rob and I sat down with the children to explain what had happened to me. We didn't go into details but explained that my breast had been removed because of bad tissue. I was going to be taking very strong medication to treat my—I don't even know if we used the word—disease. We told them the medication would make me sick and I would need rest, and all their help would be appreciated.

About a month after my mastectomy, I started eight months of chemo. I had my first dose in San Diego and then went home to New Haven for a month and a half with the kids to visit my family. My doctor arranged to have my chemo injections given to me at Yale University Hospital. In the beginning I was most fearful about losing my hair, although the doctors said there was a chance that it might not happen. Every morning I would look for hairs on my pillow and nothing would be there! Holy God, maybe I was going to be that one in a hundred that didn't lose her hair! Then a week later I was in the car, putting my hand through my hair, and a clump of hair came out in my hand. I panicked, "This is it!" My mother was shocked at first and kept telling me to leave my head alone. I got angry that she pretended my hair was going to stay in place. But for a while even I tried to stop fate. I wouldn't wash my hair so I could keep every hair on my head, but it all went, little by little. By the end of my month-and-a-half stay, all I had left on my head were very thin strands, a few wisps here and there on my head. I was never totally shiny-headed bald but it was bad enough that I had to wear a wig. I hated the wig too; it was too hot and itchy.

In the beginning it was traumatic to lose my hair. There were times I would look at myself and think, "Oh God," and look away, but I didn't dwell on it. There were occasions when I would cry or start feeling bad for myself. For the most part I just kept telling myself, "This is only temporary. It *will* grow back." Actually my hair did start growing back at one point and then it all fell out again. I didn't really ever get into an ugly period with my baldness. I even got to laugh about it when I went to see an old school friend who had a permanent hair loss disease. She was bald and I was balding and she pulled me through. To this day she is an inspiration to me. I can share anything with her and she makes me laugh. Without these people in my life, Rob and my close friends and family being there for me, I really would have been down the tubes. They deserve all the credit when it comes to my optimistic attitude.

When I left home, I had a full head of hair and now I was returning with none. My kids had seen me lose my hair but I was a little worried about Rob's reaction. At first Rob made a face when I took off my wig and then he said, "Well it's different. You look beautiful bald." He always made those supporting, encouraging remarks. Funny, I never felt self-conscious about being bald in my house. I made myself be that way. However, when I went out I would always wear a scarf or a wig. I didn't want to be stared at.

While I was on chemo I got really sick. Every two weeks I had the pills and injections and I would have two really bad days. I'd come home, have a really queasy stomach, and then I'd finally get sick. Usually I would wait to throw up to feel good. It was like come on, come on, let's get this over with. Then I was fine after that but very tired. Also I learned that if I didn't eat something with the Cytoxan, I'd get really nauseous. So I always had crackers, liquid, or water on hand every day with me. I gained some weight on chemo. I had gone from my lowest weight as an adult of 100 pounds after my mastectomy up to about 125.

Though I had worked during radiation, I didn't while I was on chemo. I didn't have enough energy. I played tennis early in the morning as often as I could, but by midday I'd be too tired to do much of anything. This was tough on my kids, particularly Mark. He had had my mother around for most of the radiation period, but during chemo he just had me and I really was out of it at times. Guilt, guilt. I couldn't do what I was supposed to be doing as a mother.

Even though I had lost interest in sex, I was sexually active through the whole chemo experience. There is nothing like a good orgasm, right? When I had one I would think, "Oh God, how can I live so long without these?" But then it would take me the longest time to want it again. But I'd always be there for Rob; we'd hug and make love. But I would try to dissuade him from getting me to have an orgasm. He'd complain that lovemaking was sort of one-sided, but I'd say, "You don't understand, it doesn't bother me. If I wanted to, I would, but it gives me satisfaction to do for you."

During chemo I began thinking about my future. I felt strongly that I had to do something worthwhile. First I considered calling the cancer society to volunteer, perhaps to offer another patient some comfort and understanding. Then I thought of my assets and what I did best. Rob and I talked about it and I wrote down what I liked doing. I always loved cutting people's hair and had been doing this for my family and friends for years. So I decided to become a hairdresser. Once I make a decision, I go for it.

The timing was great because Mark had entered kindergarten and I had ended chemo at the same time. We didn't have the money for school so I took out a loan for it. Rob was very supportive. I started school full time, five days a week. It was a grueling schedule for someone who had just finished chemo. I would leave home at 6:15 A.M. and come back after 6 P.M. But I loved it. I graduated and soon after interviewed with one of the leading hair salons in town. They liked me and I started working a month later!

Now I feel like a real professional and am so confident in my abilities. It's a very rewarding job. I am not afraid to ask questions because I certainly don't want some client suffering at my hands. I don't want to experiment on them. I know there will be days when people won't like what I do, but so far I have had nothing but thanks for the good job I have done. Do you know what that does to my self-esteem? Oh my God! I thrive on this! It's made my life!

Since I have had breast cancer, some things have changed in my life; others things haven't. The way I mother hasn't changed a whole lot. At the beginning, I couldn't be involved with the kids enough. I'd think, "What if I am not here with them tomorrow? What if I can't see my kids grow up or graduate from high school or get married? What are they going to do without me?" I felt bad for them. Now, I don't worry so much. I've lowered my expectations. I just live day to day with them.

My daughter, Becky, has always been very curious about my mastectomy and, from the day of the operation, has asked if she could see my scar. She will put her hand near my chest to check it every now and again and ask, "Mummy, is it all flat?" I say, "Yes, there isn't any more tissue left. They took the bad tissue out. As soon as it heals better, honey, I will show you." I don't want to scare her but I also don't want to lie. To this day, I still haven't shown her my scar. She's never stopped asking. The scar is not bad at all, but I guess I am still self-conscious about nothing being there and scaring her.

Soon enough, she'll know she's at high risk for having breast cancer. Becky is now eleven and developing breasts. As soon as she starts seeing doctors, they will ask her about her family history. She knows what breast cancer is but doesn't have many questions yet. I don't want her to dwell on this as a young child. Maybe I am being too protective. I wonder if I am doing the right thing on this issue. I feel guilty that I may have passed this on to her. I got it; now she may too. God forbid, I hope she won't. I had to be the one to start this whole history. So I want Becky to be extra careful about her diet and having breast exams as she gets older. I have told her that as she gets older she'll have to examine her breasts to make sure her breasts are healthy.

I am also very conscious of the possible relationship between diet and breast cancer. I never cook steaks or fatty meats for my family anymore. We eat lots of chicken, fish, and vegetables. I cringe when I see Becky eating fatty or sugary things because she has a little sweet tooth. I want her to be careful especially as she recently has gained some weight.

When I first had the mastectomy I thought, "I can live without a breast. I am lucky I'm alive and well. I am more than a breast and people are going to have to accept me the way I am." I didn't even think of plastic surgery. But after a few months, my views changed and I began considering reconstruction. Living with a prosthesis is a pain. It's comfortable enough and I do feel balanced. But I am sick of it, sick of the special bras and the buttoned shirts up to my neck, and sick of holding onto my chest so the prosthesis won't fall out. The bras are not pretty or feminine-looking. I want to have some cleavage when I wear a bathing suit. I am fed up with feeling self-conscious about it with my husband and taking everything off at night in the bathroom. Also every now and then I have a twinge on my chest, and I go to check it out and completely forget that I don't have a breast there. I think it's there and then I remember, it's not me anymore. I am ready to have something to check out.

Recently, I had an experience that made up my mind to have reconstruction. I went to have a facial. The facialist asked me to pull my bra strap down because she wanted to massage my shoulders. "Oh," I thought in terror, "she is going to see that I don't have a breast." I tensed up and my hands clutched to my breast so nothing would fall out. Then I realized this was no way to live.

I have talked to other breast cancer patients who have had reconstructive surgery and they are all pleased with the results. At the moment, all I want is the breast and not the nipple. I suppose after a while, after the new breast is part of me, I'll want the whole thing! I am also considering reconstructive surgery on my other breast so both breasts will be matched. My remaining breast could be built up more! Though I am scared about having another operation, this all seems worth it to me, because breast reconstruction is something I am doing for myself. My oncologist said, "That's great, let's do it. You deserve it." Rob is very supportive of this move, too, because he knows I am not comfortable and he would like for me to feel better.

I've seen the plastic surgeon once. In the meeting he mentioned my skin was a little taut, and that in order to prepare for plastic surgery, I should push and pull the chest skin each day for a few months. If all goes well, within a year's time we can schedule the operation. If I have to take a couple of weeks off from work to do this, I am doing it!

I feel good about "fixing" this problem but I am not so sure I can fix another one I have. Since the recurrence, my sex life has seriously changed. First, Rob and I haven't come to a comfortable place about touching my scar. I can't tell if it's more his discomfort or mine, but he still shies away from touching me there. I told him I probably wouldn't feel as self-conscious if he did touch or massage me, but nothing has happened. Second, I stopped having periods in early 1985 and they never came back. No doctor is about to give me estrogen to start up the process again, because they are concerned the hormone might cause a breast cancer to grow. It's a double-edged sword, I guess. I am lucky I am not getting estrogen because it could feed any tumors I might still have. Yet I am menopausal at age thirty-six. I have mood swings, hot flashes, and vaginal dryness. It's funny that this didn't really happen all at once. During the past six months it has gotten worse.

Having intercourse is the worst of all. I just dread it actually. I honestly can say I would be just as happy if I never made love. It's painful, even when I use tons of jelly. I feel so bad about this and ask myself, "Is this what I have to go through the rest of my life?" But most of the time, I just want to be held. This means so much more to me than having intercourse sometimes. I don't get aroused at all other than just having loving feelings. Nothing sexually stirs in me. Rob's worried that maybe he doesn't excite me anymore. How do you say to someone, "Sexually I don't have it anymore"? Yet telling him is very difficult because he is the most wonderful person I know and I could never live without him.

Even if Rob and I don't have intercourse, but relate to each other sexually in other ways, after a while I feel I *should* have intercourse. I feel obligated, which I know is bad, but I hate to think if Rob doesn't get it from me, is he going to go elsewhere? I worry that he's going to lose interest in me. So I try to be satisfying to him. Sometimes I have to be a little more dramatic. Not that I fake! I have never faked! I just make more noise.

I often wonder if Rob thinks, "Wow, if I could have a woman with two breasts, wouldn't it be even better?" Although he has done absolutely nothing to lead me to believe that he has these thoughts. It's my own thing; I know it is. In my insecurity, I sometimes ask, "So what if you meet someone exciting?" He jokes around with me, "Yeah, what if?" I feel jealous that he might look at other women, but men are *always* going to look. I mean I *look*! It's ridiculous. But I notice women's bodies so much now, more so. I guess it's wishful thinking.

Recently, I have felt better about my sexual feelings, because the talk shows I've watched and material I've read reassure me that I am not abnormal. Oprah Winfrey had a show on women's level of interest in making love. What a relief to hear I am not the only woman who would be happy with a once-a-month lovemaking session, and most of them haven't had breast cancer!

I don't think a woman can lose her femininity because of breast cancer. From time to time, I feel this little pang of self-consciousness and think maybe I am less than a "whole woman," but it doesn't have to do with my feminine qualities. To me, femininity is being gentle, soft, nurturing, poised, and nonaggressive. When I see an assertive woman, I don't usually think she's feminine. Yet I know it's important to be assertive and I'm trying to incorporate that quality as part of my definition of feminine. I also believe a feminine woman pays attention to looking and dressing well and is not sloppy. Not that you have to wear frills; a woman in jeans and a T-shirt can be very feminine.

I have never felt that I was less desirable or less feminine because of breast cancer, except perhaps when I lost my hair. Now I think I project femininity and have a good attitude about me. I'm more trendy and feel really good about how I look when I am dressed. It's funny because I was never a clothes horse before. I was wearing school uniforms for the first eighteen years of my life. Before breast cancer I had three pairs of shoes and they went with every outfit I had. Now I have to have red shoes to go with my red blouse, and yellow shoes for my yellow skirt. Clothes are more important to me now. I never wore makeup before either. But when I lost my hair, I wanted to compensate for the hair loss. So I relied on using a scarf and wearing makeup to highlight my face.

I think the breast cancer patients I know are feminine. One lady, the Reach to Recovery volunteer who came to see me in the hospital, was an inspiration to me. She was an attractive, forty-year-old woman who was very comfortable with her one breast and her sexuality. I didn't look at her as a one-breasted lady. I looked at her as a pleasant, warm, and witty woman whose whole style was feminine. It didn't matter to me if she had one or two breasts.

What strikes me more, about the women with breast cancer I have met, is that they are all still *living*. When a friend recently told me that her thirty-four-year-old sister died from breast cancer, it sent a chill up my spine. I couldn't control myself; I just started crying. This was reality; women do die from this disease. Having another recurrence is always on my mind. I could die from this disease and I am far more concerned about that than I am about how I look.

I believe it's your attitude that determines how you come out of the breast cancer experience—how you feel and think about yourself. I believe my brain controls my health and well-being, so I keep trying to think good thoughts, such as, "I am going to lick this." But you don't do this alone. I have been so lucky to have such supportive and loving people along my journey. I was fortunate that Rob was and is a wonderful and affectionate husband. I have had a number of good doctors, especially my oncologist, Dr. Shelton, who has always been so encouraging. Throughout chemo, he'd tell me how sunny and beautiful I looked. That meant so much when I was feeling low. At my last checkup a month ago, he noticed my new haircut and told me I should be a model!

I believe I was a good role model for my friends. I didn't know anyone who had breast cancer when I got it. My friends have said they admired my stamina, strength, and attitude through this experience and that they could never get through like I did. They tell me if life ever gets a little tough for them, they think of what I have been through and back off from feeling sorry for themselves.

I get lots of phone calls from women who are about to have biopsies or breast cancer operations, and I feel good about myself as a woman because I can reach out and share with them. You can't say, "Don't worry" to them but you can say, "Take it one step at a time." I save books and articles on breast cancer not only for myself but for anyone else who might need them.

Because of breast cancer, I am more self-confident and comfortable with myself. I care less about what others think and do what I want to do now. I used to be much more unselfish and would do for others at my own expense. Now I take care of me and have more to give to everybody else. I also am working and have my own income and can do and buy more things, not that I do this at the expense of others. I still have perspective and my life is more positive.

Sometimes when I am tired, I break down with Rob and tell him I don't realize how much pain I have been through. When I look back at the lumpectomy, lymph node operation, radiation, mastectomy, and chemo, I feel like Wonder Woman. I feel good about myself. I have accomplished this great feat, overcoming very tough times. I have been to the lowest point in my life and brought myself back to a high level of functioning. I am proud that I survived all this.

I continue to live a normal life. I've had cancer twice and they've caught it early both times. It's been two-and-a-half years since my recurrence and I am feeling fine. How lucky can I be?

The day after I had the mastectomy, there was an incident that really changed my attitude about life. Dr. Carlton told me I might need to have *another* surgery to remove more chest muscles. He was taking my case to the Tumor Board for review. Right then, my whole life flashed in front of my eyes and I thought, "When is this going to end and why is this happening to me again?" It was then that I had a very serious talk with Rob about what would happen if, God forbid, this cancer finally got me. It sounded so morbid but I needed to know how the kids were going to be cared for and what he was going to do. We chose the people we wanted to help out with the kids and planned my will. Then a day later, the doctor called to say the Tumor Board Review Committee recommended that I have only chemotherapy and no further surgery. He apologized for putting us through another ordeal. I nearly passed out.

That phone call opened my eyes to the fact that I am only living day to day here on earth. By God, I am going to enjoy life and my family! Even my attitude about money has changed. I was always worried about saving every penny. But we're not struggling that much, so if we have a few extra bucks, we do something with it. If I want something I like now, I get it! Why don't we buy things that we can enjoy living with now? Life is short and you can't put anything on hold; you just go for it. I am not waiting anymore for anything. I'm going to make the most of my life *now*.

6

Kate

"Breast cancer put me more in touch with the androgynous side of me. Maybe I am more of a man in terms of strength because of my scar. A man's scar is a sign of virility, proof that he has been through something that has made him stronger. A man can be proud of his scars. I look at my mastectomy scar that way instead of thinking of it as something ugly."

In late 1981, at the age of thirty-five, married and the mother of two young children, Kate found a lump in her breast that turned out to be a stage two breast cancer, with lymph node involvement. Treated with a modified radical mastectomy, she then underwent chemotherapy treatments for more than two years, which she completed in 1983. Kate's experience shows what impact the crisis of breast cancer can have on an already fragile marriage. Finding her husband unable to meet her emotional needs during her treatment, she was driven by a tremendous hunger for life and a strong desire to know that she was still attractive with one breast. Thus, Kate sought out and developed new relationships with both men and women. Though her husband stayed with her until her treatment was completed, her marriage ended in divorce. As a result of these experiences, Kate developed a positive body image and emerged as a stronger and more self-determined woman.

I was always curious about what was going to happen to me physically during adolescence, but my parents, brought up in Europe, did not volunteer information about this process. They were quite conservative people who believed that human bodies were fine until one was eleven years old; then bodies and sex were awkward subjects not to be discussed. I got this message quite clearly from my father. I guess these standards were also my mother's, but since she was very modest and shy, she wouldn't usually offer her opinions. In 1960, when I was twelve, I had started my period and remember thinking, "How am I going to tell my mother?" I assumed she would be upset that I already knew about it. But when I told her, she was proud of me and helpful. I learned about human reproduction from reading voraciously and from my two older brothers, who loved to fill me in on the hidden details of life.

In my early teens I was awkward and horsey, but I knew deep inside existed the girl I really felt like: tall, graceful, beautiful, and interesting. I just couldn't make the outside match the inside. My body was gawky and my hair never looked right. I felt very different from my peers who seemed to know all about boys, makeup, and dancing. I grew up with other values, many of which I now appreciate, but as a teenager in this culture it's hard to be different. Individuality is not exactly prized.

My parents had definite ideas, not modern, on how I should dress and wear my hair. Wearing clothing that signaled sexual attraction was not acceptable to them. Practical and sensible shoes (boys' oxfords) and clothing were valued. I learned that girls were expected to be modest and not flaunt themselves. The first time I ran into this clothing problem was when I wanted a bra. My mother said I didn't need a bra and I remember feeling self-conscious about not having one when many of my schoolmates did. My breasts *were* small but later they developed quite nicely. But at the time, I always felt out of it and dreaded when schoolboys ran their fingers down my back to see if I was wearing a bra, only to find nothing.

I wanted to be attractive and look and be like everybody else. But I was not allowed to go to parties and my parents wouldn't even allow me to read teenage magazines. They would say, "How can you read *Seventeen* when you aren't seventeen yet?" There was definitely a culture gap going on. I thought my parents' rules were boring, limiting, and far too strict.

I was an introspective, fairly shy girl. Since my brothers were four and six years older and operated as a team, and my sister was six years younger, I lived in a somewhat private world of my own, writing, drawing, and painting. Our family loved nature and we spent lots of time together hiking and camping. My parents wanted us to become self-reliant individuals and not to follow the crowd. The things that marked me as different from my peers at the time became sources of my strength later in life.

My parents sent me to boarding school in Switzerland for two years when I was fourteen for two major reasons: to lessen the influence of American teenage culture on me and to have me experience life in another country. I found that being different was not so much of an issue there. I think European culture focuses less on cosmetic concerns and there is less peer pressure to be alike. I actually had more freedom in many ways and liked living there.

When I was sixteen, I returned to the United States and attended a coed boarding school. Though I missed Switzerland and my friends, I adjusted quickly because suddenly boys had discovered me. I think my dad thought I had been a grump and kind of mousy, but suddenly all these boys were calling and I bloomed. Once on a camping trip, a boy wrote, "Kate has a hot bod" on the inside of a truck. Graffiti about me! I was surprised that I could be seen as such a desirable item. I don't think women should be treated as sex objects, but I enjoyed the attention.

Following graduation from high school, I attended a women's college and studied art and theater. I had a number of relationships with men and worked closely with a theater group that became almost like a family to me. After college, I attended art school for two years, because I really wanted a professional career in photography. During art school, I dated a number of artists and then met David, who was completing his Ph.D. in psychology. He seemed very grounded, stable, and secure. We seemed to complement one another and got married in 1970.

Over the next few years, I became well established as an artist, exhibiting my works nationally and teaching photography at a liberal arts college. My husband and I became partners in an art gallery, and parents.

I didn't have an easy time with my pregnancies. My first ended in a miscarriage, but my second produced a boy, Neil, after twenty-seven hours of labor and a C-section. But after Neil's birth, it was a tough year. Our gallery closed, I stopped working, the baby was a screamer, and my time was totally taken up in child care and recuperation. It took me a long time to feel strong and healthy again. I couldn't believe how my life had changed in such a short time. Three years later, I had an ectopic pregnancy and emergency surgery. Shortly thereafter, I became pregnant again, this time with my daughter, Lizzie. She too had to be delivered by a C-section.

These few years were terribly strenuous physically. Raising two small children, I found my energy level low and my immune system knocked flat. Though I strongly believed in doing things naturally and really enjoyed the connection of my breasts and feeding, I had problems nursing my daughter because she wasn't gaining weight. I had enough milk, but couldn't understand why things were not working out. At my worst moments I thought she would die. By the time I found a doctor who told me that she was not nursing properly, it was too late to retrain her.

But I was very happy with my children. I was a warm, caring mother but not the earth-mother type. I am nurturing with children and a good mother to them. As wonderful as I found mothering, I also found that my time and thoughts were always fragmented. There was always somebody who needed something and I didn't feel that the rest of *me* was being taken care of. My photography projects went uncompleted, even though I had the best of intentions. There just wasn't enough time. I finally decided that I would take the time to be with my children, and work would have to come later. But I did feel that I was losing time in my career and that people would forget who I was.

Like many mothers, this was a very asexual time for me. Though my sensuality was subdued, I still felt attractive. You don't feel too sexual when you have to wear shirts that somebody can spit up on. Smelling like peanut butter most of the time has its drawbacks too. When you nurse, your body is not your own. In order to be sexual, I really think you have to be able to focus on yourself, even just a little. I think one of the reasons I finally stopped nursing was to give me back my body.

Although I wouldn't characterize my husband and myself as traditional people, we did play traditional husband-wife roles: He was the money earner and I was the wife/mother. We had a very good relationship, though not without difficulties. Since David was a psychologist, there was always a feeling that we should be able to "work out" our problems. Yet he would do all the talking and I would do all the listening. I always had the feeling that he was the doctor and I was the one being diagnosed. Over time our roles became unhealthy: He was the paternal caretaker and I was the childlike, flighty artist.

After a certain period in our marriage, we had become better friends than lovers. Because of the role resentments I had, it was hard for me to be open with him. As I found out later, he felt shut out when the kids were small. I learned later that he was having other sexual relationships. Sexually, we were warm and caring but the passion had cooled. He wanted me to be more initiating and I wanted him to be less aggressive, more sensual, and playful. Actually, I don't think sex was the core of our problems. Our communication patterns weren't good. I wasn't too concerned about all this at the time because I felt that if anybody else took any part of me, there was going to be nothing left. A good night's sleep was more desirable than sex.

After ten years of marriage, David and I had drifted apart. He was involved with his work and I was involved with the children. I felt overwhelmed at home and had fears he didn't understand. I suspected he might be having affairs, but couldn't imagine myself struggling as a single mother, and so didn't ask too much. I hoped that once the children were beyond the toddler stage, my life might return to some semblance of control and our relationship would enter a new phase. It was about this time that I began seeing a psychologist because I wanted to look at what was happening in my life with David and my career. I needed to understand the meaning of art in my life too. The sessions were productive and creative at first. It was a place where I could go all for myself, with no interruptions or demands.

Then in 1980, when my daughter was almost two and my son was five, I discovered a small lump in my left breast while taking a bath. I hadn't done breast self-examination regularly because I thought I was too young to do it. I was only thirty-five years old. But I had just learned from my mother that my maternal grandmother had died of breast cancer when she was forty-four. I always thought she had died of TB, since she had been treated for this. I was really surprised. So I had gone home and examined my breasts. This small lump concerned me a little but it felt like a premenstrual problem. I made an appointment with my ob/gyn for a month or so later. But I worried about the lump and continued to examine my breasts each day. Then I found a much larger mass about the size of a fifty-cent piece. This lump was higher on my chest and had a different quality to it. I was scared and called immediately to get a checkup. But it was New Year's weekend and I couldn't get an appointment for another four days. It was a very long time to wait because I think I knew already.

I went alone to the gynecologist and he was concerned too. He said at the very least I should have a biopsy. I remember feeling terribly alone and scared. He sent me to a general surgeon, who examined my breast with his enormous fingers and talked to me while he stared at the ceiling. I was sure his hands could not do delicate work on my body and I left in a daze. I had to pick up my son from school and talked to some friends there about what had happened and got a referral to a surgeon who specialized in breast disease.

My husband and I went together for my mammogram, which was normal, followed by a needle aspiration, which revealed nothing. The surgeon said he was pretty sure the mass wasn't malignant, but just to make sure an outpatient biopsy was scheduled.

The biopsy was very frightening because I hadn't had any time to read about what happens to a woman when she has one. I always sensed deep down that the results would not be good. Following the biopsy, while I was in the recovery room, my breast was extremely painful and felt as if it was on fire. Blood began seeping through the bandages and I thought the stitches had broken loose. Was I bleeding to death? As it turned out, I wasn't, but it was hours before the doctor came and by then I believed I was literally coming apart. I spent the night in the hospital for observation.

When I got home and saw the results of the biopsy, I was shocked. My skin was bruised and purple; my breast was swollen and hurt. I looked as if I had been hit by a Mack truck. I asked my husband to take pictures of my breasts, which he did. They are the last pictures I have of my breast and they are tragic-looking. I still find them extremely sad to look at. This biopsy experience was far worse than seeing my mastectomy scar for the first time.

When I learned the results of the biopsy, I wasn't really surprised. The diagnosis was breast cancer and four lymph nodes were cancerous. My major fear at the beginning was of dying, then fear of abandoning the children, and fear of the unknown. There was so much unknown. Was I going to be crippled? Would it spread all over my body? What was I going to look like? Was there going to be a big hole in my chest? Had I contaminated my children by nursing them?

Though my doctor told me all the treatment options for breast surgery, I had already decided on a mastectomy. Even though I was very scared of more surgery, in a way I was looking forward to getting rid of my breast. My breast was hurting and was badly bruised and swollen from the biopsy. I thought, "Oh God, let's get rid of this. It's better the breast than my hand or my eyes, which I need for my profession." This sounded so rational at the time. It wasn't until later that I discovered the implications of the loss of my breast.

I remember thinking, "This is my cancer now. I *am* a cancer patient." I didn't blame my body for doing something bad and never asked the proverbial, "Why me?" To me, cancer was more like something unexpressed, trying to get out, like creativity that had not been given its free rein. I saw cancer as the negative side of creativity—something growing wild and out of control. For a while I blamed my family for not telling me about my grandmother's breast cancer.

I didn't have a lot of time to obsess about the mastectomy itself prior to surgery. I read as much as I could absorb, which wasn't much. Lots of time was spent making arrangements for the children: My sister came to babysit while I was in the hospital, my mother came to stay with us later, and friends provided the kids with rides to and from school. My husband and I walked together every day and cried a lot. His fear of losing me was great. I even gave away the family dog because I knew I couldn't care for him and no one else would. The dog later haunted me in my dreams. It really was a time of paring down and only keeping on what was manageable. It was like making preparations for a long journey.

Following the modified mastectomy, I was very protective of my body and breast area. I really wanted to take care of it. Looking at my scar for the first time was handled quite naturally. One of the nurses was changing my dressing, and I was curious and looked at my chest. I was expecting the worst and was happily surprised that I didn't have a big hole in my chest. All I saw was a neat, thin, black line of stitches. Somehow since the breast is round, I imagined that when it is removed all that is left is a deep round hole. I think most women imagine having this sunken chest, which is all scooped out. No one had told me what I would look like.

Though I was sad for my body and breasts (at the same time as the mastectomy, I had another biopsy on the right breast, which was negative), the scar was not ugly; it was quite beautiful. My friends were surprised, too, when they saw my scar. It was funny to see how my one side looked like a boy and the other side looked like a girl. In therapy, I had been interested in androgyny. Looking at my chest, I thought, "Well, there you are!"

But weeks later, I was more emotional. "Oh, God, what did they do to me? Where is my breast? In the hospital trash? Is it in a jar of embalming fluid? What did it look like? Was it in pieces or chunks? Couldn't I have taken it home and buried it?" It felt to me like the dead baby a mother wants to hold and see. I needed to mourn for my lost breast. I needed some physical closure by seeing it and putting it in the earth. It was very primitive. I never was able to verbalize those feelings and was too embarrassed to bring it up to anyone.

While I was still in the hospital, two Reach to Recovery volunteers came to visit. One woman had had a mastectomy, and the other, a mastectomy and breast reconstruction. They gave me some cotton padding for a bra and talked about prosthesis. Before surgery, I thought reconstruction was an option for me because I didn't like the idea of wearing a prosthesis. Then the volunteer with the new reconstructed breast lifted her blouse and showed it to me. Unfortunately, her surgery had been recent and her scars were red and ugly. Looking at her, I realized a reconstructed breast couldn't have any feeling, which is the only reason I wanted one. I wasn't so sure about reconstruction after all. So I took the cotton padding home and started fooling around with it to see what a prosthesis might look like. But I didn't like the way I was going to look.

At first I was not physically up to shopping for a prosthesis. At home, my sister and I tried various inventions of socks, using peanuts and buttons for nipples. Then I went to a prosthesis display at the American Cancer Society. I walked in and saw these breasts in all different shapes and sizes, made of rubber, plastic, and fabrics, just lying out on a table. It blew me away. I wanted to do a sculpture out of them, then remembered *I* was the consumer. When I was finally ready to buy a prosthesis, a good friend and I went to a lingerie store and spent hours trying to find the perfect breast and the perfect bra to put it in. Philip Roth or Woody Allen should have been there because you have to go with a sense of humor. I found the best model I could but it didn't have a nipple, which bothered me, since I sometimes wore clothing—light blouses, for example—that subtly revealed the shape of my nipples. I hadn't worn a bra in years, and all of a sudden, I had to wear all this equipment if I was going to wear a prosthesis.

Part of me really didn't want to bother with this prosthesis at all, but I was still concerned with looking like my old self. I was determined to find the sexiest possible bra to put this rubber tit in. I wore it because I thought it would make me *feel* like I *used* to look and at the time it seemed important. I only wore the prosthesis for three months and then stopped wearing it forever. I realized it wasn't making me feel any different, so who was I doing it for? By that time, I liked my body and scar and didn't want reconstruction. I thought reconstruction was a superficial change and I felt proud of my scar. I had gone through a tough experience and there was nothing to be ashamed about.

Actually, it was a funny situation with my son that prompted me to literally toss the prosthesis out. About three months after surgery, we went on vacation to Mexico. Neil and I were in the hotel pool swimming. I was wearing my carefully chosen bathing suit with my prosthesis in place when my son yelled across the pool, "Hey Mom, do you have your fake breast in?" We were totally surrounded by people. I laughed and said, "Yeah." I took it out and threw it in the bushes. I thought, "Who cared? Who needed it?" My son's attitude clarified something I was beginning to sense: I did not *need* to look like I did before.

About a month after my mastectomy, I started two years of adjuvant chemotherapy. My treatments consisted of daily pills and injections for one week every six weeks. Though my oncologist, Dr. Hamel, was highly recommended, I did not like his bedside manner. But I wanted a doctor with strong credentials more than a friend, so we began two years of a difficult and testy relationship.

I was scared of the long-term effects of chemo, such as getting leukemia, and asked Dr. Hamel, "Am I going to be here when my children are teenagers?" He replied, "Well, don't you want to be here for them now?" Then I asked him if chemo was going to change my sexual life. He sort of huffed and puffed, seemed uncomfortable, and said, "We really don't know anything about that." In spite of his poor response to my questions, I felt I didn't have much choice with the extent of my lymph node involvement so I decided to have the chemo.

My first treatment made me terribly, terribly sick. I thought I would die from the vomiting and diarrhea and almost quit right then. My doctor changed the scheduling of the tablets I was taking and that helped. After that, I still felt nauseous but wasn't lying flat on the bathroom floor twenty-four hours a day. In addition to feeling sick, which put quite a damper on my energy level and my interest in *anything*, I lost weight.

I was very worried about what chemo was doing to my body. Over the next two years, I totally stopped menstruating. At first I thought it was temporary but my periods never returned. Everything started changing. Here I was thirty-five years old, aging rapidly, having hot flashes and weakened muscles. I was going through menopause. My vaginal tissue became extremely sensitive and raw. I was shocked. Nobody told me that these side effects would happen. I am still concerned since menopause is now a permanent condition due to my lack of estrogen. I always thought I would enjoy getting older and feel good about it. This, however, did not feel good. I sure wasn't ready to be put ten years ahead of my biological schedule. I felt as if I looked fifty to one hundred years old.

My anger about all this was directed at my doctors, sometimes with good reason. I am sure David caught his fair share too. He thought it was a generic anger at male authority like doctors. Perhaps I should have switched oncologists. My doctor thought I asked too many questions. Most of his patients were older and more resigned and did not make demands on him for information. He had the classical pat on the head for me. But when people tell you a doctor is the best there is, you assume you are endangering your life to go elsewhere. Now I think a different, equally qualified person would have made the process more tolerable.

I had felt so differently about my surgeon, who was an excellent doctor and sensitive to my concerns. Funny, but he was more intimate with me than any lover because he had his hands inside my body close to my heart. I even had a couple of sexual dreams about him. I couldn't believe I'd be attracted to a man who wore polyester pants, but yet, my God, look what we had been through together!

While I was going through all this, I needed all the information I could get my hands on, especially the emotional and sexual dynamics of breast cancer and breast loss. I had so many questions that I kept asking and not finding answers. I didn't question my doctor's ability or knowledge; I just asked questions he'd never dealt with. But I didn't push too far because I wanted my doctor to be nice to me and take good care of me. There were a couple of nurses I spoke to who were a little helpful, but ultimately there was nobody capable of answering my questions. Information wasn't coming from the medical world. It's amazing. These medical people are dealing with you for two years, as you experience incredible changes as a woman, and they don't say *anything* about the possible impact on your life. Their reality is, at least you are not dead. They can deal with questions of the dying, not the living. I was dealing with both the fear of dying and warting some help in living.

To make myself feel better during chemo, I did some visualization techniques on my own. I couldn't imagine little white knights gobbling up the bad-guy cancer cells, so I worked with imagery from the field of photography. Light became my healing symbol. I felt it had power within me. It's what I am always drawn to and what my work is created from. I also used the image of a garden I was tending: clearing, weeding, and recycling the unwanted growth into nourishment for new flowers.

About a month after my diagnosis, I began writing poetry and kept a journal of my frequent nightmares and dreams. My first dreams introduced me to the death figure. In one dream, David and I were lying in bed and I saw a black-gloved hand at the window. Someone was trying to break into our house with a tripod and a camera/gun combination. David got up and tried to smash through the window at him. I reached for the telephone to call the police and got a recording. By this time, the figure was in the house. At first, he was going to let David buy him off; then he looked at me and changed his mind and took out white rubber gloves with red and black dots. He was going to rape and murder me and photograph the whole thing. I challenged him, "You're just a dumb kid, trying to take pictures of all these dead women so you can have a major exhibition. Big deal." He gave up and went away.

This black figure in time became less threatening to me, and eventually he became seductive, teasing me and trying to get me to talk with him in my dreams. My interest in him increased and he became familiar, almost an ally of mine. In some dreams, I actually became him.

I tried to give myself emotional treats in between chemo treatments. I took little trips to the mudbaths, had massages, and bought lots of clothes because I felt like spending money. I felt I deserved it because of all I had been through, plus I thought, "I may not be around to do this next year." Sometimes the clothes shopping felt good; other times it was depressing. I never knew what to do if a saleslady walked into the dressing room while I was trying things on. I avoided group dressing rooms. Occasionally, an older saleslady would say, "My God, that happened to me twenty years ago," and she'd tell me her breast cancer story. Other times, I was protective of myself and wouldn't let anyone in the dressing room.

I rearranged the way I dressed. Growing up in the sixties, I was used to wearing T-shirts and tank tops with no bra. I couldn't quite pull that off anymore, unless I was with friends. I went through an experimentation phase of what looked good on me. I found I couldn't bring myself to walk around in a tank top with one breast moving and nothing moving on the other side. So I wore tank tops with an open shirt over them, tied at the waist. Or I'd wear a shirt with the top few buttons undone so there was a suggestion of cleavage. I never had much cleavage anyway. It was funny that there was nothing to reveal and yet the hint of the undone buttons suggested otherwise.

On the one hand, I felt quite good and didn't want to hide anything, so I didn't mind that I looked different. On the other hand, I didn't want to be so obvious that it was the only thing people would look at. I thought everybody was looking. I certainly was. I have over time been less concerned about how I look and pretty much wear anything I want. An aunt of mine who had a mastectomy after me said, "Nobody notices, and if they do, they're fascinated."

Recently, I was on a walk wearing a slinky T-shirt and a couple of teenage kids whistled at me. It tickles me. I always think to myself, "You jerks, there is only one, you know." Sex is really all in your mind anyway.

During all these operations and treatment, I had a frustrating time with mothering because my children needed to be taken care of and so did I. I wished my mother could have spent more time with me, but she didn't live close by and was needed at her home. But she called and wrote frequently. She hired some household help for me, which was nice, but my children still wanted and needed me. I felt very close to them and at the same time terribly guilty for my short temper and anger at their demands. I'd think, "Oh God, here I am, maybe dying, and I am spending all my time shouting at them. What could be worse?" I missed the feeling of holding a child to my missing breast. I couldn't have them comfortably lean against me. It felt bony and hurt.

At first the kids kept their distance from me, but then came closer and closer. Since my husband and I were pretty open about our bodies around them, my operation did not change that. We told them why I was in the hospital, and shortly after surgery, I showed them my scar. My daughter kissed the scar because, she said, "It was an 'owie.' " Her act of love and acceptance moved me so and still does. I think it's good for children to know about this process because it can happen to anybody. It could happen to somebody they love; it could happen to my daughter.

When I first came home from the hospital, David was very affectionate, warm, and protective. He was never freaked out by the physical aspects of my disease. Our lovemaking was tender, really. I don't ever remember thinking he would leave me and we never even talked about it. I knew it was okay. I would hope that I hadn't married a man who would leave because of a lost breast.

Having loving male friends come see me helped too. We had close friends, Gerald and Anne. When I was in the hospital, Gerald came alone to see me. It was one of the greatest gifts he could have given me, not to come hiding behind his wife because this is a woman's disease. He came and said, "You are beautiful and I love you." I was so touched. Another time, one night when I was totally wiped out and couldn't sleep, a male nurse came to my room with tea and toast and talked with me. It turned out he had been a cancer patient too. It was those small moments that meant so much to me and reinforced that I was okay.

However, as time went on, David's and my relationship did not fare well. His attitude was, "We're going to make it all right," which worked for him but not particularly well for me. His need to be an "us"—a unit—was very strong. Even though I needed help, I also wanted to be independent.

Suddenly my perspective on life was very different because of cancer. I had a tremendous zest and hunger for life. During chemo, I really didn't want to do anything except what was really important to me. I couldn't just focus on us. I wanted to meet life head on, be alive and experience everything! I wanted to meet new people and become my own person again. David wanted to be the only one to fill my needs. Maybe he couldn't give enough to me; maybe I didn't want it from him. In any event, it wasn't working. I also was surrounded by a very strong women's network consisting of mostly single parents. They provided me with tremendous nurturing and caring, helped me with the kids, and were always available. I began to feel that they were doing things for me and the children that David wasn't.

I sought out other relationships, placing myself in a number of difficult situations, sexually, which I don't think I would have gotten into but for the cancer and the risks of having chemo. I was testing out everything, thinking, "What have I got to lose?" My sense of sexuality during chemo was briefly heightened too, due to one of the drugs I was taking. I was on tamoxifen, which made me feel constantly premenstrual and horny. After stopping the drugs, these side effects disappeared.

What really surprised me was how sensitive my scar tissue was to touch, especially when the skin was new. At first the scar was numb over a very large area but then the feeling came back. I found being stroked in this area was wonderful. It tingled and was quite erotic. These sensations seemed to come out of nowhere and numbness.

Out of all this experimenting, I developed an intense sexual relationship with a woman friend, Marianna. This relationship, which started about eight months after surgery, had a great deal to do with my healing process. It allowed me to get away from everybody else's needs. It was a place where I could be loved just for me, and cared about with no strings attached and no responsibilities. It was almost like a vacation, a major time-out. I felt I needed that after all my pain and suffering. I wanted to do something kind for my body. I was driven and remember thinking I could not say no to this woman and this relationship. I thought, "Well, even if David finds out about this, my involvement with a woman isn't as bad as if it were with a man." Not true, by the way.

I had never been sexually involved with a woman before. I didn't view myself as gay then or now. I do believe much of it had to do with breast cancer and what it had done to me. I needed so much. All the nurturing and caring that many women automatically seem to give was forthcoming from my lover. She mothered me, yes, and gave me a kind of unconditional love that seems so important to healing.

It was incredibly erotic and necessary for me. The relationship I had with Marianna was so wonderful in its intensity and body satisfaction. It was also as if I were reclaiming my breast when we were together. I didn't know whose body was whose and where mine ended and hers began. There wasn't anybody else who could touch me and make me feel okay at that time but her. It was a life force that was not only part of my healing process but also part of my grieving process.

I really believe that in loving her and her body, I was living and mourning something I had lost. In trying to explain my behavior, David later said, "Oh, your mother wasn't nurturing enough so you needed a mother." David's statement really infuriated me. Although I am sure there are elements of truth in what he said, the fact is, the experience helped me get to know and value my body again. It was like holding up a mirror to myself.

I also had a couple of experiences with men because I wanted to see if I was still attractive and desirable. One time I got involved with a guide on a hiking trip. He started flirting with me and I flirted with him. I had never done this before and it seemed such a male thing to do. I became the aggressor, stalking this man all day. I knew we were going to make love before the day was out, and I decided it was okay because I'd never see him again. I wondered how I was going to tell him I only had one breast. Later in the day we went for a walk together and ended up in his tent, taking off our clothes. He mentioned that he was accident-prone and had a lot of scars, and I said, "Well, you know I have a couple of scars I want to tell you about—umm—a mastectomy." He kept on taking off his clothes and said one of his mother's friends had had one too. It turned out to be a positive experience for me because he confirmed that my new body was okay.

My fantasy during this time was that soon my relationship with Marianna would end and then I would come back to David. It didn't happen, but that was my fantasy. Though it drove me crazy to be in both relationships at once, I really needed them. Looking back, I really don't know how I ever managed to sustain all that activity.

All during my treatment, I was in therapy. Then I asked David to join me in some sessions. I told him about Marianna. He, of course, did not understand. He couldn't tolerate or bear the situation and said he would stay with me until chemo ended, a year from when I told him. Getting back to a normal life with David did not occur. Therapy didn't help us and my relationship with Marianna did taper off, but according to my schedule, not his.

I finished chemo in January 1983 and David moved out in April 1983. I really thought the separation would be temporary. Though I didn't want him to leave, I also could not say that I wanted him to stay. I did not want to get divorced. We had been together for so long and I thought, "People survive wars and we could grow through the pain." I wanted time to get beyond cancer. But it never worked out that way, and though we tried to make it work, we were unsuccessful.

It still took another three years to get divorced after that. Having cancer was like a rehearsal for the pain of divorce that followed. I can't say that my marriage broke up because of breast cancer; it's not that simple. The children now live with me and David sees them regularly. We still share a primary concern—our children. I wish it could have turned out differently for them, because I don't want them to think when things get tough it's okay to leave the scene.

It's been three years since my chemo treatments ended. At first, it's hard to stop thinking, "I am a cancer patient," because for a long time you think about it all day, every day. Then I'd go for days without thinking about cancer and mastectomies. I might even be undressed and pass by a mirror and not stop and stare. All of a sudden cancer became a small part of my consciousness, which is really amazing because somehow I thought that would never happen.

There have been some long-term side effects from the chemotherapy that have affected my sex life. There had been more physical changes postchemo than during treatment in some ways. Everyone tells you about the short-term effects: hair loss, vomiting, and weight changes. But no one says, "Five years from now you might still be having trouble going to bed with someone." I have severe estrogen deprivation due to drug-induced menopause. There is no way doctors are going to give me, a breast cancer patient, estrogen supplements. Having sexual intercourse is sometimes very painful—it feels as if I am going to split. Even using lubricants, the tissues are sensitive and raw. It starts chafing and I have to tell my partner to stop. It's awful. I feel much more vulnerable about this than about the mastectomy. It is much more difficult to tell a new lover about how painful intercourse is, as compared to telling him I have one breast.

I went to a gynecologist to see if there was something besides lubricants that could help me. He suggested I use a rubber dilator twenty minutes every day. But it feels silly and I have only used the thing once. I suppose if I become seriously involved with someone, it will become an active issue for me. My hope is that I will get involved with somebody whom I can really trust and who cares enough about me to work it out together. Though I haven't had a serious relationship since my divorce, I have dated a number of men and no one has ever been disturbed by my breast loss.

Right now I am on a sexual sabbatical. First, because I am much more protective of myself and more cautious and selective about partners. Even if everything were easy sexually, I would be hesitant to get into a heavy relationship. There is so little space in my life for others because of my work and taking care of my children. For a while I considered joining an arts groups for singles or answering an ad by a man looking for an "Amazon Warrior." Did he really know what he was asking for? I fit the bill.

Marianna and I maintain a slightly awkward friendship. I ended the sexual nature of our relationship before my divorce. I wanted to grow on my own and didn't want to keep secrets from my children. Nor was I committed to "coming out." I still have close friends, both male and female, and think it is important for my children to know a variety of adults and role models.

The children are now seven and eleven years old, and we have a good relationship. The worst time for mothering was when David left, as I was struggling, hurting, and angry. I also didn't have much time left for the kids because I had to go back to work full-time as a photographer, and since I had been out of my profession for a few years, I didn't know if I'd be paid enough to support the three of us. I took on a second job teaching. But now we have developed a life together. We camp and hike a lot and discover ways of doing things that don't cost too much money. We are a family, the three of us.

I think I am a better and stronger person because of breast cancer and, therefore, probably a better mother. Through all of this I feel more in touch at a very deep level with my femaleness and my womanness. I appreciate women far more than I used to. I used to spout feminist rhetoric, which is easy to do when you are safe. But now I don't have such a safe life, and I have a much greater, truer understanding of what it means to be a woman. I feel very closely bonded to my daughter and see and feel more of the continuity of the generations of my grandmother, my mother, me, and my daughter.

I have concerns for my daughter's future. She does too. Sometimes she can't go to sleep because she is afraid of cancer. Other times she is unconcerned. I certainly don't hush it up and say it will never happen to her because I can't say that. We talk a lot. I tell her that breast cancer is a concern for many women, and because of me, when she is older, she'll be that much more careful, doing breast self-examination and having regular checkups. I've told her when she starts growing breasts I will show her how to examine her breasts. Every so often she'll say, "Tell me again, Mom, why did you have your breast cut off?" I'll explain the whole thing even though she's heard it a million times. My basic explanation is that there was a bad lump in my breast, and if the breast hadn't been removed, it would have spread and made the rest of my body very sick. So the bad part had to come off. The important thing for her to know is that I am now well because I had a mastectomy.

Even though I have deepened feelings about my identity as a woman, I feel more *human* because going through an experience like this transcends gender. In some ways you could say that I feel more of a man for having gone through this. Breast cancer put me more in touch with the androgynous side of me. Maybe I am more of a man in terms of strength because of my scar. A man's scar is a sign of virility, proof that he has been through something that has made him stronger. A man can be proud of his scars. I look at my mastectomy scar that way instead of thinking of it as something ugly.

I enjoy the body I have now, though it's aging faster than I would like. It was important after my surgery to be attractive and still be considered desirable and to prove it. Now I am more interested in getting on with my life, rather than checking myself out in the mirror all the time. I feel attractive and I think one looks how one feels.

Cancer changed the circumstances of my life so much. But I would never say I wish I hadn't gone through it. I value this experience immensely. I hope I don't have to go through it again but don't think I would be so afraid if I did. Though I gained much from this, I also lost some very important things: my marriage and my breast. I got back part of my soul.

As a result of breast cancer, I am a stronger woman and more self-determined. I care less about others' opinions. I feel content and yet am still very open to adventure. I am more concerned about having enough space for myself, so that I can be available in the long run for others. I am more nurturing now toward adults than I ever was before. I find myself reaching out to people who are going through something traumatic by trying to be there for them. I feel a strong drive to give something back. I can never repay those people who helped me so much, but I can pass on the love they gave me to somebody else who really needs it. It's one hell of a journey.

7

Terri

"Throughout my whole cancer experience, I felt there were teachings for me. I never would have *chosen* to be taught this way but I like the changes in me. I guess I had to go to the edge to get there. It transformed me."

In late 1983, Terri, thirty-six years old and single, found a lump in her breast that was diagnosed as a stage two breast cancer with lymph node involvement. She underwent a modified radical mastectomy and immediate breast reconstruction. She was given six months of chemotherapy treatments, which ended in the fall of 1984. From the beginning of her experience, Terri became an active and persistent participant in her treatment plans. She was an information seeker: researching, reading, meeting with doctors, and weighing the pros and cons of the different treatment options. Despite the cultural biases she confronted about plastic surgery, Terri chose to have immediate breast reconstruction following her mastectomy. As a result of the adverse side effects of her chemotherapy, Terri reached out to other cancer patients for information and emotional support. Recognizing the powerful effect that support had on her own and others' recovery, Terri became committed to helping other cancer patients through the often lonely experience of diagnosis and treatment.

*M*y brother and I were basically raised by my mother because my father, an army officer, was away on assignments for months at a time. His job changed so often that we moved almost every year until I was fifteen years old. So my mother was really a single parent who was, in the best sense of the word, a wonderful homemaker. She knew how to make a home a home, no matter where we were living, whether it was Hawaii, California, or Japan. Mom also knitted and made clothes, cooked food for marvelous dinner parties of twenty, and always made holidays and birthdays special. Having that sense of home was really important when you moved around a lot.

Because Mom provided us with a sense of continuity, I had a very grounded childhood. She was strict but fair and loved us unconditionally, as opposed to my father whose love was very conditional. She wasn't physically demonstrative but we always knew we were loved. My brother and I were both very close to her. This was particularly important because my father was a very heavy drinker. Every time he returned home, he would disrupt our family life. Dad wanted to be the classic military father: ordering us around and expecting obedience, but it never turned out that way. We were too used to being without him. It was always a readjustment when he came home and a relief when he left.

When I was younger I always wanted to be and look like my mother. She was a beautiful, blue-eyed blonde with an incredible hourglass figure and large breasts, which embarrassed her. Unfortunately, I didn't look anything like her. I had brown hair and was thin.

But as I got older I changed my mind about being like my mom. I didn't want to be like her because she was smothered by my father and never stood up for herself. All I saw was her pain and I didn't want to suffer like that. From about the age of twelve, I told her to leave my dad and she actually tried two or three times. But she didn't have any outside support, financially or emotionally, to do it successfully. She finally got a divorce when she was fifty-two while I was in college.

When my dad was gone, life for me was fairly normal. When I became twelve, my girlfriends and I became more interested in boys and the development of our bodies than we were in studying. We were very excited about getting our periods. My mother had told me everything about the topic in a positive way and I really wanted it *badly*! When my mother was young, no one talked to her and she thought she was dying when she got her period. Finally, when I was thirteen, the big event occurred. About that time, too, my breasts started to sprout. I thought, "Oh boy! I'm going to look like Mom." But it didn't turn out that way. But even though my breasts weren't big, I was proud of them. I liked showing them off in understated ways but was never the type to wear tight sweaters.

As a teenager, I was basically a good kid with a rebellious, wild side that emerged from time to time. I was very bright but I was never the kid with the 4.0 and glasses. I didn't hide the fact that I was smart. God, I was opinionated even then. Even though I was a popular person in high school and always had older boyfriends, I didn't think I was very attractive. For starters, I thought feminine meant being petite and I was large and tall. Then a bump developed on my nose and kids started to call me names like "Hook," which was so devastating to my growing and shaky self-esteem. So in tenth grade I had a nose job, which was a big deal back then. I started thinking I was cuter after that.

I still remember poring over millions of *Seventeen* magazines trying to figure out what a woman was because I had no idea! One article I read tried to teach flirting and I wasn't at all successful. I'd try to dress up and act like the popular girls acted—you know, a little helpless, a little flirtatious and coy—but it just always came out wrong with me. I was a tomboy with an adventuresome spirit, who wanted to play with my brother and his friends but who also liked wearing dresses. I wanted the freedom of being a boy and the luxury of being a girl, but I was aware from an early age that there were restrictions on my behavior as a girl. I didn't think that was fair, ever.

When it came to dating, my parents were strict. My father basically wanted to lock me up until I turned twenty-one. When he was home, he wanted no part of my dating and wouldn't even meet the guys. My mother would interview (grill) the boys, making sure she knew exactly what was going on. The message I got was, you'd better be a virgin when you get married.

Another message I got was that women didn't have careers. In spite of this, when I was in high school I wanted to be a psychiatrist. A counselor told me, "Oh, you don't want to go to medical school." She convinced me I wouldn't perform well in medical school. Since I was always helpful to others in school, I thought I would be a psychologist because I was the person everybody came to with their problems. But it was clear to me I planned on working when I grew up. I didn't want to be stuck like my mother.

The first years of high school were total agony for me and the worst time of my life. For the first time in years, my father was stationed at home for a three-year period. The family almost broke up then because my father was drinking heavily and had become a nasty drunk, not physically, but verbally violent. I was yelled at a lot and used to believe what he said to me during those times. Later I learned that my experience growing up in an alcoholic family was typical, but at the time I didn't realize it. Because I was unhappy, I questioned the meaning of life a lot at that point. I felt lonely in my search in that no one wanted to talk to me about it.

To escape the confusion and pain at home, I convinced my parents I wasn't happy at the local school and got shipped off to a girls' boarding school my junior year. This plan backfired because I hated the new school. The teachers told us what to do every minute and I had trouble accepting authority. I came back home again and spent my senior year at the local high school.

After graduation in 1965, I began my freshman year of college. Going to college in the late sixties suited my personality perfectly. I had always been a challenger. In growing up, I always felt at war with injustice. My mother said I was born like this. At age four, I questioned the reasons for Alcatraz when we drove by it. If one kid was being picked on, I would be there, risking life and limb to save him. Not surprisingly, I was politically active during college, especially after Bobby Kennedy was shot, and was involved with many causes: Vietnam, civil rights, and the women's movement. Throughout college I still searched for who I was. I knew one thing: I didn't want to be like my mother who had made a career of being an unhappy military wife. She was kind and loving to me but she had no identity of her own. I wasn't sure what I wanted but knew I rejected the old female model. Sexism disturbed me greatly.

During my sophomore year in college, I was introduced to the realities of sex by getting pregnant by my boyfriend. It was clear that we were not going to get married. Abortion was illegal at that time and I didn't know what to do. So I called my mother. She was very nonjudgmental and said, "This is your decision and one that you are going to have to live with. I will support whatever decision you make." She came with me to Mexico when I had the abortion. I know it was very hard for her to go with me, given her upbringing and background. We never told my father. We kept most things from my father actually. I felt sad about having the abortion but never regretted my decision.

After graduating from college in 1969, I spent the next seven years working in social welfare programs and traveling in Europe. I finally settled down in San Diego, working as a community organizer. During this time I was involved in a long-term relationship with a man named Nick. Though I was very much in love with him, he was into drugs, and when I got pregnant by him in 1977, it was the beginning of the end for us. I wasn't ready to settle down and knew I was never going to be the homemaker type. So we went through counseling and I had an abortion. We broke up soon after that.

When my relationship with Nick ended, I decided to leave town for a while to start afresh. I moved to Oregon for two years and worked again in the social welfare system, but I was burned out after working so many years with such hopeless people. There had been a growing emptiness and loneliness in me from my mid-twenties—a black empty void—that continued to plague me. My self-image was not really good and I hadn't learned how to take care of myself. Even before I moved to Oregon, I had started drinking to fill the loneliness with wine, lots of wine. Nick and I had been a perfect combination: He was doing drugs and I was drinking. I think from the very first time I started to drink I was concerned because of my father's history. I am sure I had a genetic predisposition to alcoholism. Obviously, I wasn't concerned enough to realize the damage it was doing to me. I also hung around with drinking people—others who looked worse than me—so I could kid myself that other people were drinking much more than I was. This is really a sign of alcoholism.

In 1983, the year before my diagnosis, I was still feeling very bad. I started to think more and more about how out of balance my life was, not only from the drinking but emotionally. The void just seemed to be getting bigger. Work was not as challenging anymore. My answers in the past had been found in work and in causes. I had a lot of anger in me. I wasn't dating anyone. I wanted something different in my life and decided to get my master's degree in teaching, and through some financial support from my family, enrolled in a program. At this time I looked okay and wasn't drinking on a daily basis. However, when I did drink I started having blackouts.

I started going to Alcoholics Anonymous but wasn't ready to surrender to the whole thing. I intellectually battled it as many alcoholics do, saying, "It's okay for them, but not for me." To take this simple program to heart was too simple for me; I was too bright, I thought. So I went in and out of AA. Then I had gum surgery, which involved a growth in my mouth that was tested for cancer. Waiting for the test results, I got drunk. I was more afraid than I had ever been in my whole life. It was not cancer. A close call.

Soon after that, on an October day, I was sitting in my living room coming off a hangover, watching my gynecologist on a local talk show talking about breast self-examination. I thought, "Oh God, I have an appointment coming up and she's going to ask me, 'Have you been doing breast exams?' " Maybe I did it once every three or four months. So I did the exam along with the TV instructions, and lo and behold, there it was. I found a lump. I shivered with sheer terror. It was the most all-encompassing terror I had ever known and there was no question in my mind it was cancer.

I didn't know anything about breast cancer except that Betty Ford and Happy Rockefeller had had it. I just knew I had it; it didn't matter if I was only thirty-six years old. I proceeded to get a bottle of wine and get drunk. I remember crying and thinking, "Oh my God, I don't want to screw around anymore and I can't, I won't, go through cancer dealing with alcoholism. It's too much to ask of my body. Cancer's going to be hard enough. I can't do it."

I now knew I had to stop drinking—I had had three-month sobriety periods before—but this was to be total surrender. I remember thinking, "I will go through this with as much courage and dignity as I can, if my compulsion to drink is removed." It was. I just quit drinking that day. That was the last time I took a drink, three years ago on October 1. That's now my AA birthday.

My decision to stop drinking was really a minor miracle because I hadn't yet had the lump checked out. When I went to my gynecologist she said, "Hummm, I think you should go see a surgeon but don't forget that 80 percent of the lumps are benign." Yeah. I made an appointment with a recommended surgeon, Dr. Callahan. I was worried about this visit, because I didn't trust or respect the medical establishment very much and thought Western medicine dealt only with symptoms and sickness, and had nothing to do with health. Moreover, I had an image of some man cutting off my breast. I went into the surgeon in a feisty, defensive mood, actually on the offensive, filled with a week's worth of readings on breast cancer. He did a needle aspiration. There wasn't enough tissue in the sample for a definitive diagnosis but he said it looked suspicious. We had to do a biopsy.

I had the biopsy as an outpatient, surrounded and supported by my friends from AA. Even though I was expecting to hear it was cancer, that didn't mean I almost didn't faint when the doctor told me it *was* cancer. Immediately I told Dr. Callahan, "Okay, by law, you are supposed to tell me all the options for my treatment." He nodded, said he knew what the law was, and gave me the options: lumpectomy and radiation, modified mastectomy, or a modified with immediate reconstruction. My immediate gut reaction was, "You can forget the mastectomy right now; I am not having a mastectomy." I was feeling my feminist oats: "I am not going to believe that this *has* to happen. I am going to learn about this and *I* will determine the outcome." He told me to take some time to think about it; I had time. How much time? He said a week; I said three; he said you can have two weeks. We compromised. After leaving the doctor's office, I walked to the elevator with my friends and told them I had cancer. They asked if I was okay. I said I was fine and then my knees collapsed, and my eyes welled up with tears and I thought, "Oh, maybe I am not fine." I was in shock.

For the next two weeks, I searched for any information on breast cancer I could find. I asked my gynecologist for suggestions on who to contact and talked to a reconstructive surgeon, an oncologist, and a radiotherapist. I interviewed breast cancer patients and read the books on breast cancer and then attempted to sift through all this information and digest it. I did this all in a state of shock. There was an added problem of my having no medical insurance because I had been in the process of changing careers. I was in school; I had thought, who needed it? I was healthy and young, right? Much of that two-week time was spent trying to get insurance and seeing if my parents could get the money together for me. Thanks to my doctors, I was put on emergency medical insurance.

In my search for answers I met Dr. Sanger, a reconstructive surgeon, and the minute I saw him I felt at peace, trusting him intuitively and instantly, which rarely happens. He said he could do a mastectomy and immediate reconstruction. Because I trusted him, I thought maybe it was safer to have a mastectomy and reconstruction. I figured if they could make a breast for me, why not? I really thought if I had a mastectomy the cancer would be all gone. Then I would put it behind me. One big surgery and it's finished—huh! No more fear of recurrence! I didn't know then that you always live with the fear of recurrence.

I finally made my decision, based on emotions, facts, and fears. I didn't think I could live with radiation because it scared me. In addition, no one seemed to know the long-term effects of radiation on somebody my age. I decided to have a mastectomy and immediate reconstruction. I thought if I did the immediate reconstruction, my body would still be whole—different, but whole. I don't know if I would have picked the mastectomy if the reconstruction didn't go along with it. Not that immediate reconstruction surgery was easy. There were multiple surgeries to undergo.

The whole week before the surgery, I said good-bye to my breast. From the moment I found the lump I held my breast a lot, remembering what an important part of me it was. I liked my breasts and had wonderful years loving them. There were many years I went braless, feeling free and loving the way my body was. I got a lot of pleasure out of my breasts sexually, erotically, sensually, and visually. But they didn't define me any more than any part of my body defines me. I would say if anything could have defined me, it would have been my mind. I still lived more in my mind than in my body. Many women think, "Oh my God, the worst thing that could happen to me is to lose a breast." To me, the worst thing would be to lose my mind. But we never know what the worst is, do we? You live through what you get dealt.

So it was okay to lose my breast. It was sad and I was sad. I don't remember worrying that I was going to be deformed because I was having reconstruction. I'd met twice with the plastic surgeon before my mastectomy and knew what was going to happen. What was most important to me was that the cancer would be gone. If I lost a breast and the cancer was gone, then it would be fine. I kept telling myself I was going to get through it all, that this was just one little crisis. I was not drinking and that was really important. I had more support from my community of family and friends than I ever imagined possible.

I had a modified radical and the lymph nodes removed under my arm. Unfortunately, after the surgery I had excruciating pain even though I was on morphine. Due to alcoholism, my response to drugs was totally different than most people's and it took a great deal more to kill my pain. Since I had not gone through any withdrawal from quitting drinking, I guess that was my payment. We waited—it seemed forever—for the test results. I had two positive lymph nodes and it was a stage two cancer, which meant that the cancer wasn't gone. Of course, more treatment was needed—chemotherapy—my life was more at risk and my breast loss was suddenly not very important. I really cried for the first time that night.

After learning that I had to have chemo, I hit a low point during my stay in the hospital. Then an old friend whose wife, Debbie, had died from breast cancer came to visit me. I told him I needed chemotherapy and was feeling kind of sorry for myself. He said, "Listen, I want you to know chemotherapy was never an option for Debbie, and if it had been, maybe she would be alive today. There are a lot of women who weren't given the gift of chemotherapy, a lot of women who went before you. You are being given that gift, so on behalf of other women, please look at it as a lifesaving gift to you." What he said just flipped it right around for me. Any doubts I had about chemo and really feeling sorry for myself left in that moment.

My next step was to meet with a recommended oncologist about chemotherapy. I didn't oncology-shop because I trusted my medical team and they said this doctor was one of the best. I also didn't have the energy anymore to look around. But, as usual, I read books on chemo before I met Dr. Peters. Dr. Peters wanted me to start chemo in two weeks' time, I started asking him a million questions, and he told me to shut up until he was finished, because if I didn't listen I wouldn't hear. Smart man. Go home and heal; then we'll talk.

I went to my mother's home to recuperate. Mom was supportive, strong, loving, and terrified, trying very hard not to show how scared she was—but I knew. I found myself always saying I was fine, trying to make others feel fine. I spent the next three weeks sleeping and reading all the books on breast cancer I could. I was most interested in how other women got through the experience of breast cancer. I remember learning so much from Rose Kushner's book (*Alternatives: New Developments in the War on Breast Cancer*, Warner Books). I was railing against the lack of information given to me about this experience from the medical profession.

On my first visit after surgery to Dr. Sanger, the plastic surgeon, I had all the bandages removed, which was really the first time I had seen my chest since the surgery. I looked at it and thought, "Ahhhh, my God, my breast is gone," and tried to remain calm and cool. There was only a tiny breast mound in its place. I left the office with my mom and in the elevator my knees buckled and I passed out. Dr. Sanger said later I was on emotional overload. I didn't think; I just reacted. Then, later in the afternoon, Mom and I went to see *Terms of Endearment*, not knowing what it was about. Halfway through the movie Mom turned to me, "I am so sorry. I didn't know this was about breast cancer." But you know, it was good because it was the first time I really cried about having breast cancer. It was okay to have breast cancer because it was in the movie. It was okay to cry.

Over the next year, 1984, breast cancer seemed like my entire life. Three weeks after surgery I started chemotherapy, six months of Cytoxan, methotrexate, 5-FU, and tamoxifen, and the saline injections began in my tissue expander for my breast reconstruction. Chemo was so foreign to me. I made the mistake of looking up my drugs in the *Physicians' Desk Reference* and they all said, "Warning—toxic—death—if administered improperly." With the first chemo treatment I felt as if I gave up total control of what was going on in my life. I thought I would pass out the minute I got the injection. After the first time, I also started looking and waiting for the side effects because I'd read all about them.

The second time I had some nausea but I learned how to deal with that by keeping food in my stomach. Boy, did I keep a lot of food in my stomach. By the third treatment, my hair was thinning, though I never lost all of my hair. I was terrified of hair loss, thinking I would be ugly. I didn't want to suffer another loss. Then I noticed my eyelashes were coming out! So I went to the store and bought false eyelashes. I didn't have a clue on how to put them on and never did.

Then other side effects started happening. I used to call the third day after chemo, "the chemo blues." It happened so regularly with each treatment, I knew it was caused by chemo. Knowing this helped because it meant *I* wasn't depressed; it was a drug-induced mood, which meant it would leave me. So it wasn't that bad.

After three months I noticed that my comprehension abilities were almost gone. It would take me twenty minutes to read a paragraph in a book, and even then I didn't understand it and couldn't remember it. I couldn't think of words. I got really, really annoyed that I couldn't think. I prided myself on my intelligence and I couldn't even think.

After my second treatment my periods stopped and I started getting horrible hot flashes and night sweats. It was like being on constant premenstrual syndrome. Here I was, menopausal at age thirty-six. I kept hoping my periods would come back but they didn't. It's said one can deal with individual losses well, and then one will come up and pow, *all* the losses are relived. Menopause snuck up on me like that. It wasn't just that I couldn't have children; it was also that my body was aging before its time. It was changing *again* and it was out of my control. Not only do I lose a breast, but my vagina dries up, my skin ages, and my bones get brittle? I was really angry. But I also accepted that chemo offered me the best chance for recovery.

Then I started to gain weight, 20 to 25 pounds. I felt that I looked horrible. I was heavy and had no energy. I could gain 5 pounds in a weekend without changing my food consumption. The weight gain affected me more seriously than the breast loss. Maybe I was experiencing a cumulative sense of, "Oh my God, who is this person?" The self-image and self-esteem problems that occurred with my weight gain were the worst things for me about my breast cancer experience.

I gained where I had never gained weight before in my life—my upper arms looked like those of a weight lifter's. My neck and waist got thick. Even my calves gained weight! "Oh my God, what *is* happening to me?" I kept thinking I should be able to stop the weight gain. Was I now to be blamed for something else? Why did I crave cheeseburgers and ice cream when I never ate them before?

Finally, I talked with other breast cancer patients who had the same crazy food habits and were gaining weight too. I was not told to expect this problem because at the time there wasn't a lot of knowledge about how chemo affects weight. The doctors kept explaining my weight gain away by saying I was more inactive and undergoing hormonal changes, and "Oh, a little extra weight is healthy for you now." I did my own research and finally found a couple of nursing journal articles that documented weight gain in women who were given CMF chemotherapy. I felt better knowing that I wasn't to blame for the weight gain.

When I was going through chemotherapy, I was helped tremendously by going to a seminar by Steven Levine. Finally, someone who was willing to talk about cancer and fear of death and how to handle it. I finally felt I was in the right place. I told him about my problems with chemo. "What you need to do," he suggested, "is visualize the chemo helping you. You don't have to do the armies killing off cancer cells scene. Just don't put your body at war with itself; rather see chemo as helping you to get well. It's part of you coming in to help you." After that, I didn't look at chemo as this horrible thing I had to put up with.

At the beginning of chemo, I isolated myself from everyone. I just wanted to curl up and take care of myself. I didn't date or have any relationships during chemo although there were male friends in my life. Though I had a very strong support group, I had a lot of trouble asking for help. Are you kidding, *I* didn't need that! I thought of myself as Wonder Woman. Somebody told me, if I got graded for cancer, I would have gotten an A. I put on the famous, "I'm okay," because the few times I said, "I am not okay," I noticed people had a low tolerance for that. Also I didn't want the, "Oh, poor Terri routine." I wanted acknowledgment, not pity.

I started talking to other women who were going through chemotherapy. We'd developed a phone support network. It was the most important component of my recovery—talking to other breast cancer patients. Also because I attended tumor board meetings and was becoming quite knowledgeable about breast cancer, I shared information with them. Since I was a few months ahead of others in treatment, I told them that when they got depressed, for instance, that was a normal cancer experience. Nobody ever says to you, "This is a normal cancer experience." Probably because the whole experience is abnormal!

I believe we have funny ideas about how we should get through a cancer experience. There seems to be no place for depression, anger, tears, or burdening family and friends. Therefore, cancer patients don't feel they have permission to talk about these things. The expectation is that you are just a strong and wonderful person who tries to go right back to your life as if nothing is happening. We cancer patients believe we should behave that way. So when the depression, anger, and tears inevitably come, and when you get mad at family members who for the one hundredth time have sent you an article on some cure for cancer and you could stuff it down their throats, or when someone says, "Oh, you're so courageous, aren't you something," being able to share with other cancer patients becomes *crucially* important.

Other breast cancer patients understood me and wouldn't laugh whenever I thought a pain was another cancer. They wouldn't say, "Oh, you're a hypochondriac. Why don't you think positively or why do you think of the worst?" I used to think, why couldn't I *handle* all this? My friends said, "Why should you? Why don't you just use this time for healing? Stop listening to everybody else." I acknowledged that I was given this gift of time to heal and rest, a time to go inward, and I did. I finally decided that it was okay to do that.

All through chemo, I was very anxious to finish my reconstruction. I wanted a new breast so I could feel whole again. In fact, reconstruction gave me something to look forward to through my cancer experience. Even though surgery wasn't recommended, I pushed for the operation. Four months after I started chemo, my permanent implant was put in. A few months later I had the final surgery to put the areola and nipple on.

At first, the process was a wonderful curiosity to me; I was fascinated by the art and science of reconstructive surgery. I used the professional detachment way of learning, standing back and observing myself. While chemo was not so great, reconstruction was interesting and fun, even though it hurt and was painful. I looked forward to going to the doctor! Dr. Sanger was so important in that he made me feel we were in it together. He saw me and my breasts probably more than any other man has ever seen me. He did a lot for my self-esteem by telling me how attractive I was all the time. Other people would say, "Oh God, you look so good," but they didn't know. He *knew* what I looked like. I would have gone through more feelings about breast loss and feeling deformed if it wasn't for that man.

At the beginning, Dr. Sanger told me my new breast would not look like my natural breast. I thought, "Oh well, it will look great; I will have high firm breasts." Little by little, after I got out of fantasy land, I understood that medical science can only go so far, but the end result was okay with me. It's now hard for me even to remember what my breasts used to look like. But you know I never had to wear a prosthesis and deal with something foreign outside my body. It was only inside my body that there was something foreign.

It was a long, slow process in accepting my new breast, incorporating this foreign implant as part of my body. It was like adopting a child and making my reconstructive breast my own. I wasn't hiding in the closet with my new breast though. I showed it to women who were thinking about having the surgery. I'd say, "Look at this—isn't this amazing that they can do this?" I even showed my male friends how my breast looked at the different stages. Yet when my friend Shawn, who had seen me through the whole process asked, "Let me see the end result," I said, "No! I don't want to show it to you." He laughed at me and said, "Well, it's finally becoming your breast! So your natural modesty is back again." I was normally a very modest person. It wasn't okay for him to see my breast anymore. It was mine.

Though I was glad to be finished with reconstruction, I wasn't so sure about finishing chemo. When I first got breast cancer, I decided, why not do this with as much acceptance and class as I can? I didn't have much choice. I thought I'd give myself a year to go through chemo and reconstruction, but then that was it—one year out of my life and I would be back on track and normal. That was my theory. I thought I had grappled with life and death. But with the end of chemo came new fears. With no more chemo, I was afraid there were no drugs in me to fight the cancer anymore. All I could think was, "Oh my God, now my estrogen will start producing and then the cancer cells will find the estrogen receptors and it's *boom*—a recurrence!" By that time I knew from reading there were no tests to pick up microscopic cancers. I think I learned too much for my own good.

In the meantime everyone around me was saying, "Your cancer treatment is over. Go and enjoy life! Aren't you happy?" I wasn't. I was sad from cancer and I was not enjoying myself. I was not making something out of my life. I jumped off the deep end and went into a depression.

It was like posttraumatic shock syndrome. I had been dealing with everything so beautifully and gone through all the surgeries, chemo, and reconstruction. Finally, after it was all over, it was time to fall apart and that's what I did. Even the cancer state of feeling special was all gone. But I felt I had come so far and I wasn't willing to live my life in fear or let the depression get in my way. So I went into therapy, a therapeutic journey, for a year. I am so glad I did it. What I needed to hear constantly was the answer to, "What is insanity and what is having cancer? Why am I so scared? What is this terror? Are my feelings normal?" When you go through something like this, any unresolved issues in your life come right up to the surface, whether it's your childhood, parents, relationships, or yourself. Things you have always accepted in your life are no longer acceptable.

Confronting all these issues was very uncomfortable, scary at times, and somewhat lonely, but I learned how to deal with them and my aloneness. I had to find my own answers and realized I couldn't expect a relationship to save me or give my life meaning. I had to tough it out and learn to live with me alone, making sure I knew who me was. Finally, after a year, the fears started lifting. Surprisingly, I found that having a relationship was very low on my priority list but learning about what I really wanted out of life was high.

About the same time I was finishing therapy, I finally lost the 25 pounds I had gained with chemo. But one of the results of my weight loss was that my breasts no longer matched. I was living with it. I didn't think it bothered me until I went to see Dr. Sanger and he said, "There really is a difference in the size of your breasts." So this year, 1987, I had both my breasts redone so that they would match better. I did it knowing that it would be at the most a couple of weeks of pain, and then I would forget the pain and have the results I wanted. I think my match is very good now and I feel great about how I look too. When I stand in front of the mirror, I see a breast that has many scars. I am not ashamed of them but I don't feel like walking with a banner either. My reconstructed breast is rounder and firmer than my natural breast and the nipples are different. I can feel the skin, which is still my skin. In terms of a sexual response, there isn't a whole lot—a transplanted nipple is not connected to anything to make it feel. But it's a part of me and the important thing for me is I can wake up in the morning and put on a regular bra and forget about it. There is no way to tell I have had this surgery. The only other time I think about my breast is when I massage it in the morning. I have to do this to keep it from capsulating, hardening.

For me, having immediate reconstruction was something very positive I did for myself. My body and me feel more whole. Feeling your body is whole again is very important. It's not to look pretty or sexy; it is more basic than that. The thing that annoys me is how society treats women who choose to have reconstructive surgery. When I went through reconstruction, I came up against everybody's sexist attitudes, "Aren't you happy with yourself; aren't you just glad to be alive? Why do you have do this cosmetic surgery? You're vain to want this. Why don't you just accept the way you look? Why fix something that no one will notice?" Then people say things like, "I don't know how you could go through all that—I could never do what you did." There is this implicit statement that you are a fool to consider it.

Our cultural attitudes create a crazy-making situation for women. On the one hand, they tell you it's vain to want to look good, and on the other hand, they tell you without a breast and being whole, you are not attractive and sexually good. Why should women think they are vain to want to restore balance in their body? It has nothing to do with vanity. It has to do with wholeness. Why should we even have to explain this? What is most important is what a woman wants to do for herself. Our culture does not support catering to women's needs and wants. You would think that everyone could identify with what it must feel like to lose a body part and wanting it back. If someone is replacing an arm or a leg, nobody says it's cosmetic. It's restoring a body part. Up until a few years ago, Medi-Cal wouldn't pay for breast reconstruction because it was considered cosmetic surgery, but they would pay for penile implants. Do you think one man would ask another man, "Why would you want a penile implant?" No, they'd understand in two seconds. The medical insurance companies certainly did. The old social attitudes have not caught up with modern technology.

On the other hand, it is very important for some women *not* to have reconstruction. By accepting their one-breasted state, they reject what others say that we, as women, should or should not be like. Like not wearing bras or not shaving our legs. I think women traditionally have been very good about denying themselves their wants and needs, and not being decision makers in their lives. There were times when I went through this last reconstruction, when people asked me why I was putting myself through so much pain. I thought maybe they had a point; why was I doing all this? I asked Dr. Sanger if it all made sense. He said, "You tell them we're doing it 'til we get it right." My feeling is however you want to see your body and accept it, it's okay. We should have enough room in life not to be judgmental about each other. This is all a part of women learning how to care for themselves: taking back and owning their bodies again.

I feel differently about women now. I've always had women in my life, but after breast cancer I learned what friendship really meant, particularly because I wasn't involved in a relationship with a man. My life was so busy and cause-oriented before that I didn't have time to honor my friends *or* myself that much. There was too much to do and not enough time to be. My women friends taught me that I was acceptable the way I was.

At the time, I could not be the strong independent woman who could do everything herself. I really needed people more than ever and they were there for me. My women friends talked with me about my body, my fears, and my pain. Their strength helped me get through it. Thank God our society finds it very acceptable for women to share their feelings and fears. I don't know if men feel as much permission to do that or have as much practice as we do.

What was surprising was that the men in my life became more loving because of my breast cancer, not less. Why? First, I let them in more; second, they responded to my vulnerability and wanted to protect me. I think lots of breast cancer patients think men can't handle this, that all they care about is staring at and feeling breasts. It's macho not to handle it. I was certain my women friends would never walk away from me but I wasn't so sure about some of my male friends. Some of those men did disappoint me but it had nothing to do with my breasts. They couldn't handle a life and death situation and they ran. But the fact is that most men are not obsessed with women's bodies, any more than women are with theirs. Having breast cancer breaks down the barriers of everyone's role expectations.

What is interesting to me is that I am a far more feminine person now. I define femininity as feeling at home with being a woman, a female person, inside and outside. It's being comfortable with who I am as a human being. I am softer and more gentle now. I never let myself be that way before. The nurturing, giving part of me has been freed up. Before, I felt to survive I had to be independent and tough. I looked angry; I *was* angry.

Before I was sick, I thought I knew how to be feminine. I paid attention to what I looked like and was always well dressed, hair in place, and my makeup on. Everything else about me was extremely masculine: my out-spokenness, my intelligence, my fighting for causes. I probably still show that side too much, but in this male-dominated society, you need some "macho" to survive. I was trying so hard to be masculine that a lot of my inner feminine qualities were sacrificed. I would now characterize all these qualities—strength, nurturing, softness, intelligence—as human. Every man and woman needs to be both gentle and strong. My masculine and feminine parts, my yin and yang, are more in balance now. It's ironic that I am now working in a traditional feminine profession: counseling.

There have been constant challenges to my health since I finished chemo. The challenge always seems to be learning how to take better care of myself. I think this is a very human thing to do. It's also a feminist thing to do, bringing energy inward instead of putting the energy out all the time. It's very womanly of me to nurture myself. Believe me, I didn't have the faintest idea how to do this before I had cancer. Before breast cancer, I didn't ever really take good care of myself. I worked too hard, I drank too much, and I found all the ways I couldn't put myself first. I kept really busy doing things that didn't mean much. My life was full but I never spent much time with myself. I still have to look at all the ways that I wasn't gentle with me.

I am now much more honest and open about how I feel. I accept myself as I am. I learned that I am not Superwoman. I had been a doer. I always had to contribute and it wasn't okay just to be a person. I needed an identity with a label of worker or student. Learning that it was okay to be just me, with no labels, was one of the major things that came out of my having cancer.

I am now able to forgive myself. I no longer hate myself for drinking. After the diagnosis, the compulsion to drink went and it's still gone. It holds nothing for me anymore. I never even wanted a drink throughout my treatment. I also used to say, I'd feel so much better if I were thinner. "When I am thin again," I'd say, "Life will be great!" Sure I feel better when my weight is down but the same problems remain. I still get terrified if I take cancer tests. It doesn't matter if I am a thin or a fat person. The weight doesn't matter; the age doesn't matter; those aren't the answers.

I have confronted myself honestly about some of my losses, like being menopausal and unable to have children. I did some real mourning about not being able to have a child. But having children in my life was never a high priority for me, and I am now unwilling to make time in my life for a child. It wasn't so much having the child as it was that I no longer had a choice. When confronted with the fact that I can't have it, I want it more. I now accept it but that doesn't mean that when I am with my god-child I don't get a twinge. I certainly don't feel less a woman for not being able to have children. There are a lot of things in life I will not be able to experience, and having a biological child is one of them. But I feel sad when I say that, because I have a feeling that there's a lot of joy that goes with raising your own child, and I've had to say no to a vital part of life.

When I first went through menopause, I was concerned about aging but I am not worried about getting older anymore. I feel just as attractive as before. I also have wonderful older female role models in my family; all the women have accepted aging beautifully. I can't imagine my mother worrying about getting older. She welcomed her gray hairs. I have gotten to the point where I really believe that whatever beauty or attraction I have comes from within.

Getting older and having breast cancer has also changed what I value in sexual terms. Since I value myself more now, having casual affairs, which I thought was adventurous, is out for me. That old lifestyle of being sexually flamboyant is out. Why bother now! It takes too much energy! I would rather stay home and read a book. On the other hand, for the first time I want to share my life with someone. There's now room for someone and there really wasn't before. Everybody says, if you have gone through the cancer experience, you can go through anything. I don't think that's true. It was difficult but this particular experience is just one of life's challenges. On balance, it wasn't that hard. To me, losing a child or a spouse is much tougher than what I went through. But what happened to me was a gift. I learned lessons that changed my life for the better.

Throughout my whole cancer experience, I felt there were teachings for me. I never would have *chosen* to be taught this way but I like the changes in me. I guess I had to go to the edge to get there. It transformed me. The crucial lesson I learned was to do what was most important to me. What's most important to me is helping others, because the happiest times of my life have been when I was sharing—laughing, giving, crying—with someone. During chemotherapy, I started counseling other breast cancer patients. I loved it and knew I was effective. Out of this counseling experience has emerged a full-time career for me in meeting the needs of cancer patients through the development of cancer support programs. These programs are my babies! To stop this now would be like stopping in the middle of labor! I love what I'm doing.

Finally, I have shaken off that ridiculous veil of immortality. We live in a culture that believes we will be young forever. Sometimes, people ran from me when I had cancer, because they had to look at their own fear of death. To accept that I was mortal meant that they were too. Everyone is always betting on tomorrow, but putting things off in life is not cool. People faced with cancer get this gift of knowing we must live every day to its fullest. Having confronted the possibility of my own death from cancer, I learned how to live. All I have is now, today. Today I am happy. What more could I ask for?

8

*Barbara Rosenblum**

"Many women internalize other people's way of looking at themselves. Breast cancer challenges that by making you deal more with your *personhood*: what kind of person and woman you are, and what are your ultimate values. With breast cancer, a woman starts owning her own life."

In late 1984, Barbara, a forty-one-year-old gay woman involved in a long-term partnership, was told she had a stage four breast cancer with lymph node involvement. She had discovered the lump almost a year before and had been told repeatedly that it was noncancerous. Following a breast biopsy, Barbara had three months of chemotherapy, a modified radical mastectomy, another three months of chemotherapy, five weeks of radiation, and an additional twelve months of chemotherapy, which she completed in 1986. She was treated again with chemotherapy after having had a recurrence in 1987. Living with advanced breast cancer, Barbara quickly realized that breast cancer was not about losing a breast; rather it was a disease that involved the loss of life, *her* life. Faced with her mortality, she explored what she called the deeper issues and questions about personhood

---

*According to her wishes, Barbara's real name has been used in her story.

and the quality of life. She asked, "Who am I and how will I deal with the time I have left?" Barbara died in February 1988. She was forty-four years old.

*T*he most important thing in my family was to have a good mind and to use it to get out of poverty and succeed. I grew up in New York in the 1940s in a Polish immigrant family with my mother, father, and younger sister. Though we were poor, I never remember feeling deprived. My mother was a very plain woman, a hardworking housewife with a second-grade education. My father, who in his early years in this country was a janitor, was a very demanding man. Later he got into small business, and though he wasn't the best of businessmen, he was a good thinker. He was very bright and fast. I would describe us as plain people who believed it was important to work hard and use your brains. When I was growing up, my father didn't treat me or my sister really as boys or girls. He didn't know how to relate to girls so he related to us as potential workers. He'd talk to us about the importance of working all the time and moving up. The quintessential story about my father was when I was in the seventh grade and did a lot of painting and posters at school. Once I showed him a poster I had brought home. He brought out his drafting materials from his military service and showed me that my poster was off one-sixteenth of an inch. He had high expectations.

My parents also raised me to be independent. It stood me in good stead for life. But I think one of the reasons I never got married—I only lived with men for long periods of time—was because I found it extremely hard to depend on somebody.

We certainly were not a family that spent time looking in the mirror. I think survival was more at hand. I never had the sense that spending a lot of time on what I looked like or what I wore mattered much. So I never spent much time fussing in front of a mirror. Even when I was ten and noticed developing breasts on my chest, and had gotten my period, my body wasn't a focus for me. I just didn't pay much attention to the changes. I was a little young for all that development to start. My parents didn't talk to me about sex and puberty, so I was not as ready and informed about these changes as I should have been.

I never went through what I would call the natural developmental process for a young teenage girl: putting curlers in my hair, putting on makeup, trying on different clothes, or getting ready for a date. I wasn't very interested.

I was not brought up to believe that femininity was very important. My mother was not a fussy woman and literally had no vanity. She never used

makeup and wasn't interested particularly in clothes. So clothes didn't
mean too much to me either. Since we didn't have much money, I used to
wear a lot of hand-me-down clothes. I remember my sixth-grade wardrobe
consisted of three skirts and four blouses. I would alternate wearing the
skirts and blouses from week to week.

During high school I had a very active social life. Like many kids, I was
a tormented adolescent and chose to hang out with the bohemian kids in
school. I was the arty type, looking and dressing like a beatnik and wearing
black clothes all the time. We all wore our hair long and straight. We
looked depressed. I remember I hated the look and texture of my hair. It
was long and stringy, fine and thin, and not exactly an advertisement for
Breck shampoo.

Throughout my high school years, my parents encouraged me to use my
brains. I was fortunate to have a number of teachers who challenged my
mind. One woman, my English teacher, was and still is very influential in
my life. She was just an absolute idealized image of what I wanted to be
like. She was smart, had her own opinions, was independent, and had her
own personality, even though she was married. She was a feminine,
good-looking woman, who dressed well, not in the commercial sense, and
cared how she looked. She was more assuredly feminine from the inside
than on the outside. Even after she had four children, she remained very
much her own person. She'd always talk to me about reading and literature,
and tried to help me develop because she believed I had talent. She was a
nurturer—not in a schmaltzy way—but in a demanding way: "I have high
expectations for you and I believe you can do it." Then, as now, I was
surrounded by and attracted to competent women like her.

After I graduated from high school, I attended college for a year in New
York and got A's and F's. I realized that I wasn't emotionally ready to go
to college. I was one of these kids who had to go and prove herself in the
real world before she could go back to school. I dropped out of school and
worked for a record company for a while. When I was twenty-three, I did
go back to college. I was more mature and settled and was living with a
boyfriend. I went to NYU and it took me nine years to get my B.A. I
worked part-time and went to school the rest of the time. I really loved
learning and decided to go on to a Ph.D. program in sociology at North-
western University, where I was given a scholarship. Got a scholarship to
go spend four years freezing!

My education, particularly my graduate education, provided me with the
ability to do what my father so wanted for his kids. Having a higher
education is one thing that provides you with the opportunity for growth,
and my experiences led me to be much more sophisticated than the people I
grew up with. I got exposed to different ways and now carry myself

differently. I am comfortable with everybody in any class. I think that social class and my mobility up has been a very important theme in my life, more important than my femininity.

In 1972, I completed my Ph.D. in sociology and moved to northern California with a man named David, with whom I had fallen in love. We stayed together for more than seven years. Soon after we arrived, I got a position as a professor of sociology at Stanford University and remained there for seven years.

David was a photographer-artist and being with him was almost like being married to my father. He wasn't a good moneymaker but was intelligent and really a plain, nice, and simple guy. After seven years, my ambition got in our way. I was very ambitious, for me and for him—too ambitious for him. I wanted to be a professor and he was more conventional and wanted a wife to stay at home. Of course, I feel I should have seen the differences growing but didn't. In any case, in 1980, when I was thirty-six, I made two big changes in my life. I changed my job *and* my lover in the same year. That was hard and heavy. I was reevaluating what I was doing with my life. I took a new job as an administrator with a small nontraditional college, running their special programs. Toward the end of my relationship with David, I began a relationship with a woman. Although I was always interested in women before and had had small sexual encounters here and there, this particular woman, Sandy, really changed my life. Sandy was older and more experienced and came along at a time when I was a little confused about what I wanted. She really actively pursued me and I went for it, and since then, my life has been very different sexually, socially, and emotionally.

It's funny to change your sexual orientation because I was with men for most of my life. I didn't think about sex too much. It wasn't an important part of my life. I had a very normal, high sex drive but thought that sex was a natural part of making love and being with a man and being part of a relationship. It was no big deal. I wouldn't be shy about making the first moves. Sex was very easy for me, and I never had any problems or traumas and was never dysfunctional. Everything I ever did with my body felt very natural and there was no shame associated with it. From the minute I started making love, it was terrific, except for a few hits and misses when I was young and learning about my body.

It always felt very biological; some times of the month I was more horny than other times, like right before my period or during ovulation. But sex was never a thing that I spent a lot of time doing; it was not an event. Some people spend lots of hours making love and they are really into it. I was never like that. I did it for a half hour and then went to sleep! It was just organic. Making love did not make me feel more or less feminine; it just felt good.

Being in a lesbian relationship is very different than being in a heterosexual relationship. For me, the big difference is not just sexual—it's emotional. I always felt lonely with men in some ways—there is a heterosexual loneliness in male/female relationships. You are always trying to get close and understand each other. In a lesbian relationship, you understand each other too well and want to get away from one another. It's true! So it's emotionally very different.

Sandy and I developed and still continue to have a very engaged, somewhat turbulent, relationship. I fight with Sandy more than any other person in my life—intellectually and emotionally. We have an active, intellectual relationship. We always talk a lot because we're both writers and researchers, and we've written and published together. Emotionally perhaps we're overly fused, but I never feel lonely with her and have always felt she's on my side. I never felt that before. It's a wonderful, wonderful feeling to have somebody on your side.

Right before my diagnosis in 1985, Sandy and I had been together for five years. I was very satisfied with us. I was also working hard, was very busy and engaged in what I was doing emotionally and intellectually. I really liked my job although there wasn't much prestige. Since my job never paid enough, I was in the process of beginning a small business as an editor and manuscript consultant—writing book reviews for newspapers or giving papers at conferences.

My breast cancer story is a tragic one in that I found the lump a year before it was diagnosed. I first discovered this lump myself in early 1984 and went to my HMO (health maintenance organization). The doctor felt it, said it was a fibroid cyst, and not to worry. I went back a month later as it was still there and growing larger. I saw a second doctor who said, "I don't feel anything unusual and yes, it is large." I insisted on a mammogram. He did the mammogram and it was negative. We learned later that the radiologist read the mammogram wrong—it *was* cancer.

But then they told me there wasn't anything wrong. So I waited another six months and the lump was still growing. By now my breast was almost twice as large as the other one, so I went to a surgeon at the same HMO who was supposed to be a breast specialist. She felt the lump, stuck a needle in it, and said, "Hum, I don't think there's cancer here but it's something. Why don't you stop drinking coffee for three months?" I went to three doctors, none of whom recognized or diagnosed the problem.

Soon after that doctor's visit, I went to New York for a conference, and while there noticed substantial skin changes on my breast, which to me was really serious. I called Sandy from New York and said, "Something's happening. I am very scared. Get me the best breast diagnostician in the city." She found him and this new doctor performed a fine needle aspiration and sent the results to my HMO doctor. It was cancer, stage four breast cancer, the worst stage of breast cancer you can have. It was eleven months of a delayed diagnosis.

When I heard this news, Sandy was in Winnepeg at a conference giving a presentation. When she called me to find out the results, I told her I had cancer and cried and she said, "I am coming home." That was such a testimony of her devotion to me. Nothing was as important as her coming home. I felt very good about that. Sandy came home about thirty-six hours later.

Obviously we had some treatment decisions to make. We met with the HMO team of doctors who told me I had to have immediate surgery, this kind of chemo, and so on. I said, "What a minute! You just messed up on my diagnosis. You didn't even give me a test yet to see how far it's spread and you're taking me to surgery? No way. I'm getting a second opinion." I went to see a genetic counselor in San Francisco and I think she saved my life. She told me, "There are other doctors who will do your treatment differently and you owe it to yourself to get a second opinion." *Then* I got very angry, very upset and agitated, because I knew it was screwed up and the doctors had made a big mistake. I also didn't know who to trust. Before I got sick, I trusted my body and I also trusted doctors.

In my case, too, there was a betrayal of both my body and the medical profession. I am not even sure that I trust any doctor now. To be done in by medical incompetence, especially coming from a family background where competence is so valued, freaked me out.

I went for consultations with three oncologists and they all recommended the same thing: Get the most aggressive chemotherapist I could find. I left my HMO plan and got a whole new team of doctors and went on a different treatment protocol. If I had followed the other guys, I would be dead.

Of course, I filed a lawsuit against the HMO and had a very good case, unfortunately, for me and them. I won before we even went to court; that is, we settled out of court. I am set for the rest of my life, but my life, well, the statistics are not too good for me. There is only a 25 percent chance that I will live for five years. Maybe now there's a greater chance because I've had chemo, but frankly I don't know what my prognosis is right now. I believe I have a good chance to outlive the prognosis. Maybe I will be one of those twenty-five out of one hundred women who survive stage four cancer.

Anyhow, I am much more positive now with this new team of doctors. I go to high-class doctors that charge a lot of money, $250 for a consultation, but they spend an hour with me and know what they are doing. It makes a big difference in your peace of mind.

The week I got my diagnosis, Sandy and I pulled together twenty-five friends in our living room and told them what the diagnosis was and that we were going to need their help. They were great and really came through. They took me to the hospital, drove me to chemo, made phone calls, and went shopping. Our friends became our support system.

When we started going through all the doctor visits, Sandy was extremely cooperative and actually very involved in my treatment plans. At first we did everything together and she wouldn't let those doctors touch me without her being in the room and their answering to her. She was with me for all my scans and tests. She came with me at first for the chemo treatments. But when she did I would get all anxious because she would be anxious, and we would amplify each other's anxieties. It was better I went by myself. Then, too, she had to go back to work because we didn't know about our money situation. Slowly we adjusted and tried to return to life as normal so that Sandy could go back out on the road.

Of course, all your relationships are never really normal again. So many doors open with this disease. For example, my relationship with my parents changed—I fell in love with my parents—they were wonderful, warm, supportive, and upbeat. They had a very positive attitude, always saying, "You gotta have hope and they'll cure this." It fills my heart to be around them, especially my mother who's so strong in a crisis.

Strangely enough, at the same I was getting chemo, my mother was given a diagnosis of cancer and she started chemo too. She's got a great attitude. I went with her to one of her chemo treatments and she took it like a champ. She didn't even get anticipatory nausea, as I sometimes did, before she went into the treatment room. It was no big deal to her: "So, they just give you a shot." My mother has been quite a role model for me.

My first treatment for breast cancer was chemotherapy. In order to reduce the size of the tumor, the oncologists started me on three months of preoperative chemotherapy: Adriamycin, 5-FU, and Cytoxan. On this chemo regimen, I got sick for five days every three weeks and I threw up a lot. You feel as if you have the flu for three days, and by the fifth day, you can finally walk around. My second regimen was with Cytoxan, methotrexate, and 5-FU, which is insidious because CMF makes you drag yourself around. You are not throwing up but you have the nausea. I found it better to just throw up and get it over with.

But I never threw up alone. Most of the time during chemo, Sandy was with me when I was nauseous, and then I had my friends there to help me when she was gone. At the time I said to myself, "You know, it's more important who you throw up with than who you sleep with. Throwing up in front of somebody takes such trust and intimacy and dependency, like letting them hold your head or getting you to the toilet. It's easier to go to bed with someone and make love than it is to throw up in front of somebody. I swear to God." I never was so vulnerable when I made love.

After the three months of chemo, I had a mastectomy, then three more months of chemo, and then five weeks of radiation. Now I've been on another twelve months of chemo on CMF and my last cycle is next month. All I can say is that surgery was a piece of cake, radiation is not such a piece of cake, but it's nothing compared to chemo. Chemo is the worst.

There was never any choice for me about having the mastectomy because my tumor was large. I had consulted two radiation oncologists, both of whom said I was not a candidate for a lumpectomy. As soon as I had the mastectomy, I joined a support group and was very surprised that everyone talked about reconstruction. I was worried about my *life* and thought, "God, my breast doesn't count that much. My femininity is not in one breast." I could easily wear a prosthesis. I was also afraid if I had a recurrence and it was under a reconstructive implant, then nobody could find it. I just wanted to keep my chest exposed. I do have a very high chance of recurrence, given my diagnosis. Later on, I understood better why reconstruction is an important issue for some women, after I got this letter from a woman friend with breast cancer who said the worst thing about having breast cancer was going to bed with her husband. With her husband, she always wore her bra and prosthesis. I thought it was very sad she couldn't take the prosthesis off. Her husband probably got turned off when he saw her scar. I always thought that the scar should be touched, massaged, and looked at. Not to have your lover touch your scar would be awful.

I was never concerned about the loss of my breast affecting my relationship with Sandy. I was glad I was with a woman at this time because I think there is a difference between having a lesbian lover and heterosexual lover when you have lost a breast. It affects how you feel about yourself. Sandy was really attentive to me all through the mastectomy experience. She was in the hospital every day from nine in the morning until seven at night. We looked at the scar together, we heard the news together about the number of lymph nodes involved, and she helped me drain the fluid from my hemovac and take showers and baths.

She made it very clear to me through jokes and looking at the scar that she was extremely comfortable. She said things like, "They are going to call us the three-breasted robin." And we'd laugh. Sandy listened to me when I complained but didn't indulge in my complaints. The loss for me was not as bad as somebody else who has nobody around. I think about these people who don't have lovers and I don't know how they do it—even if you never make love—it doesn't have to be the greatest romance in the world. But even to have a friend, a brother or sister there, to have somebody there with you is really important.

My mother cried when she saw my scar. I was showing it to her and saying, "Look at what a good job they did. Would you like to see it?" She cried and said, "I see that they did a good job but it pains me to know that you had to go through this." I felt connected to her, but wished she hadn't cried.

The side effects of all this surgery, radiation, and chemo does take its toll: shopping for and wearing a prosthesis, losing your hair, getting sick, gaining weight, being tired. First, because of the radiation and surgery, I couldn't be fitted for a prosthesis for at least eight months because of tenderness and skin changes. When I finally did go to buy a prosthesis, it was the first time I had really looked at myself. It was like looking at a stranger when I saw myself in a three-sided mirror and I freaked out. It really hit me when I was outside in the world.

The side effects from chemo have been bad for me. I have been extremely proud of myself about my mental strength and attitude to tolerate chemo. I know I have a good chance of survival because I can tolerate chemo. But I have gained a lot of weight with chemotherapy, more than 25 pounds. Sandy has been fine about my weight, joking around, saying now I look Rubenesque and how she loves chunky women. But being this overweight is very uncomfortable and has taken a long time for me to really cope with it. Up until now there has been a direct relationship between what I do with my body and its weight. I could swim and diet and then I would lose weight. But now, no matter what I do, no matter how much I eat or don't eat, exercise or don't exercise, my body seems to have a very peculiar metabolism all its own. It feels very much out of control. I have to just let go and cope with the fact that I now weigh 162 pounds. For months I have been avoiding reality by wearing my old, large-size, sloppy-type clothes. This weekend I am going to a store that specializes in clothes for larger women. It is just a part of life that I have to accept. I am just hoping that when chemo finishes, I can start to do more exercise. I hope I have the energy to exercise. I am learning to live with all this.

Some time in my life, when my cancer is very advanced, I am going to be in a hospital weighing 85 pounds, and, in view of that, this weight gain doesn't mean that much. But you can't avoid society's notions about being overweight and the value of thinness. I wish that I could be my normal weight, which is a little plump and chunky.

The hardest part of chemo for me was losing my hair. I lost it all in the first twenty-eight days of chemo. My hair had been long and curly from a perm. Even though I got a very short pixie haircut, my hair came out in clumps. It's emotionally very difficult to comb your hair and have big pieces of it come out. I bought a wig but never wore it—I hated the feeling of it—it was too hot. So I just wore a lot of hats. Then at one point I went around bald. When my hair grew in a little bit, about ¼-inch-long hair, it felt almost stylish. With the hair back, I could worry about the weight!

What bothered me a lot were the things that nobody else can really see. It's said sometimes that when you have an invisible, hidden kind of disability, like having a mastectomy, it's harder on the individual because she appears normal to the outside world, but inside she knows she's different. One thing nobody else noticed is the way in which my fingernails became discolored from the chemotherapy. There are black stripes on them. When that problem started coming up, it really pained me. I had a very hurt, vulnerable feeling. "Oh my God, this has to happen, too?"

Because of this long bout of chemotherapy, I have gone into a premature menopause and have hot flashes and all the other components of menopause, like drying out of the vaginal tissues. Sex becomes a little uncomfortable with all this.

So sex has become very distant to me. I look at it as I never have before. I have noticed that my sex drive has changed tremendously. Before I used to really know during the month when I would feel sexy—you know, clues and signals—and now I don't know. My body doesn't or can't tell me and I don't feel sexy so often.

For instance, in the old days I would lubricate if I was excited. Well, I can be excited now but I am not lubricating—does that mean I am not excited? You turn to your body to tell you how you feel about something. I don't think even when I finish chemo that my body will do the same thing anymore. I don't know for sure, but I was told it is unlikely that my periods will come back. I think I will be menopausal from now on and have low estrogen levels.

In spite of all the awful side effects of chemotherapy, I have a lot of anxiety about going off chemo. Because as long as I am on chemo, I don't have cancer. In preparation for going off treatment, I've requested a meeting with my oncologist for a case review. Between now and then, I am trying to find out about all the other research trials that are going on. Are there endocrinological or immunological therapies available that I could possibly engage in?

As I move out of treatment, I think a lot about living with the changes that breast cancer has made in my life and my body. What's changed? What's affected me? For starters, today's *New York Times* "HERS" column was about how a woman's pregnancy made her and her husband closer. I thought I'd write a column in answer to that, "How My Breast Cancer Made Me and My Lover Closer." I think mainly that when couples have a shared experience, whether it's a baby or a life-threatening experience, they have an opportunity to grow together.

Because Sandy and I are so close and talk a lot, we understand how this has impacted both of our lives, so we have made changes together. I have really felt it's not just me, it's us, and that's made me feel less alone. I think my relationship with Sandy has helped me accept the shape of my body, minus one breast, more than I could have accepted it alone or with a man. Some studies have shown that lesbians tend to cuddle, lie around, talk, and be affectionate but not have hot sex. That's more descriptive of Sandy's and my relationship. I need lots of touching and just want to be held, and I get plenty of it. But in all fairness, too, I think you have to look at this in the overall context—my breasts were not that sexual for me to begin with. Sometimes I ask myself, if I were with a man, would I feel any differently? There might be more pressure with a man because I think men bring a lot of sex drive to a relationship.

Right now my body feels very foreign to me, very uncomfortable and unfamiliar. I don't look the same when I look in the mirror. I have a different shape. I am a little bit shy about my body now. For instance, I would like to go swimming at the YWCA, but there are only public changing areas. I am hesitant about taking my bathing suit off there. Then I think, "Screw it, these people are going to have to deal with it." So this week I'm planning to become a member of the Y and start swimming.

I am slowly getting over this stuff. Recently, I was in the Caribbean with a male friend of mine and we met some other people at dinner who we liked. We all got drunk, smoked some dope, and were having a fine time. Then somebody suggested, "Let's go skinny-dipping." My friend Peter said to me, "You have to tell them ahead of time so they don't get freaked out." It didn't even occur to me about my operation. I thought I just would take off my clothes and go skinny-dipping. But he was concerned. So I told one of the women, "Look, I want to tell you I have had a mastectomy." She said, "You know, I thought you might be on chemo because your hair was so short." To the acute observer, you don't have to explain too much. Nobody's been upset so far. It's really been fine for others.

You can't help but think about your femaleness, your womanhood, with this disease. Breast cancer, more than any other life-threatening illness, challenges a woman's femaleness. It's a female hormone-related disease and it takes place in a part of the body that is associated with sex, sex drive, appearance, and cleavage. Since having breast cancer, I feel I am not more or less a woman; I am a woman in a different way. I think there are three things that I associate most with being a woman: first, her sexuality; second, her being a powerful person in her own life; and finally, a cultural way of being traditionally female by dressing in a feminine style and wearing makeup.

In terms of my femininity, I think I have gone down on the sexual dimension and up on the dressing and conventional dimensions. In fact, I may have gotten more feminine in the conventional sense of paying attention to my body and breasts. I was told my whole life what a pretty girl I was, and now when I look in the mirror, I see that I am a pretty woman, a good-looking woman. But most of my life, I really experienced myself as very plain. I wore plain clothes and had a plain face. I am now more aware of my appearance. I'm wearing more makeup and earrings, and dressing more like a conventional female than before I got cancer.

I never liked to go shopping before because clothes were a necessity to me rather than fun. Now since I have this money from my malpractice suit, clothes are becoming fun. I haven't thought too much about why the changes have occurred. Maybe I am compensating for the extra weight. I am just taking care of my body more. I am decorating it more. Before I just took my body for granted and never paid any attention to it. It was right there on automatic. All the good stuff was in my brain and I carried my body with me. But now I pay attention to my body.

Breast cancer opened up areas of my life as a woman that I maybe wouldn't have explored. I look at the possibility of my eventual death and ask, what is the way I would like to go toward that? To be as complete and integrated a human being as possible and to have a sense of integrity and wholeness. The only way to do that is to explore all parts of myself before that time. It's a sense of "I am many things; I am many parts; they are all part of me." That includes various aspects of both my femininity and my masculinity, whether it's dressing up, being sexual, powerful, assertive, soft, independent, or dependent.

I saw a movie about a forty-nine-year-old anthropologist from USC with asbestos lung cancer who only had six months to live. The way she chose to live was by continuing to be an anthropologist, studying Orthodox Jewish life in Los Angeles until two weeks before she died. What she did was to strengthen, deepen, and continue to build upon all that she had been. She was very successful all her life. She wasn't about to give that identity up. She clung to it until the end.

When I saw that movie I thought to myself, "Is that what I want to do—be a sociologist until two weeks before I die? No." I want more openness in my life. There are many things I haven't done, projects I haven't completed, and there are things that I have underdeveloped in myself.

So now I am exploring different ways of being a woman, coming to terms with my total womanhood, not only with my lover but with male and female friends. Right now it feels like dress-up; I feel like a little girl about five years old putting on Mom's shoes. For instance, I toyed with the idea of having children before I got sick. I never had a really strong urge to have children in the abstract. I had a number of significant relationships in my life, but in only one of them did I want to have a child. But the minute I got my diagnosis, I wanted to do all the things that I didn't have a chance to do up until then, like having a child. You want to break right through any limitations that are put on you. I have already explored the powerful, important woman part of me, but I have had a long struggle with allowing myself to be dependent. This disease has opened up the dependency parts of me.

When I started to throw up with chemo, I *had* to be dependent on others, and, believe me, when you are on your knees at the toilet, you really know who's independent and dependent! There's no ambivalence about that issue. I have also been a good worker my whole life, but I haven't been a good player because I have always been stressed out. I just haven't been relaxed. I always did things that were productive, not just because they were fun. I have had a hard time with intimacy and commitment, and that part has changed too. I have come to terms with being dependent and having somebody take care of me. I have come to peace with my transition to lesbianism, which was very hard for me because I had been a heterosexual for a long time.

You know a life is like a trajectory that can be quite narrow. Breast cancer has deepened, broadened, and opened up my life. That's the way I decided to live with this disease, by deciding who I was and how I would face these ultimate questions. It really clarified a lot of things for me. Now I can and have accepted so much more.

When I was diagnosed at age forty-one, I believed that I was just statistically the first among many of my women friends who would get breast cancer. This injected me with a sense of purpose in the way that I handled having this disease. I wanted to be a role model and have tried to conduct myself in a way that others can follow. Like many other women who have had breast cancer, I have counseled other women with this disease. I've called them and told them that I was here for them if they needed me.

If a woman faced with breast cancer asks me how she is going to get through this assault, I can say a number of things. Part of it depends on how she already *is* as a person. She will not become a different person overnight. First, I think to get through this experience she needs to know her own coping strategies, look at her past and see how she has coped with other problems, and that is probably a very good predictor of how she might cope with this disease. She should get to know herself. Second, she should think about those coping strategies and how satisfied she is with them. Are they functional for her? Did they limit or help her? Sometimes a strategy is good but it limits your options. One of the things I would recommend that every breast cancer patient do is to see how other people have coped or are coping with the disease. I did it and it helped me a lot.

Women with breast cancer always seem to ask me how I feel about reconstruction, though sometimes they feel shy about asking. Though I, of course, think it is perfectly right and normal to want a new breast, my impression is at bottom, every woman who faces breast cancer faces the loss of her own life. Even if you have the cleanest bill of health, with breast cancer there is always something hovering over you. So, sometimes femininity can be a disguise or defense against dealing with the deeper issue of facing your life. Many women want to focus on their breasts alone, because they are invested in having a conception of the disease as local, rather than systemic. But if they understand that breast cancer is a systemic disease, which I think it is, then things change. Many women have to go through their concerns with their femininity first and resolve that issue, either with reconstruction or whatever. Then maybe they will get to the deeper questions about life. I think that is the ultimate place to go with breast cancer.

But I don't mean to say that every issue about femininity has to be a defense. I do believe there are real issues about femininity to be dealt with and the way that men respond. I think women's fear of losing their femininity is culturally induced. I understand that many women are acting out the culture's commercial notion of what it means to be feminine. You see these ads with a woman slowly putting on her panty hose, shaving her legs, putting on her makeup, and we all think women have nothing better to do but take bubble baths all day. It's no surprise that women who have had breast cancer fear that they are now damaged goods and that nobody will ever pay attention to them. How can they get a boyfriend? What kind of guy is going to be attracted to them? What can they give?

If I didn't have Sandy, and just started a relationship, would I tell a man/woman I have five years to live? What kind of a person is going to get involved with me? I wonder about that. There are intersecting issues that aren't clear because you have to deal with your life and your femininity at the same time.

There are a lot of hidden gifts in having a life-threatening illness. If you've been ambivalent, you get clear very quickly. You just deal with your issues because there's no time. When I was told my diagnosis, my doctor said, "Well, I guess you will begin to deal with the quality-of-life issues." I thought to myself, having been a very self-conscious person who's been in therapy for many years, that I had been dealing with quality-of-life issues all the time. Breast cancer's not just the beginning of the quality of life. But what is sad is that for a lot of people it's only when something catastrophic happens to them that they then feel they deserve to live. I would say that when you face your death, you begin to live. Then you feel you deserve everything and can laugh deeper, cry louder, spend more, eat richer, and goof off more. Do everything with more vitality. You can even be depressed better! It all becomes more; it's an edge. It makes me feel more alive. It's a gift.

Many women internalize other people's ways of looking at themselves. Breast cancer challenges that by making you deal more with your personhood: what kind of person and woman you are, and what are your ultimate values. With breast cancer, a woman starts owning her own life.

9

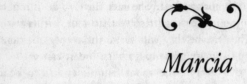

Marcia

"But I've survived cancer so far with few disruptions in my life. There was no room in my life for cancer, because the problems and limitations of others in my family were far greater than mine. This has been a great equalizer."

In 1971, Marcia, forty-five years old and married with four children, was diagnosed with a stage one breast cancer. One day after her biopsy, she had a radical mastectomy, followed by six weeks of cobalt treatments. Seven years later, in 1977, Marcia felt a lump in her shoulder that was surgically removed and discovered to be a second cancer, a fast-growing sarcoma. Treated with chemotherapy for eight months, Marcia completed her treatments in 1978. Tackling the losses resulting from her first breast cancer treatments, Marcia returned to her normal routine of taking care of her family and working within two weeks. Even though she had a recurrence, more cancer surgery, and chemotherapy treatments, Marcia still maintained that there were far worse things that could happen to her. As a veteran cancer survivor, she measured her losses less by the impact they had on her appearance and far more by the effect they had on her ability to function on a daily basis. She found living with breast cancer paled when she compared it to other chronic diseases, such as her daughter's mental illness. Marcia's age and experiences enabled her to be more accepting of life's tragedies and made her focus on what she wanted to accomplish each day.

I was seven when my mother died. She was thirty-five. She was sick for about two years and spent a good part of that time in the hospital. I can remember sitting in a car outside the hospital waiting for her to come out, so she could come home and spend twenty-four hours with us for a holiday. She had a melanoma on her back that had spread into her lungs, because the doctor treating her only removed the growth and never examined the tissue. It was the classic wrong way to handle cancer. The family was very angry with the doctor, but, of course, in those days I don't think they would have been able to stop it anyway. In the 1930s, cancer was very hush-hush and something bad. Cancer then was like AIDS is today. I was told never to tell anyone my mother had died of cancer. If my brother, sister, or I talked about it, my aunt would shush us up. At the time, I was so young that I had no fear of cancer, but as I got older I became terrified of the disease.

After my mother died, my brother, who was six years older than me, and my sister, who was two years older, and I went to live with my mother's sister, Sarah. My mother really wanted her sister to take care of us, because she knew my father was incapable of raising three young children. He didn't put up a fight over us either. My father lived until he was eighty but I had very little contact with him during my life.

Even though we viewed ourselves as orphans, our parents' families made us feel a part of their conservative, well-to-do Jewish world in Baltimore. We felt very secure and were surrounded by aunts, uncles, and cousins who always included us in their activities. My Aunt Sarah was quite Victorian in her outlook but she didn't inhibit me at all as I was growing up. She never talked to me about menstruation, though she was practical and very matter-of-fact about everything else. Sex education was not on her agenda. Perhaps part of the problem was I beat her to the discussion by starting my period and developing breasts when I was ten and in the fifth grade. To be ten years old with fast-growing breasts was embarrassing. At first I was quite self-conscious. I have memories of being at swim parties and trying to hide my breasts, which spilled out of my bathing suit. Bathing suits in the 1930s were not made for young girls with large breasts.

But by the time I was fifteen, I had grown into them and was comfortable with my body. I was also very athletic, which I am sure helped my body image. I enjoyed all sports but the one thing I really excelled at was swimming. One of my uncles, recognizing my talent, brought in a well-known swimming trainer to coach me. Soon after, I was in swimming meets and did quite well. Later swimming would become a major part of my life.

Growing up a teenager in the late 1930s was tame compared to the 1990s. Though I went to a private girls' school, I had a very active and natural social life: going to dancing classes, parties, and playing sports with boys all the time. I was always more interested in sports and books than boys, although I always had one boyfriend. I was a wholesome bobbysoxer, saddle shoes and all. I didn't care about clothes or material things at all. I was attractive, though pudgy, very bright, a little shy, and had long, black hair, which was my outstanding feature. It seemed that everywhere I went, someone said something about my very long hair. My hair gave me a tremendous amount of confidence. It was my mark, what made me different.

When I was a senior in high school, I decided I wanted to become an engineer, but after my first year of college, it became clear I was not mechanically minded. I became an English major. Had I not married, I am sure I would have pursued a writing career and gone to graduate school, but *c'est la vie.* I met my husband during college. We were from similar backgrounds and I was crazy about him. Peter was a very bright, sweet, kind young man. We got married in 1949. I was a virgin when I got married and so was he. Of course, in those days there was no question about having sex before marriage for a good girl. Peter was quite a lover and we were like puppy dogs—very playful and all over each other. We really enjoyed one another.

I always knew I was going to be married and have children. When I was young and asked what I wanted to be, I always said, "I want to play mama with a baby." Peter and I had four children, two boys and two girls. I would have had more except with my last son I was sick and was scared to try again. I loved being a mother and raising the kids. At the time, I didn't think about working because most women didn't consider career *and* marriage as an option.

For the next twenty years, Peter and I were very happily married. I felt we had an ideal marriage except for a few in-law problems. I would describe our family as stable, normal, and almost golden. Everyone was healthy, happy, and active. After the kids were in school, I started working with the YWCA and helped them develop a community swimming program. This led to a professional career for me in coaching and educating other people in the field. I started to become well known for my work, so I was very satisfied professionally.

Then everything started to unravel. In early 1970, my youngest daughter Sue became mentally ill. We were totally unprepared for it, and we certainly didn't understand how a seemingly healthy young woman could suddenly be so ill. We took her out of college and had to place her in an institution—the first of many over the next fifteen years. Needless to say, our family was under great stress, emotionally and financially. It really tore us apart.

With this crisis it became clear that Peter and I handled stress differently. There are two ways of handling a crisis—fight or flight—and I fought, he fled. He couldn't accept that one of his perfect children could be ill and went into a depression. I have always been a fighter and storm trooper, and it seemed I was the chosen one to fight this time. However, being left alone to make decisions about Sue made me a target for lots of anger, both my daughter's and my husband's. Often after I made a decision, Peter would disagree with me. It was a very lonely time for me and I resented the lack of support. I think my marriage survived at the time because of our daughter—we had to stay together for her sake. Of course, you blame one another, too, for the problems and feel like bad parents. Our relationship was very strained. I don't think Peter touched me for a year after Sue's diagnosis. It was hell.

For the next two years, we saw social workers, psychiatrists, and psychologists. You name them, we saw them. Counseling was crucial for us in learning how to handle the ongoing crisis. Because I was so upset, and trying to just get through each day, the doctor gave me Valium and Seconal tablets and then sleeping pills to help me get through the nights. I am convinced that the biochemistry of my body changed due to all that pill-popping.

After two years, the situation was much the same and I had gone into a deep depression and was seeing a psychiatrist alone. This reactive depression was the most frightening experience I had ever been through. I was practically suicidal at one point. I wanted to give up. The worst part of depression is you can see no way out. But slowly I came out of it. Peter was very solicitous of me during this time and that helped me.

Right before my diagnosis, I was coming out of the depression. Personally, I was not in a good place. Luckily, I had some positive things in my life: I felt good about myself professionally and thought I was still an attractive woman. My children were doing well. I was forty-five years old and my body image was still intact. I very much enjoyed the company of men and still loved dancing and flirting.

In 1971, three years after my daughter became ill, I found a lump in my breast. I was very conscious of breast lumps as I had had a number of biopsies before but all had been benign. I immediately went to my internist who believed the lump was nothing to worry about and told me to come back in six months. However, given my family history of cancer and my fears, I went to another doctor, a breast specialist, who said, "You don't fool around with a lump. Let's take it out right away."

I went in the next day and had the biopsy. Nobody was worried about the lump being malignant, including me. My attitude was, "No problem, it's going to be benign again. Oh, what if I wake up and have only one breast?" I was really being cavalier. When I woke up and still had two breasts I thought, "Oh great! I'm fine." Then the doctor came in and said, "I am sorry, it was malignant. We've caught it early and we've removed all the cancer, but we'll have to do a radical mastectomy tomorrow. We'll probably have to give you cobalt treatments as well." I had no choice, really. This was a time when there were no choices of treatment for a woman with breast cancer.

My reaction to the diagnosis was funny. I didn't feel devastated. I was glad I was alive but wasn't fearful about dying. I didn't even *think* about dying. I wasn't afraid because the doctors were so reassuring about finding it early and getting it all out. My reaction was also tempered by the presence of my family doctor who was a personal friend. He was in the hospital room when I'd been given the diagnosis and was so upset about it that I was more concerned about him than me. I kept telling him I would be okay. Having him so worried about me helped me.

Surprisingly, what I felt was tremendous relief. I was finally being punished and paying the price for being a bad mother and it was now over. "Okay God, you've punished me." I felt as if a heavy burden had been lifted from my shoulders. It's strange because I had been so depressed before and then this experience brought me out of it. I had felt so alone before and now *I* was being taken care of for the first time in years. I needed the nurturing. It felt good to be allowed to be weak for a while. Having cancer was like a catharsis—it gave me a new lease on life.

Maybe another reason I wasn't really upset was because I felt I was already living on borrowed time. Since my mother had died at thirty-five, I felt I wouldn't live past thirty-five either. I think what affected me more was having an increased fear of cancer and wondering how I'd deal with issues of survival.

The doctors told me late in the day of my biopsy about the radical mastectomy, and I was too doped up to worry before I was under the knife again the next morning. I don't remember crying that night. When I woke up from surgery, I thought I was going to feel bad but I didn't. I honestly think if we hadn't had the crisis with our daughter that it might have been the end of the world for me. But I'd already hit bottom so I couldn't go any further down. Getting a diagnosis of cancer is nothing compared to being told you have a mentally ill child. What is the loss of a breast compared to lifelong mental illness? Our family problems helped put things into perspective for me.

I was overwhelmed by love and support from family, friends, and acquaintances. It also never occurred to me that no one would pay attention to me or not love me anymore because I had breast cancer. I got more attention than I ever expected. I hate to admit it but I liked all the fuss after so many years of dealing with others' problems. My husband and kids were wonderful. I received letters from people in the community that I barely knew. A friend of mine with breast cancer came to visit me and showed me her scar and prosthesis, which was very helpful to me. After three days in the hospital, I got antsy about unfinished work so Peter gave me a Dictaphone and we set up an office in my room. Soon my secretary came in to help out and I held meetings with my staff there. I was back at work in my office two weeks after I got out of the hospital. I really felt that I acted as a role model for recovery in that I went back to work so quickly. It also made me feel better about me.

When I first looked at my scar in the hospital, I didn't like the looks of it at all. I cried and thought, "I have lost my lovely zaftig!" Radical mastectomies aren't pretty to look at because they remove so much of the chest muscle. The first day I took the bandages off, Peter saw the scar and said, "Oh, it's beautiful," meaning it was a beautifully done operation, which it was. The doctor had said it was the best operation he ever did. But it wasn't beautiful to me then. After that I never really grieved for my lost breast. I adjusted to my new chest. Periodically I was sad but it just was not a major, terrible loss for me. It was the exact opposite of what you would think would happen. I remember I still felt young and attractive and thought I was a woman men could flirt with.

A few weeks after surgery, I started six weeks of cobalt treatments. The radiation experience was easy and I was never uncomfortable. I didn't suffer any burns. The same nurses cared for me each treatment, the room was kept warm, and music was played as I lay on the table. Until I finished cobalt treatments, I couldn't be fitted for a prosthesis but that didn't mean I didn't wear anything over my scar. I always felt it was very important that I wear *something*. I stuffed cotton and lambswool in my bra, used white socks and whatever worked to fill up the space temporarily. I really believe you should not call attention to the breast area, particularly if you are big-breasted like I am. You look so lopsided and funny without balance.

I will never forget the time when a friend, Mary, a new mastectomee, came to our swimming club. She wasn't wearing a prosthesis because she hadn't been fitted yet. You could see she was flat on one side. I grabbed her and took her into the lady's room and told her to stuff paper towels in her bra, saying, "Don't ever appear in public like that. You'll call attention to yourself. After you've had surgery, people are fascinated and always stare or look at you, so you be sure that you are matched." She didn't know that; she needed somebody to tell her.

As soon as my treatments were over, I went by myself to a local lingerie store where the salesladies were used to fitting women like me. They were just lovely. As a matter of fact, I am using the same prostheses that I bought there in the early 1970s. I think I bought seven models. I refuse to buy the new ones: I don't like the feel of them and the new models are too expensive. The only thing I didn't like about the mastectomy was how high my scars were. I couldn't show off my cleavage anymore. I had liked my cleavage and was proud of it. When I shopped for bathing suits, I had to be careful because I didn't want the scar to show.

It's funny what having a mastectomy does to you. You do everything not to call attention to your chest because you know people are always watching you. You start dressing better. It became very important to me to dress properly, and it was the first time I started spending more money on good clothes. Also, to lift my spirits, I paid more attention to myself generally. For instance, a few gray hairs had appeared on my head and I started coloring my hair. I wanted to look better after breast cancer, not worse. The last thing I wanted was people looking at me and thinking, "Poor Marcia" or have them think my life was over. It wasn't.

After my surgery, my relationship with Peter didn't change much. I didn't spend a lot of time looking in the mirror because he handled it so well. He was very accepting of me and it didn't matter to him if I had one or two breasts. Our sexual relationship probably improved because we hadn't been in the best place right before I got sick.

Following the end of cobalt treatments, my life became routine and normal again. Our daughter continued to have problems, which kept us all in a constant state of "What's next?" but it was incorporated as a given, as part of our ongoing lives.

Professionally over the next year I did very well, becoming a director of a statewide fitness program for youth and taking on additional responsibilities as a swim coach for a high school. The kids I was coaching all became a part of our extended family and it was a wonderful new part of my life.

In 1974, Peter had a heart attack from which he recovered but he decided to go into semiretirement. I remember we felt then that three strikes to one family was enough. Then I started having serious vaginal bleeding problems, and given my history of breast cancer, the doctor suggested I have a hysterectomy. Some people might think, "Oh, this woman has lost her breast and now her uterus. What's left of her?" No, it was a relief to me. It was like having labor pains. You know that the pain and suffering is limited; it's done with after the delivery. You're glad when it's done. I was glad to stop the bleeding problems and having periods. The operation scar itself was tiny.

Then in 1977, when I was fifty-one, I felt a lump on my shoulder. I don't remember being particularly upset but went in to see the doctor. He decided to do a biopsy, under a local. After about an hour of probing, he said, "Nothing is there. Nothing to worry about." About a week later, I went to have the stitches taken out and my family doctor was on duty, covering for my vacationing internist. After looking at my shoulder he said, "Marcia, I don't like the looks of this. We've got to operate again to see what's going on."

It was cancer, a fast-growing sarcoma that would require further surgery. With this recurrence, I was more afraid than with the first. It appeared the cancer wasn't related to my breast cancer, but it was suggested that this might be a result of the cobalt treatments. "Well," I thought, "it's too late to do anything about the cobalt." I was scheduled to attend an important weeklong meeting in Los Angeles the next day and decided to go. I was more worried about the meeting than the surgery. As soon as I got on the plane, I realized I was going the wrong way. Two days later I was in the hands of a medical oncologist at a cancer center in Philadelphia.

The operation was handled well. Part of my shoulder blade was removed and I knew this time I would have some physical limitations. With the mastectomy I had no handicaps. I felt lucky, because like the removal of my breast, this second operation involved an external part of my body, rather than any vital organ. Again the doctors said the cancer was limited and everything had been removed. Again I didn't have a bad time with surgery, because I was so active in my life and work and my support systems were strong. My family again came forth with lots of love and support, gathering around me. My children would call every day and Peter was always with me at the hospital.

I did have some problems with my left arm after the second surgery. I got arm edema and stiffness, which I still have nine years later. Of course, I now had limited movement of my shoulder and arm. The hardest thing for me, the first year after surgery, was realizing what I couldn't do anymore. If I reached for my briefcase, I couldn't pick it up without losing my balance. Relearning how to balance was tough. Having to do arm exercises for months to regain strength is very painful. Periodically I went for physical therapy to learn how to do such things as putting on a coat. I also used a Jobe sleeve and still do—that's like an ace bandage for the arm—that keeps swelling from accumulating in the arm. Whereas I could still swim freestyle with my problems after the mastectomy, all I could do after this was a dog paddle.

For someone like me, who has been physically active her whole life, to be unable to do these things was an adjustment. But I started swimming as soon as I could after the operation. I felt secure and accepting of myself. I think my attitude was evident because everyone would tease me as I swam, "Well, you never could do the crawl well anyway."

Of course, with my second cancer, none of my doctors wanted to take any chances and it was recommended that I have chemotherapy for a year. They said it was optional, an insurance policy. With the mastectomy I had no choice; now I was given a choice. I did some research and consulted a number of oncologists. I had major concerns about the long-term effects of chemo. One oncologist said, "Well, ten years from now we'll know what to do about these effects." I didn't think so but I decided on chemo. I did it reluctantly, of course, but I was scared not to do it.

The real trauma of this cancer experience was that year of chemotherapy. Chemo was the most devastating experience, medically and emotionally. I never thought of myself as ill with cancer. I was never sick before or after the mastectomy. It had been very mechanical and my life had marched on. Not true of chemo; chemo was hell. Chemo was not therapeutic; it produced illness. I hated it. I cried every time I had it and did not trust it at all. I felt so vulnerable.

To keep up my work schedule, I had Thursday treatments, took off Fridays from work, and then was sick all weekend. Monday I would be back at work. I remember being very sensitive during that time at work. If something upset me, I would cry very easily. This was hard for me because I ordinarily am a strong decisive person. I also felt under pressure because I wanted to keep my job. You wonder if people are thinking, "Is she going to make it?" There was also financial pressure on me because there was a need for my income.

The first few times of chemo, I was so violently ill we had to call the doctor in. Throwing up for over twenty-four hours is killing and even the antinausea drugs didn't work. On top of this, my chemo injections were given to me in a cold, sterile emergency room setting, with different personnel each time. The nurses offered no tender loving care and were horrible. One time right after an injection, I was having a really tough time and feeling very sick. At that point, my family doctor came in to see me. He lay down next to me on the bed and just held my hand. Talk about bedside manner! He was hurting for me the whole time and I was worried about him worrying about me! His caring attitude is what I expected from the people who were treating me. Later, I wrote a long letter to the hospital and the doctors, protesting their poor treatment of cancer patients. They have since changed their treatment program, but in those days cancer patients didn't have an organized voice, and there were no support groups or resources available.

I considered quitting chemo *so* many times. Chemo drains you to the point where you are only existing. The surgeries were nothing, but the chemo treatments finished me off. The fight went out of me at the time. My whole life was planned around chemo treatments. I was wearing a wig and feeling lousy about my body.

As it turned out I didn't complete the whole year. I was so miserable that I asked a consulting oncologist if he felt it was necessary anymore. He told me the chemo was only an insurance policy, and though it had been recommended, he thought everything had been taken care of with the surgery. I was a little shocked because I had based my decision on this "fast-growing sarcoma," which I guess hadn't spread yet. So I stopped chemo after eight months.

I, of course, experienced the most unpleasant and usual side effects of chemo. Besides being nauseous, I lost weight, my energy, and all my hair. I wore a wig for eight months, which always felt unnatural, and when my hair grew back in, it was all gray. I had decided, because of the carcinogens in hair dye and my fear of recurrence, that after chemo I wouldn't ever color my hair again.

I didn't color my hair but suddenly I looked older. My hair had been my pride and joy, and the loss of it was far more traumatic than losing my breast. I could fake the breast but not the hair. Losing a breast didn't change my sense of sexiness at all, but the change in my hair color did.

After my mastectomy, I colored my hair and felt young, but the moment I had gray hair, I felt differently about myself. At first that was very hard. I was no longer *the* attractive Marcia with gorgeous dark hair. I think gray hair makes you look older, feel and act older. The two things that I most identified with my attractiveness, a full bosom and my hair, were gone. But for me, the hair change was the worst.

I also noticed that men reacted differently toward me. Before I would be at dances and older men would always come to the table and ask me to dance. I loved dancing. But after my hair color changed, they didn't ask me anymore. Now I am amused; then it was difficult. I can understand why women color their hair to keep themselves looking young. I am sure if I hadn't had cancer I would still be coloring my hair, especially as a professional woman. But I am not taking any more chances with possible carcinogens.

After two bouts with cancer and a hysterectomy, I still believe that I am a feminine woman. My looks may have changed but the other qualities I associate with my femininity haven't. I feel less attractive but I have adjusted to that.

Losing a breast never made me feel unattractive and it didn't make a real difference in my sexual life. It never occurred to me that Peter would be less interested in me because of my only having one breast. He was always a one-woman man, devoted to me, and had never checked out other women. He told me I was attractive all the time. If you want to hang around with someone who judges you by your breasts, you're in trouble anyway.

When I first got cancer, I had been married for over twenty-five years. Peter and I had gone through many changes in our sexual relationship because of children, work, personal concerns, and just getting older and slowing down. Our lovemaking after twenty-five years was a lot more quiet than when we were nineteen. If anything, after breast cancer, our sexual feelings were more intense. You're glad to be alive; you're thankful for being loved and being able to love. Now, after forty years of marriage and some disabilities, the older married sexual life has become more servicing and caring for one another. What is interesting is that Peter's heart and other medical problems have affected our sex life much more than my having breast cancer.

Sex is only a small part of a total relationship. We were so lucky to have many years of satisfying sex, and how many people ever had even five years of that? I feel fortunate. I think if you've been satisfied sexually, you can look for other things in your life as well. I used to wonder how people lost themselves in grandchildren or work; weren't they frustrated? Now here I am totally in love with my grandchildren and never busier in my professional life. Now it's a kind of relief—who wants sex, who needs it? I'd rather dance! Certainly there have been times when I miss the old lovemaking. I have felt sadness and bitterness and thought why did this all happen to us? But I can't stay there, for what purpose? Being sexually involved and being attractive were two things that were important to me at one point in my life but that has changed. Part of this change was due to chemo and the other part is aging and the circumstances of my life. It's just different now.

But I am the same woman that I was before cancer in other respects. I am the classic Jewish mother who's always nurturing people, too much so probably. I continue to play the role of supermom—wife, mother, and homemaker—although I can't cook very well. I still like doing for others, flirting, dancing, and having men fuss over me. I still want to make others comfortable in my home. I believe that it is an important feminine attribute to look well and not be sloppy. I do dress well but really don't think about my body image anymore. I have never been the kind of person who was a clothes horse and spent lots of time shopping or having manicures. I don't want to spend my time that way.

I was never the delicate flower type and actually don't remember thinking or worrying about whether I was feminine or not. I don't suspect I would have been considered your traditional feminine woman because I have always been a mover, a shaker, and a fighter. I am a more modern feminine woman in that I have worked for many years. My kids always said I didn't need to be a woman's libber because I always did what I wanted to do. But feminism has never been a cause for me as I have never identified with women as a group. I strongly believe you make things happen for yourself as an individual. I want to be liked for my own sake, not categorized in some way because I am a woman. Still, I have never felt my outspokenness and my femininity were mutually exclusive, because I believe that you can be a feminine person *and* be assertive. Being assertive to me is part of being a person and has nothing to do with masculinity or femininity.

Because of cancer, my feelings about myself as a woman have changed, but the new definition involves my changing role as a woman. It's been nine years since my second cancer and almost fourteen since my first. I feel in a way it's probably been a blessing for me to go through cancer because it's helped me be more accepting of the aging process. I found it's a relief to be older. It's a relief not to be checked out all the time by men. It frees you up to do what you want to do and be worried less about the fight out there. I am not playing the competitive game anymore. I may have needed the attention years ago but it's no longer necessary.

I loved being a young woman and a mother. I loved being an ambitious, hard-working woman. Now I love being an older woman who's a grandmother and all the wiser. I feel I *am* a grandmother type—it amuses me because I never thought this would happen. I sometimes look at myself and see my dowdy old Aunt Sarah! Socially I used to be the belle of the ball—sought after and danced with—and now I am "the old lady." If I tried to be something else, it would be inappropriate. I am not ashamed of my age and make no secret of it at work.

At work, I now play the role of mentor. I have been highly successful in my field and have been responsible for many new and innovative programs over the past thirty years. I have been satisfied with my career, but as time goes on, I am more and more ready to let go. I want to write and spend time traveling, seeing my children and grandchildren.

It's for all these reasons that I think the issue of femininity or a woman's attractiveness is generally more of an issue for younger women with breast cancer. If I had been a younger woman with breast cancer, I think it would have been more difficult. My looks would mean more to me if I was still single and dating, or trying to climb up the corporate ladder. If I hadn't had any children, I would be more concerned. I'd probably consider reconstruction too.

But as a sixty-year-old woman, I now accept and live with the physical changes I have undergone. I have never considered reconstruction because I don't want to fool with my body medically or cosmetically. I am adamantly against it. I don't understand why other women would want to fool with their bodies in this way. My surgery is done and I have healed. I don't need it for my ego or self-esteem or looks. I don't need it to make me feel better. I am what I am and am comfortable. I am flat on one side, so what? Maybe someday I will be flat on the other! I have been using a prosthesis for over fifteen years and haven't had any problems. Because I am large-breasted it looks funny to be unbalanced, so I feel more uncomfortable without my prosthesis than with it. I don't think it's attractive to look at me or anybody else lopsided. I also don't need people staring at me.

When I had my radical mastectomy, no one ever talked about breast reconstruction. It wasn't an option. Now it's talked about all the time. I am not so sure I like people making so much of the reconstruction business. It seems to me they are premising their belief on the assumption that women need two breasts. Perhaps they should focus more on the fact that a woman can get along fine without a breast. One's sexuality does not hinge on a part of the body. It just never occurred to me that I had less value as a person or a woman because of the loss of my breast.

The biggest changes in my life did not come with the mastectomy but with the recurrence. I became far more concerned about my health and far less concerned with my looks. I think generally, the older you are, the more health concerns become a priority in your life. The question is, am I healthy and am I going to survive? Maybe that's why sex and other things in my life became less important. Once you have a life-threatening disease you *know* you can get it again, which I did. You hope you won't, but you know damn well you are more vulnerable than other folks. Suddenly, your priorities are much clearer.

Though I have survived a long time, I continue to have a healthy fear of cancer. If there's a sore that doesn't heal or a pain in my eye, I go bananas. I am very sensitive to how my body feels when I am under stress and do everything I can to take care of it before it becomes a problem. I believe strongly that it is the responsibility of anyone with a life-threatening illness to take better care of themselves, not less. Sleeping enough, eating well, exercising, and dealing with stress is crucial for good health.

I manage stress in my life better now because I have been through so many crises. I used to spend many nights waking at 3 A.M., facing all my worst fears, overwhelmed with the losses and feelings. But I'd get up the next morning and get on with my life. You have no other choice. You just do it. You get back into circulation. I've learned to do this through experience, reading, education, support groups, and therapy. Not being afraid to seek professional help is key. I have my own chop suey recipe book of coping styles. For instance, I have incorporated some behavorial psychology techniques to help me—like using *stop* thinking. I have a bad or depressing thought and think *stop*! It works. Appetite comes with eating, so I make myself eat. I make myself call a friend when I'm a little down. I reach out to others. I internalized these methods and use them when confronted with problems.

Because of my age and experiences, I have also become more accepting of life's tragedies, the ups and downs of life. I am satisfied with life but I expect less now. Less satisfies me more. My experience has taught me that we all have to suffer and work out our own problems. I used to feel that I had to solve everybody's problems, help everyone in trouble, and put out the fires. Now I realize I can't, nor do I want to.

Women traditionally have felt that they are responsible for everything, particularly when things go wrong. They take it on themselves to try and solve others' problems. It comes from being a mother and a wife, all those years of protecting and nurturing. I can't do that anymore. Having breast cancer points out quite clearly that you are only responsible for yourself. You can only control yourself, and whatever will be, will be. You cannot waste your time worrying about things over which you have no control. If you can help a situation—fine—but you learn to detach yourself and accept it when you can't change anything. Living with the uncertainty of cancer and fifteen years of mental illness in the family and being unable to solve that situation has taught me this lesson.

I've gotten to a place where I am very accepting of myself and nurture myself by planning each day with what I want to do. Planning to get what I need in my life is very important. Nurturing me involves sharing with my family and friends and babysitting for my grandchildren. These are the things I need in my life. My connecting with others is the way I nurture and take care of myself.

I also make only short-term goals. One of my goals was to make it to sixty years old. I did it! I go through stages of bargaining, telling myself, "Well, if I can only live to sixty, that's all I want." Now that I made sixty, I am a pig, greedy for life. I want to live until I am seventy! I have all these wonderful grandchildren and feel so close to them. I want to see them grow up. My life is filled with working and my family and friends. These are the joys of my life.

There is no question that having breast cancer is a humbling experience because you are so vulnerable. I feel that I am more of a person for having survived this. But I've survived cancer so far with few disruptions in my life. There was no room in my life for cancer, because the problems and limitations of others in my family were far greater than mine. This has been a great equalizer. There are so many other worse disabilities that could happen than breast cancer. I thought I was badly off because I had no shoes until I saw someone who had no feet. If things really look bad I think about that.

When I think about women's fears about being less attractive and being abandoned because of breast cancer, I compare those fears to those of the mentally ill. There is a tremendous stigma attached to being mentally ill in this country. Mentally ill people constantly have to fight the fear of rejection: Are they less a person because of their condition? How are they going to hold their heads high when they go back to work? Will they ever get a job? Will they be able to live independently? Their self-esteem is *zero*. To me, having breast cancer is minor compared to that. For me the loss of my breast was nothing compared to my daughter's illness.

If you're a breast cancer patient having problems with self-esteem, I say, "Go get help! Join a support group, go to the Y's Encore program, or seek professional help to build yourself up." If a woman feels down about herself and how she looks, she shouldn't try and do it all alone. No, life's too short to go around feeling worthless. There's too much to live for. The fact is that many women live through the experience of breast cancer and are no less people or women. They are functioning in the world, feeling good about themselves and *living*. That is what I want women to know about breast cancer.

10

Nancy

"When I talk to people about this experience, what interests them most is that I feel good about myself, my body, and my life, *and* that I have survived so long. People want to know that a woman is alive and well thirteen years after breast cancer and a mastectomy. They want to hear that you're okay. I am okay."

In 1974, at the age of forty-eight, married and the mother of three children, Nancy was treated for a stage one breast cancer with a radical mastectomy. She had no further treatment. Unhappily married at the time of her diagnosis, Nancy needed to find other avenues of social and sexual support to help her through her breast cancer experience. With a newfound respect, Nancy took charge of her life and was able to leave her twenty-five-year-old decayed marriage. As a divorced, middle-aged woman with a radical mastectomy, she proved that if a woman has confidence in her attractiveness and body image, she can continue to have fulfilling intimate relationships. A long-term breast cancer survivor who has functioned and felt well for years, Nancy demonstrated that women are more than capable of successfully coping with the breast cancer crisis.

When I was young I was a tomboy and deeply involved in being my father's little darling. I was five years younger than my sister and was supposed to be a boy. At least that's what Dad said. Maybe that's why he encouraged me to be active in sports and taught me how to box when I was four. He'd get down on his knees and box with me. I learned all about Jack Dempsey and doing the old one-two. Dad thought it was really funny when I landed "one on the button." I was also taught to swim, canoe, ski, and skate. I played "kick the can" with the boys in the neighborhood, loved to climb trees, had dirty fingernails, and wore pants. I was *always* outspoken. As a child I was described as willful, fearless, and wild. I was very much unlike my older sister, who was timid and quite dependent on parental approval. She would always ask, "Could I?" I would always tell *after* I did something.

I was born in 1925 in a small town in Ohio, where we lived until I was about twelve. My sister, brother, and I were brought up Catholic, although as adults we never went to church. My childhood was happy, though not trouble-free, as we were quite poor during the Depression. My parents always loved and took care of me; they were supportive and available to me. If I didn't always have my father's approval, I always had my mother's. My father was a railroad man, who had gone to work after eighth grade to support his family because his father had died. Dad was a nineteenth-century "Life with Father" sort, an Irish-American Catholic man with definite ideas about feminine virtues: Women did not work; they stayed home. Women also stayed in their place. When I went to work in my thirties, my father said I was self-indulgent. Feminine women were definitely not like his mother-in-law, who lived with us. My grandmother was considered a troublemaker—feisty, stubborn—with a big mouth. One of the worst things said about me in my family was that I was like her.

Unlike her mother, my mother was feminine, well-educated, calm, self-possessed—a peacemaker and mediator. She didn't do anything my father didn't want her to. My parents' relationship was fairly simple: My mother adored my father and he adored her and they did not cross each other. If I said something disparaging about my father, my mother gave me holy hell. I never heard them quarrel. I grew up thinking people who care about each other don't fight.

My mother gave me mixed messages about being a girl: I was told to be a "nice little girl" and grow up to be the kind of wife she was; but I also was told not to. I couldn't have been such a little brat without her support.

My mother talked to me about menstruation when I was about ten. When she first got her period, nobody had told her what was going to happen. She didn't want that to happen to me. So I was prepared. When I got my first period at twelve, I had been *waiting* for it to arrive. About that time, when I was in seventh grade, we moved to Columbus. I found out city girls didn't behave the way I did. The first part of the year, I retreated from socializing because the girls in school were cliquey and totally ignored me. In response, I remember thinking I didn't want to have anything to do with groups of girls *anyway*. By the second half of seventh grade, I was suddenly noticed by boys. Then the girls didn't ignore me and I made lots of friends.

By the time I entered high school, I was full grown: leggy, wiry, with lots of long dark hair and very big green eyes. I wasn't dreamy-looking but I wasn't too bad-looking. I was a part of a group of girls, yet I was also a loner in some ways. One of my problems was that I was a very good student. One of my closest friends used to scold me and say, "Stop answering questions in class! Settle for C's if you ever want to be popular." I couldn't do it. Still I didn't have problems finding dates. Roller-skating rinks were the best place to meet guys in those days.

I got a little plumpish in my late teens, the heaviest ever in my life except when I was pregnant. I just seemed to fill out. Then during college I lost weight and got almost too thin. I remember I was going to a dance and had a very nice black dress on. It just hung on me. There wasn't anything to hold it up. My mother said, "You need to put something in there," and stuffed some tissues into my bra. I liked the effect so much I started wearing these rubber pads—falsies really. Nobody ever discovered them!

Breasts weren't a big item in my life, except as they governed what kind of dress I wore. I was very aware that there was a big division between those who could wear strapless dresses and those who couldn't. I would rather have had that pushed-up bosom look but there wasn't enough material to work with.

I wasn't womanly looking at the time. To be womanly was to have a figure like Betty Grable or Lana Turner, the sex symbols of my teenage years. Still I really didn't identify with them as much as I did with the ideal feminine lady of the time: Greer Garson—Mrs. Miniver—who was intelligent, thoughtful, soft, and a lady with grace.

I had a flaming love affair when I was a senior in high school. Mark was my first real boyfriend and I was absolutely crazy about him. Though babes in the woods, we explored absolutely every aspect of our sexuality. I don't know how we knew what to do but we had a wonderful sexual relationship. We didn't use anything to protect ourselves and I don't know why I didn't ever get pregnant. Before this relationship, I had been very straight, a virgin. In those days, there was necking and there was petting and I necked. I knew deep down that if I did pet, I would go all the way. Which is what happened with Mark.

Unfortunately, after a year the relationship broke off. College and distance put a damper on our young love. Four years later, I ended up marrying a fellow student I had met my junior year.

Larry and I had planned to marry after my college graduation but I got pregnant. After all that fooling around I finally got caught! We got married in 1947, I graduated from the University of Ohio, and my daughter was born in 1948.

Larry wanted an academic career and entered a Ph.D. program in history. By the time he finished his doctorate and served in Korea, we had two daughters and I was a full-time homemaker and mother. I mean full-scale, with-a-vengeance, bake-your-own-bread, clean-and-wax-floors home-maker. During those years I was on an emotional roller coaster, often on the point of suicide because there was no way to be the perfect housewife and mother that I tried very hard to be.

In 1952, Larry was offered a professorship at the University of Pennsylvania and we moved to Philadelphia. We had one more child, a son. When our son was three years old, I decided to go back to school, part-time, to get a teaching credential. I was going nuts at home. Larry was very supportive and I loved school. Soon after I got my certificate, I began teaching history part-time at a private high school.

It seemed like the classic all-American family story until the mid-1960s when my life began to fall apart. A number of crises occurred that affected my life as a woman and wife, a mother and a daughter. My mother died during this time. She was diagnosed with cancer, had surgery, and died two months later. She was only seventy-four. I missed her terribly.

One daughter had left home to go to college and my son was in high school. I had loved raising them and was beginning to miss having them close by. They were always terrific kids and I was particularly close to my daughter. Then my marriage began to crumble. My husband was involved in affairs with his students. I didn't know at first. I just knew something was wrong.

I was forty years old. I remember looking in the mirror and thinking, "You still look like a girl, your cheeks are rosy, your hair is curly, and you look fine first thing in the morning." I wondered what he was looking for. His house was well cared for, his children were wonderful—I just didn't understand. Something in my background told me (probably reading *Ladies Home Journal* stories) that it was my fault. I'd think, "What have I *not* done?" But I was also angry because I couldn't come up with anything. How could twenty years of marriage go down the tubes?

Larry recanted a couple of times, though he never really suffered remorse. He managed to convince me the marriage was going to work by telling me I was middle class not to be involved in affairs myself. Being the good learner I am, I tried that one for a while too.

All of a sudden this chaste housewife who had not noticed a man for twenty years started sending out signals. I am convinced we do exude something to start the process. At first, I was too chicken to do anything, but I finally started seeing other men and had a number of affairs.

For the next ten years, my marriage was like a roller coaster. We were both having affairs, yet we remained glued to each other in a pattern of game-playing that we seemed to thrive on. I don't know—maybe after such a long time, you keep hoping somehow things will work out. Fortunately, I was doing well in my professional life. I went back to graduate school, got a master's degree in education, and was teaching full-time at a local college.

In 1972, I experienced many physical problems: terrible pains in my left breast, breast lumps, and bleeding from an IUD. I was very frightened and went to see my doctor, who removed the IUD and put me on birth control pills. Eventually the bleeding stopped and the breast swelling went down, but I was still spooked. I had vivid dreams of death. In one, my mother was the pilot of a plane. I wanted to get away, telling her, "I don't want to go where you're going." I noticed the fuselage was like a casket. Then suddenly my husband came and slammed me into the cockpit with my parents and closed the door. I didn't get that message for a while. Anyway, I had strong feelings that I was on a death course. Soon after that, my father died of old age.

About the same time, a women's studies course was being developed at the college where I was teaching. My involvement with the course was the beginning of my consciousness-raising and feminism. I had already been reading books by Germaine Greer and other feminists and was very interested in the movement. I did one lecture on "The Body and How to Talk to Your Doctor." Little did I know how I was going to need this information.

During that school year, for the first time in years, I had a feeling of tremendous well-being: intellectually, physically, and emotionally. I finally had started therapy, and though in touch with my anger at my husband, was feeling hopeful about my marriage. I looked good for a forty-eight-year-old. My hair, which I'd colored since my thirties, still had a shine to it. I didn't have any concerns of aging and had no premenopausal symptoms. I looked youthful and healthy. Life was going well.

Then sometime during the summer of 1973, I was standing in front of a mirror doing my hair. I saw a shadow on my breast, felt it, and was sure I had a lump. The nipple on my right breast had inverted earlier that year, but it returned to its original position. I told Larry I thought I had a lump. In his usual unsupportive way, he told me to go see my doctor—*he* couldn't do anything. I went for a checkup and the doctor recommended I go to a surgeon. I made the surgeon's appointment as soon as I could because Larry and I were scheduled to leave the States in a month to go to Denmark on one of Larry's professorial exchange programs.

The week before I had the appointment with the surgeon, I began a wild infatuation with a very handsome man, who was somebody else's husband, of course. His name was Lee. I really went into it knowing I was going to have an affair with this hunk—I nailed him. I thought that this would be really good for me. We met for lunch and he asked me to go away for the weekend to New York with him. I said yes.

After making love for the very first time, he told me, "You have a lump in your breast." I told him I knew and was going to the doctor Monday. He was very concerned. On Monday morning I saw the surgeon who tried to aspirate my lump. No luck. She was fairly sure the lump was malignant and wanted me to sign all the release forms right then for both a biopsy and a radical mastectomy.

I wanted to know if there were any other options for me. She said, "We can do the biopsy and the lymph nodes and stop at that point. But that really is not a viable option—let's get rid of this." I told her to just go ahead with the whole works; I wanted it over with. I felt trapped. She said, "I can operate tomorrow or I can do it in two weeks." As I was about to leave the country and didn't have much time, I said I'd come in the next day and have it done right away. I really didn't give myself much time to have second thoughts. I asked about reconstruction at the time but the doctor wanted me to wait for at least a year. If there were no further problems, we could discuss it then.

I went home to pack my bag and tell my family. I told my kids, who were home visiting and were very frightened for me. Then I told Larry about the biopsy and he looked very helpless and said, "What a disappointment." I rejected him right there and then by saying, "Don't worry about me. I'll be fine." I didn't want to discuss it with him. I shut him out fairly early on in this process. He hadn't cared when I told him about the lump and he'd rejected me so many times before. He made it clear that "It was my problem." I was frightened but did not really believe it was breast cancer. I was sure I was fine.

I checked into the hospital Monday night and the surgery was the next afternoon. My doctor was a good surgeon but she had no bedside manner. She brought me out of anesthesia after the frozen section, leaned over, and said, "I am sorry, my dear. I am going to have to take it off." I am sure it was a deliberate act, so when I came out of recovery my family members didn't have to tell me I no longer had a breast. I learned later that my lump was the size of a pea and there was no lymph node involvement. They had caught it fairly early.

When I woke up in the recovery room, I had never been so miserable in my life. I was only forty-eight years old and things had been going so well. I was in touch with the fact that I had just begun to love my breasts when I lost mine. It took me a long time to like them because I grew up in Lana Turner's time. I hadn't had big tits and had a sense of physical inadequacy for a number of years. I was sad. I also questioned why *I* got breast cancer—the classic "Why me?" syndrome. I had no family history and was still young. I think it was partly environmental because when I was twelve I had a spot on my lung and the doctors used to x-ray me all the time. The x-rays in the thirties and forties were loaded with radiation. If it hadn't been the x-rays, then what? I wanted to know why.

I was also concerned about my daughters' risk of getting breast cancer. I had nursed my children until they were ready for drinking cups and was worried maybe I had transferred the problem to them. I thought, "Boy, what a heritage." I really felt guilty. Later, because they were concerned too, my daughters quit taking birth control pills and learned about breast care and doing breast self-examination. I hoped they would never have to face this disease.

The first thing my husband said to me in my hospital bed was, "It's over and you are going to be all right. That's all that matters." I remember thinking I would be climbing this mountain by myself and that was *not* all that mattered. I didn't want any comfort from him. For the first time in my whole life, I experienced the adult feeling of "It's up to you; you are on your own now." I wasn't blaming anyone. I realized it was my crisis and thought, "Thank God, I am alive. I have a whole second chance. Now what am I going to do with it?" I knew I was going to get through it all and get on with my life.

Larry visited me but only for short time periods. He really didn't want to be there because he didn't like being around sick people. However, I was very comforted by my kids, all my friends, and coworkers who came to see me the week I was in the hospital. I actually had a wonderful time there and felt like a queen. When I got out of the hospital, I looked out at the car window—it sounds so corny—and noticed how terribly green the trees were and what a beautiful day it was.

When I got home from the hospital, I felt physically good and quite strong. I did my arm exercises while I was still in the hospital and was able to raise my arm way up in the air. I wasn't depressed, nor was I in pain. But I felt very much on my own. Larry was afraid of me physically and didn't come near me. He never touched my chest. Although the night before we left for Denmark, he made some verbal overture like, "Why don't you come over here?" I went over to him and I stayed on top of him so not to put any pressure on my chest and the bandages. He couldn't do anything and I got fatigued waiting. We'd had quite a great sex life before this. I felt like asking him whether he'd slept with his girlfriend that day. My feeling was that he didn't want to sleep with me until I was better. It wasn't that he was afraid of hurting me; rather that he didn't like bandages and illness and was frightened.

Given this lousy situation with Larry, at my very first opportunity, I called Lee who was willing to meet me anywhere and anyplace. It was less than two weeks after my mastectomy when we met. He said, "I have all the luck! God, I just meet you and look what they do. They start cutting you up!" He was utterly accepting and considerate, and I was still every bit as exciting to him as I had been without the bandages and with two breasts. It meant a great deal to me to be accepted; if I hadn't had that, the rejection from my husband would have been devastating. But it never occurred to me that Lee would reject me. As a matter of fact, it was very hard for me to accept the fact that my husband was doing just that. It took me years to admit to myself that this man with whom I had three children, and with whom I had lived on more or less intimate terms for a quarter of a century, was put off by what happened to my body. You just don't think your husband is going to do that.

So I got my needs taken care of by a man who had his stuff together. But only until I went to Denmark. We'd discussed our relationship and Lee had said, "Neither one of us is in a position to make any promises." We were infatuated but not in love. We decided not to write one another that year because it was too risky. It was painful to say good-bye.

Within a month after my operation, as planned, I went to Denmark with Larry for the next year. This was a physically cold and difficult year, both personally and socially. It was also the first time that I had time to really look at my body. I was horrified by this red slash across my chest and didn't like to look at it very often. Fortunately, our bathroom mirror was very high and I couldn't see below my chin. It was a cold climate and there was no central heating or electric blankets in our home so I kept very bundled. I usually don't wear a nightgown to bed but I did then because of the cold. It was a year of being covered. Though I didn't really see my chest very much that year, I felt unattractive.

I don't remember any sex that Larry and I had. I am sure we did but it sure wasn't memorable. Our sex life had been memorable at various times in our lives—he was a great technician—but it seemed to have ended.

It also didn't help that I didn't have a prosthesis for the first year after my mastectomy. When I was in the hospital, a Reach to Recovery volunteer came to visit me and gave me a little pad filled with cotton fluff. I used what she gave me much longer than other breast cancer patients, I'm sure, because my flesh wasn't healing as fast as it should have. My doctor said I wasn't ready for a prosthesis. So I waited a year until I got back to the States to buy one.

I also desperately needed information about breast cancer. In 1973, there was almost nothing available on breast cancer for patients. For the first year after my operation, I was frustrated in my efforts to find materials so I could understand the disease and learn how to live with it. I spent time in medical and college libraries searching for answers. What did other women do? Had I done the right thing? Was I sorry? I decided that no, I wasn't sorry. I felt safe and thought that living was worth so much more than a little breast tissue. Of course, less than a year after my operation, Betty Ford had her mastectomy and *Time* magazine came out with an up-to-date article that gave me information that I hadn't read before. Suddenly, breast cancer came out of the closet. It had been lonely territory before that. Nobody talked about it.

That first year after my mastectomy, one of my major problems was loneliness. At a time when I needed support and love, all my friends were thousands of miles away and there was nobody to talk to. Being in a foreign country didn't help. I really didn't tell anybody about my operation either. So nobody knew, except Larry, and he didn't understand that every little pain to me was a brain tumor, and how frightened I was. We fought quite a bit. The only way I could sleep was to use Dalmane. As I was drug-sensitive, I'd be dopey and tired almost every day. Being removed from my work was bad too. Going back to work would have been a lot easier than what I did in Denmark—housekeeping. I went to one doctor who said I was suffering from culture shock—talk about being misunderstood! That year I was exhausted by isolation, physical problems, worrying, and a lack of social support. It was the first time I seriously thought of leaving Larry for good.

I was so relieved to come home. One of the first things I did when I got home was go shopping for a prosthesis. It was difficult because there weren't many stores in town selling them. When I finally found a store, the prostheses weren't the right size. All the salesladies did was make me look like a Sherman tank. I kept telling them, "That's not my body; that's not me!" Since I couldn't find what I liked locally, I went into New York and finally found a store that carried a prosthesis that had a silicone filling with foam rubber on the back. I bought four of them. In those days, prostheses were always round, which most breasts aren't, but it was okay. The breasts also hardened after a while too. Of course, prostheses are much better now because they're contoured and shaped to fit under your arms and made out of better materials. The one I have now is comfortable and feels like me. It clings to my body and doesn't shift around. It doesn't exactly fill in where I am flat, but to tell the truth, it doesn't have to be filled in because I have never been filled out!

The year after my return from Denmark proved to be a crucial year. It was emotionally the end of my marriage. Lee was back in my life again. I had few responsibilities besides my work, as the kids were gone. I had lots of spare time and decided to go back in therapy. My therapist kept telling me, "If your behavior changes, your husband's will have to change too." I changed my behavior. So did Larry but it was not for the better. I thoroughly frustrated him by acting in new ways, being my own person and not jumping when he pressed his demands.

I also wasn't feeling well. I was having endometrial bleeding and pain. The doctors said I had an ovarian cyst and needed a hysterectomy. I thought it might be cancer again. It had been less than a year since my mastectomy and I was still worried about recurrences. This time I was sure it was going to be malignant and I'd have to have radiation and chemo. The doctor's attitude was, "You actually don't have much use for your uterus anyway. Let's take anything we see lying around." I asked them while they were at it, maybe they could take the fat around my tummy, but they wouldn't do that! I said yes to the hysterectomy because I didn't want to take any chances. It turned out to be a benign ovarian cyst. Boy, I was dumb. I surrendered a perfectly healthy body and allowed them to do the hysterectomy.

This surgery was far more traumatic than the mastectomy. I went into immediate menopause with all the well-known symptoms. Though I was almost fifty, I had had no menopausal symptoms before. On the outside I looked the same because all I had was a tiny bikini scar. But I was a little iffy about my insides because I was reconstructed. I wasn't sure how it was going to feel with intercourse. Though I was scared, I was also eager to find out whether "it" still worked. I initiated the first encounter with Larry and intercourse hurt a little, which I told him. After that he was reluctant to try anything and didn't think it was worth the bother. He never accepted me after my surgery. Our physical relationship really deteriorated and basically ended. Of course, good old Lee came through for me.

Fortunately, my relationships with other people outside my marriage were burgeoning. I had seen how loving my friends and coworkers were after both my surgeries. I believed that people admired me and that was very comforting. People reached out to me—maybe I reached out to them—anyway, things were different because I was closer with everyone I worked with. These relationships became very important. Out of having breast cancer came a life decision to develop the friendships that had possibilities. Once you have had a life-threatening illness, in a way the ultimate has occurred, and it changes everything. You want more and receive more in relationships, particularly with others who have similar problems to yours. I recognize this quality in other breast cancer patients and we understand one another immediately. It's almost a clubby thing.

I needed my husband less and less. Early on, I believed that he was meant to be my best friend, my lover, and my everything. Like many women of my generation, I didn't have my own friends in the early years in my marriage. Larry had friends and they had wives. Their wives became my friends. But my friendships had become my own and far more important than my relationship with my husband. Six months after my return from Denmark, I filed for divorce, which became final in 1975. I'd endured enough pain, tried enough new patterns of behavior, to know I couldn't live like that anymore. I am a slow study when it comes to leaving. It took me a long time.

The marriage was not good when I got sick and it didn't get better after I got sick. What stood between me and taking action to end it was the sense that I *couldn't* have been that mistaken, that *wrong* about somebody who I'd lived with all those years. To find out that he couldn't accept my body when it changed—that "my old age" was repulsive to him—was shocking to me. Larry seemed to respond the way many women do to the loss of a breast. He behaved as if *he* was the one that lost something! I find it embarrassing that I would have chosen such a man. Angry at myself more than anything. I wouldn't blame breast cancer for the breakup of my marriage. But I think it was a catalyst that showed me the side of him I suspected was there, a shallowness and inability to accept change. I think he was afraid of a strong woman too.

What was strange was that *I* felt really confident about my body. I may have been missing some parts but knew I was attractive because I got lots of reinforcement. Besides Lee, many men paid attention to me. My missing breast didn't make a difference so I never considered reconstruction. Also, I didn't have any chest muscle and was basically frightened at the prospect of enormous amounts of surgery. The doctors would take skin grafts from God knows where. The time the surgery would consume and the risks it would entail wouldn't be worth it to me.

If I was forty-eight years old now with breast cancer, I would love to have reconstruction. But I am sixty-one and accustomed to what I am. It would have been nice had times been different but I'm not going to go back. For what purpose? I am a little envious of the women who are having immediate reconstruction. But I feel good in my clothes and don't feel bad without them either. People ask me if I'd ever have a face-lift and I say, "Why would I have surgery for any reason than to save my life?"

Besides, since my remaining breast is small, I'm not lopsided. I feel attractive with one breast. I have certainly never had any problems with dating or sleeping with anyone. It never occurred to me that the loss of my breast would be a problem and it hasn't been. It's been a matter of my self-concept and how I view myself. Since my mastectomy, both as a married and divorced woman, I have dated and had affairs with men and never have had a bad experience. I had a twenty-eight-year-old male friend— a real doll—who became my lover for over a year. Boy, did he surprise me when he asked me to go to bed! I was twice his age! We used to sit in the bathtub on cold nights and drink wine. He never had a problem with it. Some men are interested and some want to touch my scar and some just don't pay attention.

It's interesting, but through lovemaking I have discovered I have a phantom nipple. There's a place under my arm that must have been a connecting nerve to my breast that is still there. If that place is touched just right, my long-lost nipple's erected. The body remembers.

Lee is still in my life. We've been seeing each other now for over twelve years, every week. He loves his wife and intends, as he promised, to stay with her for life. At this point, I think it would panic me if something happened to their marriage. I don't really want to live with anyone anymore. I have gotten used to being on my own. I do what I want to do. I like the solitude, but like everybody, I get lonesome from time to time. I am close to and keep in touch with my kids. My life is full of the things I love—the theater, dance, and music.

I have the same fears any other single woman who's in her sixties has. I hope that I can keep on working until my retirement gives me enough money to live a decent life. Professionally, I have done well and am still learning. In addition to my teaching, I have been awarded fellowships and grants. I've written and published articles, poetry, and books.

I always thought I was feminine and still feel very much a feminine woman. I like being a woman and I wouldn't rather be a man. I have a fair degree of female vanity in that I like looking and dressing well. I like being attractive to men. I think I am feminine in my concern for and sensitivity to people's feelings. That's a strong part of being feminine.

I like my women friends better than I like any man. But I still like men and relate to them with lots of flirting. Some of my more radical feminist friends have scolded me about this flirting. I flirt! Yes, I do! I like the spark, wordplay, and eye contact that's part of a male-female relationship. That's the fun part of being feminine. There is nothing wrong with it. I lose nothing by doing it because that is not the *only* way I relate to men. Now I also expect to be listened to by men. I am on equal terms with everybody, male and female, I deal with. I am not aggressive but I don't back off.

I am very definitely a different woman because of breast cancer. My life became enriched in many ways by breast cancer. I feel I am a better person because I have demonstrated an ability to survive a life-threatening disease. I am *more* of a person.

Breast cancer, like any other life-threatening disease or painful experience, simply brings about a total change in the way we perceive our lives. Priorities get all sorted out—it may take some time to choose them—but ultimately it happens. I finally got out of a bad marriage and learned how to care for me. I know what's important for me now. I care what happens to my life day by day, month by month. I don't just do something because I want to be a good sport.

When my husband and I split up, my son said to me, "I am glad to see you're coming into your own. You're finally coming out from under the tyranny." My mouth dropped open when he said that. That was how I perceived my situation at various times, but not fully. Breast cancer made me aware of how valuable my life is and taught me that I am in charge and not to be trifled with. I am much less frivolous now. In some ways I view the earlier part of my life as being frivolous because I did not value myself as much as I should have. I let myself be used and let things happen to me because I didn't have enough respect for myself. That doesn't happen now. My life is not to be taken lightly. I took it lightly.

The first year after breast cancer, I felt my body had betrayed me. I hadn't treated it badly and didn't understand why it happened to me. I felt vulnerable in a way that I have never felt before; I still do. Once you've had breast cancer, you learn to live with the unpredictability of life. It doesn't matter how many years you've survived. I am particularly aware of this because I talk to women with breast cancer who may die. Sometimes I find it painful to talk to them because I can't say, "You'll be all right." Some will be; some won't.

A few years ago, I became really terrified when the Reach to Recovery volunteer who had visited me in the hospital, and had become my friend, died of cancer. She was a beautiful woman who was younger than I was. She had survived breast cancer for seven years. Her death occurred during the throes of my divorce, so I was particularly vulnerable to her loss. That set me back. She got past "the five years." I was past the five years too. I was very glad to hit ten years. But I am still aware that I can have a recurrence.

When I talk to people about this experience, what interests them most is that I feel good about myself, my body, and my life *and* that I have survived so long. People want to know that a woman is alive and well thirteen years after breast cancer and a mastectomy. They want to hear that you're okay. I am okay.

11

Julia

"One important thing I have learned since having breast cancer is the power of sharing. I had *never* been one to discuss my personal life with anyone, but I started talking about my breast cancer because I felt it was important to help other women. If a woman shares her experiences, she feels much better. I firmly believe that being open with others is the best way to accept yourself. Reach to Recovery is an important program because it shows that women *live* after breast cancer and that breast cancer doesn't stop you—you only stop yourself."

In 1983, Julia, a fifty-five-year-old divorcee with five grown children, was diagnosed with a stage two breast cancer. She underwent a modified radical mastectomy and had no further treatments. A woman who professionally and personally nursed and mothered everyone else, she found that she was transformed by her breast cancer experience and decided to take care of herself first for a change. Disregarding the myth that a woman with breast cancer will have difficulty finding a partner, she remarried after her mastectomy. Ordinarily not one to talk about her feelings, she learned to open up and talk with other breast cancer patients, surprised about how much better she felt when she discussed her concerns. Julia's strong religious faith played a crucial role in her ability to cope with her recovery. As a result of her religious beliefs and newfound faith in herself, she devoted herself full-time to helping other women through the American Cancer Society's Reach to Recovery program.

I was born right before the Depression in New Mexico in 1928. I was the baby of the family, the fifth and last child born to my parents. My background was mixed because my father was black and my mother was pure Navajo Indian. Though I looked more black than Indian, I was brought up with many Indian traditions. My mother, who kept her black hair in the same fashion for her entire life—braided and pulled back—raised all my sisters and brothers and me very much the same way she had been raised. Our hair was always pulled back in large braids, we ate Indian foods, and even dressed in Indian fashion when we were young. The strange thing was, at the same time, we were raised Baptist!

We were an odd family: an Indian mother, a Baptist black father, and five children, who lived with most of my mother's extended family. They all took care of us and we always felt loved. But my mother was the most important person in my life.

Since I was the baby, she spoiled me horribly, and we became very close. Too close, I think, sometimes. Though she was my mother, we were more like friends at times. I could confide in her about anything that worried me.

My mother was a very joyful and cheerful woman who was very affectionate with us all. A loving person who really cared for people, she always wanted to share with others, no matter what we had. If the neighbors didn't have enough money for food, she'd fix them meals and give them clothes. Even though she worked in a factory all day long, she always took time to help others. I am like her in many ways.

My father, a railroad worker, was a stern man who also could be very affectionate and warm. When I got into trouble, he might whoop me, but he'd only spank me on my legs, so I wouldn't really get hurt. But no one ever loved me like my father did. He always told me he loved me and how pretty I was. I felt so special and important because of that. The most valuable things he taught me were always to care for myself and not to be jealous of what others had. He encouraged me to get an education and firmly believed I could do anything I wanted. He believed in me. I was very fortunate as a child to have both my parents love me so much.

By the time I was thirteen, I was almost the size I am now. I was a tall, thin kid, with really long, black hair, whose breasts seemed to sprout up almost overnight. All the women in my family had big breasts, so I thought I would too. When my breasts started growing, Mom began to rub Indian medicine concoctions made with alcohol and vinegar on them. The medicines were used for swellings and other problems back then. It sounds strange now, but I didn't question Mom about why she was doing this, because I remember thinking my breasts were growing *awfully* fast, so maybe she wanted to stop them from growing. When I was older, she told me she didn't want me to grow up and thought the alcohol might shrink and dry out my breast tissue. I guess she wanted to keep her baby, and I think she hoped that my breasts wouldn't be as large as the others in my family. Unfortunately for her, the medicines didn't work, and my breasts followed family tradition.

I was never scared about getting my periods because Mom explained what was going to happen. Maybe I'd have a little pain in my stomach and some discharge with a little blood. She showed me the sanitary napkins—homemade at that time—and how to use them. As Mom was an immaculate lady—she had a real thing about cleanliness—she'd sterilize the cotton rags in a pot and dry them, then fold them and wrap them in plastic. Of course, being told about this event and experiencing the actual first period was a little different. I was scared when it happened and was *sure* I was going to die. In those days, I was an anxious kind of kid—everything made me jump. As I got older, I became quite a calm person though.

Once the discussion with my mother about periods ended, and I started menstruating, I never talked to anyone about it, not even my girlfriends. There were lots of secrets about reproduction and the facts of life then. Questions were not encouraged. You didn't ask your friends about it because they might say something to their mothers, who would say something to *your* mother. Our mothers were old-fashioned and didn't talk about things openly like mothers do now. I grew up thinking if I kissed boys I could get pregnant. I really believed it! My father explained pregnancy to me: "Kissing won't get you pregnant, but it leads to it. If you let a boy get that close, he'll want to go further." But, like most fathers, he never went into detail as to what the boy would do. The message was just don't let him touch you. I grew up in a very modest way—I never saw my brother or father undressed. I didn't see a man naked until I was married!

In 1941, when I was thirteen, my dad left us and moved to Arizona. Since we lived with most of my mother's family, my dad had not been thrilled with having them around all the time, particularly because of their Indian ways. He decided he wanted to get away but my mother didn't want to move. In spite of their strong feelings about each other, he left. It wasn't that traumatic for me for some reason, maybe because I was the baby of the group, and I got to live with both my parents after that. I moved back and forth from state to state throughout my teenage years. I was the only child in the family that wanted to do this, and since my mother basically trusted my dad with me, it worked.

I definitely took advantage of this situation. I gave them a run for their money when I was a teenager. I knew Dad really cared about me and would use that to manipulate him. Like if one of my dad's girlfriends did something I didn't like, I'd tell him and he'd drop her! Sometimes, I played my parents against each other. If things weren't going well with my father, or I didn't get what I wanted from him, I'd call my mom and ask to come back. It always worked! My dad was aware of what I was doing and would joke with me about making the Santa Fe Railroad rich with my comings and goings. But he never stopped me.

During high school, I decided to become a nurse. It was no surprise to my family, because ever since I was a kid, my sister and I played doctor and nurse instead of house! I was always the one who cared for people. I even took care of my dolls who, of course, were always sick with headaches and stomachaches. But they got better when I was there. My nursing abilities were always *there* inside of me. It was a personal gift of being able to give to others that later made me successful in the profession.

All through my teens, I was very active in athletics, running track, playing basketball, and being a cheerleader. I wanted to be and was in *everything*. I was too busy in the social things to pay a lot of attention to my studies, but I wasn't a bad student—I had a B average. After high school graduation, I decided to stay with my dad in Phoenix and go to college.

At the time I entered college, I would describe myself as a good-humored and good-natured person, who liked to make people comfortable. I wanted everyone to like me. I was a good friend. But I also had many successes as a kid and always wanted to be first. I was very competitive—being involved in athletics showed me that. Daddy always said to me, "You have to try to do your best," and I did. So I was a self-confident young woman and I liked myself. But I wasn't flashy or a show-off.

During my junior year, I met my future husband, Joey, through mutual friends. He was a handsome man, a real charmer who had nice manners, but my dad didn't approve of the relationship because Joey was three years older than I was. Like all fathers, he wanted me to finish college. But like many young people who were in love then and felt it wasn't right to do anything sexual without marriage, we decided to get married. At the end of my third year of college, I dropped out of school and started a new life.

We were happily married for over twenty-five years and had a good time together. Joey and I grew up together, and I became an adult with him. He spoiled me too. He was not only my husband but a friend and a brother too. In 1952, when Joey went into the service and while he was in Korea, I got my nurse's training and started working in hospitals. We also went on to have five healthy children—four daughters and one son.

The one area of our marriage that wasn't very satisfying to me was our sexual relationship. At first, I was inexperienced and shy with Joey and it took me a long time to warm up. Joey was sex-crazy—his whole family was like that—and he only wanted for himself. When we made love, he didn't take my feelings into account, so I didn't give my whole self to him. Then I also didn't want to have sex because I was getting pregnant every year. Sex wasn't a pleasurable thing to me when I was younger. Sex was something I dreaded. I never was relaxed and didn't have climaxes. I didn't worry about the fullness of enjoyment; I just did it because my husband wanted to. I always cared about other people's feelings, so I didn't involve myself. Everything else was working out in our relationship, so I didn't think too much about it.

We raised our family while we both worked. We always went to church and raised our kids as Baptists. I worked evenings; he worked days. So we were able to cover our parenting responsibilities. We loved our family and I loved being a mother. I still love being a mother. Besides my work, my life was my children and I didn't like being separated from them. I was very active with the kids' schools, mothers' clubs, and the PTA, and even serving milk at recess. You might say I was overly involved with the kids' learning. A number of my children went to a Catholic school, because I didn't think the public schools were up to par. Though I was a Baptist, I started going to Catholic masses and even took catechisms so I understood what they were learning. I always felt the church was inside of me, so it didn't matter which church I went to. To me, having the faith was the important thing.

During the early 1970s, a number of changes occurred in Joey's life and mine that led to our splitting up. The first change was that I became burned out from nursing. When I was trained, nurses cared about the patients and were dedicated to making them feel better. No matter what your status was—LPN, LVN, RN, or nurse's aid—when a patient needed something, you got it. In the 1960s and 1970s, nursing became just a job for many nurses who didn't care much about the patients anymore. Because of their bad attitudes, many patients got hurt. So I ended up taking care of everybody's patients. I got downright tired. It was too bad because I was a good nurse and I loved the work. I left the nursing profession and started a new job working for the State of Arizona's Health Department in 1974.

The second change was that Joey, who had been a part-time gambler for years, became a full-time gambler. His life was taken over by it—it was a disease, a horrible habit. He stopped going to church and doing the things we had been raised to do. I started to worry as more and more of his time was spent staying out later and later. He began to neglect both me and the children. We all asked him to stop, and he wouldn't. After two years, I had decided I was going to go out on my own, without him. After all those years, we still loved each other but the relationship wasn't working.

I was almost forty-eight years old and thought I wasn't getting any younger and better start fresh when I could. In 1976, I moved out of the house and found a place close to my job. The three youngest kids came to live with me a few months later.

Though Joey and I separated, we didn't divorce until four years later, because he always gave me sad stories about having no money for child support. I didn't push him and I was in no rush. But my husband and I kept fairly friendly relations until he died a few years later.

The worst time for me was during our initial separation because it was a big step for me to leave. But I had prayed over it and felt I was doing the right thing. The kids were devastated and shocked and saw me as the "bad guy." They never thought this would happen and, of course, there were lots of hurt feelings all around. It's hard to do that to a family.

One problem was that no one could believe we were splitting because we had been the ideal couple. I had never complained or said anything to my sisters, brothers, or friends about his gambling. I wasn't an open person about my personal business and was always reserved about myself. I didn't talk much about my feelings either. If there was anything wrong with me, no one would know it. I didn't think anyone could understand how I felt. It was funny because people always came to me with their problems because I gave good advice and always told the truth. Sometimes I was so sympathetic about their concerns that their problems became *my* problems.

Anyway, I didn't tell anyone about my separation and problems. Fortunately, a friend at work noticed how sad I was and asked me what was wrong. For the first time in years, I poured out all my problems. She understood. That was the beginning of me sharing my feelings with others.

A few months after I moved out, a man named BJ, whom I had known before, started coming to see me. Interestingly enough, he was always in the vicinity when I seemed to have the most troubles. He was there right when I needed him. BJ was a source of strength to me during this time, but also stayed in the background and didn't intrude on me. He was a smart man and sort of eased into my life. Though BJ and I continued to live apart for the next four years, we spent all our time together.

It took some time, but a few years later, my life was going well again. I was living with my two youngest kids, still working for the state, and still involved with BJ. Then, in late 1982, unfortunately my mother became very ill with cancer and I ended up commuting back and forth to New Mexico to take care of her.

She was in pain a lot of the time and suffered so. One night when she was having a bad time, I prayed to the Lord to just take her pain away and give her tumor to me. I begged him, "Just take it from her and give it to me." The Lord came to me and told me that my mother was saved and I didn't have to worry about her anymore. She died soon after that. I was so relieved to know that in her death she was saved. I was finally able to cry and let go after that. It was then that I became a born-again Christian.

A few months after my mother had died, I went to a doctor for a checkup at my health clinic. Dr. Klein told me in the breast examination he'd felt something suspicious but was not sure what it was. He asked me, "Have you ever had a mammogram?" I said, "No." He informed me, "When you're past forty, you should have them regularly, especially because you have large breasts." I was willing to have one, so Dr. Klein referred me to another doctor at my clinic who was *not* worried about this suspicious area in my breast. He said, "There's nothing wrong with your breast and there's no reason for a mammogram." He *wouldn't* order one. I thought this was all very frustrating. So I came back the next day and saw another doctor, Dr. Jordan, and told him that I had found a lump. This doctor felt the lump and ordered a mammogram, which is what I wanted. Some of these health maintenance organizations are funny places—you have to be persistent and manipulative to get what you need.

It was strange about finding my lump. Right before my mother became ill, I had received an American Cancer Society brochure in the mail on a breast self-examination (BSE) course. I had been thinking about learning how to examine my own breasts, though I didn't know anybody who had breast surgery or had problems with her breasts. I had just had a yearly physical, and according to the doctor, was fine. So I don't know why I decided to sign up for the course, but I did. But because I left for New Mexico, I never took the BSE course. I wondered now if I might have found the lump earlier.

There was a shadow on the mammogram. Dr. Jordan told me, "I don't think it's serious, but let's go with a biopsy just to make sure." Even though I didn't know at that time what a two-step procedure (biopsy first, surgery second) was, I told him I'd consent only to the biopsy, but didn't want any more surgery the same day if it was cancer. I didn't want to wake up from my biopsy with my breast gone. I wanted to go home first and then make my own decision. I had no experience with this breast cancer business, so I can't understand why I had the common sense to say all that. Luckily, there was no fight from Dr. Jordan; he agreed with me.

We made arrangements for the biopsy the next week, but for the next two months, things kept happening to me. I kept postponing the surgery—my daughter needed help with her kids, there were problems on the job, etc. I couldn't find the time. I came up with some great delays. But actually, I was frightened and remember thinking, "If the biopsy's put off, maybe it's for the best." I really thought *maybe* the lump would go away. I was only fifty-five and had been healthy all my life. I really didn't want to know. Dr. Jordan kept calling, insisting on my having the biopsy. Finally, in August 1983, three months after the mammogram, I had the biopsy.

When I came out of the anesthesia, I asked the nurse where Dr. Jordan was, and she told me, "He's left, so I guess there must not have been anything wrong, or else he would have talked to you about it." I went home thinking I was okay; I was so relieved. Then Dr. Jordan called me two days later, saying he needed to see me to check the bandage and stitches. That was the first time I got afraid. If the nurse had called me, I wouldn't have worried, but when the doctor calls, it's trouble.

By the time I got to his office a few days later, I was in a state of shock and very nervous. The first thing the nurse said to me was, "What are you here to see the doctor about?" I was so anxious, I got really upset with her. What did she mean—she had the medical record right in front of her! She *knew* why I was there. Of course, once I saw the doctor I was too scared to ask him anything. After Dr. Jordan changed the bandage, he said, "It looks good. When you're dressed come into my office." I dressed very fast.

It was only then that Dr. Jordan told me, "Well, there is a problem. I think we'll have to go for further surgery." He didn't tell me anything about the pathology report. He started talking about treatment options, saying he'd prefer to do a modified radical mastectomy. Up to this point, the man never mentioned cancer to me. He continued, "You can always have reconstruction. Besides, do you know how many movie stars have had breast cancer? Why, even the president's wife has had it. Why, you'd be surprised who's had it." He just kept rattling all this off to me. I finally interrupted him: "Big deal. I don't know all these people you're talking about. What about *me?* What's going on with me? Let's decide now." He talked about the possibility of a lumpectomy and radiation, but then he said, "If you have the modified radical, we're more likely to get it all. Although it doesn't mean that you won't have a recurrence." Then that is when *cancer* first registered in my mind. The word *recurrence.* Then he said, "If it were my wife, that's the way I'd do it." I tell you, I am so tired of hearing that from male doctors. They kill me about this "wife" solution. I wasn't his wife. He wasn't talking with me; he was talking at me.

It's funny. There I am in shock, trying to have a sane discussion about treatment of my breast cancer. My mind kept racing, and I remember thinking I didn't care about having a lot of surgery, so I might as well have the modified radical. I felt the cancer was less likely to come back that way. My breasts weren't that important to me. Our "talk" ended and I told him I'd have the modified radical.

Of course, I didn't realize what was going on until I walked out of his office. BJ was waiting outside, took one look at me, and said, "You look like a zombie. What happened in there?" I told him I had to have more surgery and BJ immediately said he wanted to talk to the doctor. I realized I had a lot of questions to ask, too, and I really wanted to talk to the doctor again. The nurse told us the doctor had left and we'd have to make another appointment. When I look back at it, Dr. Jordan didn't handle me at all well. But you don't have time to be angry because you're scared. You get angry later.

BJ drove me home. Though BJ and I weren't married yet, he was a part of me and my life and I felt he should be involved in the decision. He asked me, "How do you feel about having your breast cut off? And before you answer, remember the loss of your breast is minor compared to your life. If this will save your life, do it and don't give it another thought. I'll be with you all the way through." I said okay; that meant a lot to me. Soon after I got home, I called my oldest daughter and told her, and she cried, "Oh no, Mama, not your breast!" Slowly I was realizing that I had cancer.

You know, my first fear about having breast cancer was losing my breast. I didn't think about the cancer first, probably because the immediate thing to deal with was the mastectomy. I mean, it's the very first decision you have to make: Do I or don't I take off my breast? Then later you begin to deal with the cancer part. The reality of the situation early on is, I can identify with the real, concrete breast and losing it. Cancer, on the other hand, is something nebulous that you can't see or feel and it represents mortality. It's easier to deal with the mastectomy because it's real. The death issue is not.

I decided to have the modified radical mastectomy. First, I wanted to get rid of all the cancer and not take any chances. Of course, what you don't really know then is that you'll live with possible recurrence for the rest of your life. The doctors love to tell you, "They got it all," but the fact is maybe, maybe not. Second, about a week after the biopsy, I ran into a good friend of mine and told her about my breast cancer and possible surgery. She smiled a little and said, "I have breast cancer too. I had the mastectomy just a month ago." I couldn't believe her! I looked at her and was surprised that I couldn't tell she was minus a breast. She was wearing her prosthesis and pulled it out to show me. But she wasn't too open with me about her experience, so I didn't learn much. She thought I was being badly treated because they didn't do a one-step procedure on me! But since she looked okay, I thought having the mastectomy wouldn't be so bad.

I went in for the mastectomy in early September 1983. If you can believe it, the hospital placed me in the maternity ward and then moved my room two more times during my stay. I must admit I was very depressed at that time of the surgery. I missed having my mother around to talk to, and one of my sisters was so hysterical that she upset me. The night before surgery I thought about what it was going to be like waking up and my breast not being there anymore. But I was never into my breasts, so it didn't bother me so much about their appearance. The only thing I was concerned about was how I'd look with clothes on. Since my friend looked fine, I thought I would too. I prayed that night that everything would turn okay and I would live.

My oldest daughter came to stay with me, and when I woke up from surgery, she was there by my side. I was in the hospital for four days and my room was full of visitors, flowers, candy, and cards and that made my stay. I never had a chance to get upset or lonely because the room was full of visitors until 8 P.M. every night. I wasn't in pain. I had lots of support from BJ, my kids, and even my ex-husband was very supportive. I acted jovial and cheerful to everyone. I was so cheerful that some relatives asked me to talk to a relative who had undergone surgery the week before and was depressed. At the time, I thought, "What is this? *I'm* in the hospital and they still want me to console somebody?" I did call him and he said, "If you're a woman who can stand to lose her breast, and you're doing okay, I can stand this." I felt good about that. But after the phone calls and all my visitors had left, it was hard for me; I'd get lonely. It was interesting, but I never worried too much about dying.

After the surgery, I had to wring the pathology report out of my doctor, a Dr. Thompson. He wasn't going to tell me about my lymph node involvement. When I asked him about the results, Dr. Thompson said, "I don't know how many, but there were a few." As it turned out there were two. Today, I would automatically be given chemo with that diagnosis, but in those days they didn't treat you like that. My breast cancer treatment ended with my mastectomy.

While I was still in the hospital, I thought about what all cancer patients think about—why me? Why did I get cancer? I had come from a healthy family on both sides, except my mom, they lived long lives—all my grandparents lived into their eighties and nineties. I wasn't quite sure why I got cancer, although I heard some theories about stress. Between my divorce and my mother dying, I'd seen some bad times. As a nurse, I had learned a lot about illness, having seen lots of people sick. The one thing that stood out was that *everybody* gets sick—rich people, poor people, white, black, good, and mean people. Regardless of what they did, bad things happened to them, so I guess I wasn't unique. I'd also seen many people die, so I thought, "Well, it could be worse. I am still alive, so why not me?" After that, I really got a positive attitude about my cancer. I was no better than anyone else, and living right had nothing to do with it. I had been just lucky and was blessed to come out of it okay.

My attitude about having cancer was also influenced by a Reach to Recovery volunteer who came to visit me in the hospital. My experience with this lady was not really good. She was a very conservative, uptight, white woman who was *strictly* dignified. She was very pleasant and tried hard to convince me everything would be all right, but she didn't help me. She didn't show me her scars or share a whole lot emotionally with me. What a bad role model for a cancer patient! Right then I decided the American Cancer Society needed some help, my help. When I got better, I was going to volunteer for the program. I thought, "I am going to visit these ladies openly with a smile and more warmth than this lady is giving me." The woman actually helped me because she did such a bad job! Of course, the Reach to Recovery program requires that a woman be at least a year postsurgery before she can be trained. So though I signed up for training as soon as I could, I had to wait for a year.

But about the time I was ready for the training, in August 1984, I had experienced some major back problems that were caused by a bad disc. I had to have surgery. Being trained as an ACS volunteer got postponed for a short time. This back surgery had a far greater impact on me than my breast operation did. When the nurse first helped me out of bed after the surgery, I had no control over one of my legs. I went into shock: "What was wrong with my legs?" My nerves in one leg had been damaged in the surgery, but it was not until *after* the operation that the doctor explained that this was a possible side effect. He also failed to mention that I could have died, might not be able to walk again, might lose the use of my bowels, and be unable to have sex. Fine time to tell me! The neurosurgeon, who had no personality to begin with, really made me angry for withholding that information. I let him have it and he later apologized. But once I've been angry and have had it out, I am through with it. I don't come back to things; I just move on.

In any case, I decided this injury wasn't going to stop me from walking. I had a lot of faith I would walk again without help and I did. I had to use a walker with a leg brace at first, but within the next year I got rid of them both. But losing my breast was put in perspective when I thought I might not be able to walk for a while. You can function fine with one breast but you can't get around very well with one leg.

My faith was what got me through breast cancer and back surgery. Faith and the support of my family, but particularly BJ; his love helped me a lot. We had married soon after my mastectomy in 1984. After my mastectomy and my back operation, BJ, as always, was by my side. I couldn't have asked for anybody to be better to me. He was accepting of me and was so pleased I was living. He always told me, "You're the same Julia to me." He was really wonderful, cooking for me and waiting on me while I recuperated. Later he told me he loved my positive attitude, and we even joked about cancer together, only the way cancer patients can. I was so comfortable with him that one time after an argument I even threw my prosthesis at him! I know, too, that part of my adjustment was due to my personality. I am not timid, and I am a fighter.

Our sexual life did not change after my mastectomy or back operation. I didn't expect it to either. If it had been my first husband, things would have been different. With BJ, even though I didn't consider myself a sexy person, I enjoyed making love and felt like an equal partner. I have been more open sexually with BJ than with Joey, because BJ was accepting and gentle with me, encouraged me, and cared about my feelings.

The first time BJ and I were going to make love after my surgery, I wasn't sure if I was going to take off all my clothes or not. I thought I'd keep my gown on. My scar didn't bother me but I thought it might bother him. Then I started laughing at myself, "Girl, you're acting like a teenager! *He* knows you've had the surgery. Who are you fooling? If I start out this way, we'll have problems." Nobody talked to me about what to do after surgery; it was my own thinking about how to approach sex. So, I just took off the gown and he didn't say anything to me, and we enjoyed each other. I mean if I can't stand to look at myself, how can I expect anyone else to look at me? It just takes time. Sure, I was sad for a while, but it all comes out all right. BJ touched me all the time and even began to help me with breast self-examination each month.

After my breast surgery, the biggest problem for me was learning how to put in my prosthesis. It takes a while to get used to. Now I am using an Image prosthesis; it's a new model that fits so closely to my body, it's like a breast cast, and even matches my skin color. I can wear it for days so I don't have any daily problems at all as a result of wearing a prosthesis. I have never wanted breast reconstruction because I didn't want any more surgery. I am happy with how I look and having one breast hasn't changed how I feel about my body. My scar never bothered me and still doesn't. But if I did have reconstruction, it would be for myself and not because of what others might think.

After about a month's recuperation from my back surgery, I was itching to get involved with the Reach to Recovery program and called ACS. They rescheduled me for my training. I went to the American Cancer Society office with my walker to attend the training. They were a bit concerned about me— I didn't look like the picture of health—and called my doctor who said, "Don't worry about her, she's a fighter!" I have been involved with the program now for over four years and in the past year have been the coordinator.

Being involved with this program has changed my life and been the best work I have ever done. And I am not "strictly dignified" when I meet women with breast cancer! In my experiences as a Reach to Recovery volunteer, I've found that no one woman is the same. How each woman responds depends on the kind of person she was before breast cancer and the kind of support she has after. Besides a woman's own attitude about her cancer, the key element in getting through is to have support from friends and family. If she doesn't have the support, she'll have a hard time making it. Because it's so easy to get in a shell by yourself, be sad and depressed when something like this happens to you. Every woman will have a time for crying and feeling sad, and then she moves on and gets on with her life.

Most women adjust well and get back to their routine lives, though I have found that the women who are the least flexible in their lives have the hardest time getting back on their feet. If a woman has a routine and nothing sways her from it, when breast cancer hits her, she can't adjust because her whole life and lifestyle changes. She can't deal with it—breast cancer doesn't fit in her schedule.

These are the women I always hear saying they can't believe breast cancer happened to them—their lives were perfect. They thought they were on top of it and found out they weren't. It takes those women much longer to adjust. I have also noticed that every woman I have visited has had some devastating event in their lives before their breast cancer—like my experience, someone had died or there was a major illness in the family or a divorce. I really think that something is going on with stress and this illness.

I have counseled hundreds of women with breast cancer over the past four years. My feeling is, a woman's relationship with her family or her husband or boyfriend depends totally on the woman herself. If she's sad and ashamed of her body, then they will be too. If she accepts herself, they accept her too. Some women say to me, "I can't stand to look at this scar." A few women are so devastated that they don't even buy a prosthesis. They don't begin their healing process for themselves. I tell them to get a prosthesis, because it's at least a start to restore their body image and no one will know. I know, it *is* hard to see a scar where there was a breast before. It's a loss and you have to grieve. But I tell them it just takes time to get used to and they will adjust. You *have* to.

Over the past four years, I have noticed a difference in the breast cancer patients I talk to. They are less afraid now than they used to be and are more aware about the disease because of the information they read in the magazines and hear on TV programs. Before, breast cancer was a secret and no one talked about it. Now it's easier. I do notice it's still harder for older women to talk about it, because when they were growing up, breasts and cancer were always hidden. It's so much more open now, almost too open! Breast cancer can be discussed just about anywhere now, and at last women are beginning to realize there's life after breast cancer.

Having breast cancer really changed me. It changed my whole life. I became a different person and a different woman. I feel more secure and better about myself. I suddenly looked at life differently and wanted to enjoy it to the fullest and do all the things I didn't do before. I prioritized what was important to me and wrote down what I really wanted to do: retire from my job (I did) and do my church and volunteer work. I can't quite describe the change but it's like I am a reverse of my old self. The whole cancer process makes you very aware of yourself in all areas, not just your body. It's like when you're born again: You're still the same person; you're just doing things differently afterward.

For example, now I am much more aware that my body is not just a structure; it needs tending to. It's so important, because without the body, you don't exist. I was careless before breast cancer and took my body for granted, treating it as if it wasn't anything special. I have learned the importance of early detection. Just because you're feeling fine doesn't mean you are fine. I feel very strongly that women have to learn about breast self-examination and knowing their bodies. We women have to learn how to take care of ourselves. I do now. I am very aware that I have to care for myself by getting enough rest, eating right, exercising more, and always taking the time to just relax. Isn't it funny that I had to get sick before I really took care of myself?

Perhaps the biggest change for me was, I started thinking about myself first and others second. For most of my life, I thought I was a strong woman and I was, for other people, but not myself. Before, I put everybody before myself. There were times when my kids were growing up when I would do without and give them everything. I'd put off seeing a doctor if the kids needed money for clothing or school. I wouldn't take the time for myself if someone else's needs were there. I now have learned how to say no—that word wasn't in my vocabulary before! Now I am very assertive. I am in charge and I wasn't before. All of a sudden, I had a new awareness about me and I announced to everyone, "This is Julia! I come first!" Now I really am concentrating on me and what I want to be and do.

Now some people may say I am selfish and not very feminine. But I have never considered myself a feminine woman to begin with so it doesn't bother me. If you look at femininity like a job description, it was one job I never applied for. To me, feminine women are quiet, passive, fragile, and break easily. But I have never been that way, never been fragile. But I have been a woman, a good woman and *womanly* all my life. To me, being a woman has more to do with her heart than her breasts. I have been a nurturer, kind and gentle, have always been a lady with good manners, and have my own way of carrying myself. I don't like the word feminine because it restricts the definition of a woman. I am stronger than ever before now; would you say that makes me less of a woman? I am *more* of a woman now than I ever was before!

Since I have had breast cancer, I treasure my body more and pay more attention to it by doing things that make my body feel and look good. I treat myself because I deserve it. It's not vanity. I do things I never would allow myself to do before—like having manicures and facials—and buy things I never dreamed I would buy. I want to look good, so I buy nice clothes and gifts. I have found that I am not alone in this attitude. Many cancer patients do the same thing!

One important thing I have learned since having breast cancer is the power of sharing. I had *never* been one to discuss my personal life with anyone, but I started talking about my breast cancer because I felt it was important to help other women. If a woman shares her experiences, she feels much better. I firmly believe that being open with others is the best way to accept yourself. Reach to Recovery is an important program because it shows that women *live* after breast cancer and that breast cancer doesn't stop you—you only stop yourself.

One of my Reach to Recovery home visits was to a forty-five-year-old woman named Martha, who wouldn't get out of her bed. She'd been hiding in her bedroom for at least a month since her mastectomy. When I walked into her room, she was in her bed, hiding under her bedcovers. Martha was so scared and fearful of being rejected that she hadn't told her boyfriend or her friends at work about her illness. She had barely looked at her scar. I told her, "For a while I thought my world was coming to an end, but I told everybody at my job and my family and friends about it. Believe me, nobody feels sorry for me. I got married after my mastectomy and am still with my husband. My kids are fine. I am fine. After surgery, you just learn to adjust. I am not saying you don't feel sad that you have lost a part of you. I felt sad for a time, but I moved on." Then I showed her my scar and my prosthesis, which I usually don't do, but she needed to see it. Then we looked at her scar together. She started crying, and I hugged her and told her to get out of bed and start moving. We started talking about her experience. I encouraged her to call her boyfriend while I was there and she did. He thought she was mad at him for something. He was wonderful to her. Within two weeks, she was out in the world again. That's the power of sharing. When you see that happen, you have to reach out.

The sad thing about that story is lots of mastectomy patients do not feel they are whole or acceptable without breasts and society makes them feel like that. It causes them to shy away from people because they believe they will be rejected. Many women don't know how to tell their children, boyfriends, or husbands, or friends.

My experience is that most men, most *people*, don't care if their wives or girlfriends have one or two breasts anyway. But what kind of relationship do they have if they can't talk and share with their loved ones? And the single women, well, it is harder to start up a relationship but it's hard even if you don't have breast cancer.

I think it's better to find out up front if someone has a problem with you and your cancer, rather than get hurt later. If a man does reject you because of breast cancer, who needs him anyway? Who's perfect? For those women who worry they'll never be involved again, remember me—a fifty-six-year-old woman who remarried *after* she had breast cancer.

What's crazy is, women are more concerned about what everyone else thinks and aren't really caring about themselves. Women don't have confidence in themselves and in their mates. What's wrong with women that they think their mates won't stand by them? You have to have more faith and trust in who you are.

The bottom line in breast cancer is there are bad times, yes, but it's going to get better. It totally depends on a woman's attitude and how much she wants to improve the quality of her life. I am not saying everything's rosy, but once you have this disease, you live with it and you understand there's always the possibility it will come back. You realize the five-year survival mark doesn't mean much. But it's that knowledge—living with her mortality—that's going to make a woman's life be even better after breast cancer. Because she is going to care more about herself than she ever did before, and do what she wants to and enjoy what she has. We all want to survive and make each day count. Being a survivor is what counts.

My faith has played a big role in my survival. I am not into a special denomination even though I go to the Baptist Church; I just have a faith in the Lord. My faith and positive thinking are quite powerful! It helps me keep out bad thoughts. I have been tested twice now and survived. The doctor said I wouldn't walk after my back surgery but I did. I now have real confidence in my body and myself, but I had to have the faith to have this happen. And though I strongly believe in my ability to keep myself healthy, I also firmly believe that going to doctors is very important. The doctors wouldn't have gotten so advanced in treating illness if God didn't mean for them to. So I go in with my faith for checkups. If a doctor operated on me for a suspected recurrence, I know the cancer wouldn't be there. Though recurrence is in the back of my mind—I know it's there—I don't worry about it. I refuse to receive bad thoughts about a recurrence and never have for five years.

After I started talking to women in the Reach to Recovery program and saw how much I helped them, I have become more and more open! I was raised to listen and now I talk too much! I am more active in the community than ever before, working with all kinds of cancer patients. Cancer is my baby—it plays a huge role in my life from which I get fulfillment and great satisfaction. There's no prestige or money in it for me; it's just close to my heart. As a born-again Christian, I have more faith in myself to express what I feel and I have confidence to know I am saying the right thing.

I don't go preaching to other people about this; only if they ask me, do I talk about it. But I think my light is shining. The Lord resides in me and I have peace. It's all about love, really. If you don't love yourself, then you can't love others. Since I have had breast cancer, I have a lot of love for myself so it's easy to share. Sure, helping others takes a huge commitment but you get what you give out. So I am rich in giving and getting. I am a wealthy woman and I feel wonderful.

12

Hemlotta

"I was fortunate in that I had no preconceptions about breast cancer; I didn't know what it meant or how to behave. Breast cancer didn't mean horror and death and loss of womanhood to me, so I was not fearful. Therefore having this disease has not threatened my being a woman at all."

A happily married seventy-four-year-old woman with grown children and grandchildren, Hemlotta had lived a rich and full life by her own account, when she was diagnosed in 1986 with a stage two breast cancer, with lymph node involvement. She had a lumpectomy and a lymph node operation, eight weeks of radiation, followed by seven months of chemotherapy treatments, which she completed in the spring of 1987. Her strong Hindu faith played a significant and positive role in how she perceived herself and her experience with breast cancer. Accepting that death is a natural part of life and concerned more for her soul than her body, Hemlotta faced her life-threatening disease with acceptance and little fear for her mortality. Her involvement with yoga and homeopathic medicines enabled her to get through radiation and chemotherapy treatments. Breast cancer taught Hemlotta that no matter how old you are, you can still learn new things about life.

I was born in India in the same province where Mahatma Gandhi was born, in 1912. I was the seventh of eight children. My parents had an unusual marriage in that my father married my mother when he was fifty-five and she was twenty. In 1922, when I was ten, my father died. I remember his funeral well. They washed and bathed him in our house, as was custom, and then he was cremated. I can recall very little about my father, but one thing he always said was his daughters were also his sons because we served him so well. For an Indian man of his age, his attitudes about daughters were unusual. My father left the family with good fortunes and I believe I was lucky to be born in this good way.

After my father died, my mother was a great influence on all of us in the family. Though my mother loved my father deeply, she was never one to get upset by calamities. She was a very strong woman, very religious, and had great faith in God. She was also very intelligent and always up-to-date on world knowledge though she only had a third-grade education. She interpreted the best of the scriptures in her own way too. A very loving and good mother, she, like my father, shared an enlightened view of what her sons and daughters should do. She always said to all of us, "Go ahead and do what you like in life." Although when my brothers indulged in bad activities from time to time, she could get a little hot-tempered but would always say to them, "I still love you." I think I was so fortunate to have had my mother as a role model.

Soon after my father died, my mother and eldest brother decided to send me to an English girls' school in our district. As you can tell, my mother was very reformed in her thinking about education because girls were rarely educated in those days. I attended the school from elementary through high school and graduated with a high school degree. So I grew up speaking both Indian and English.

It wasn't until high school that my breasts grew and I don't remember feeling one way or the other about them. I had a strong reaction to my first period, which arrived when I was fourteen. I had no idea what periods meant. My mother, who had explained nothing to me before this, made me feel easier about the whole process, explaining that the bleeding was a most natural thing and not to be afraid of it. She also said, "You are not to come downstairs during these times; you must sit up in the room." So during my first period, I sat and read on the third floor of our house. I never questioned why; I just took life as it was. In those days we did not have tampons. So in the way of my mother and sisters, I learned to double up my petticoat and wind it around and through my legs and then wash and change it every day. I did this for years. I didn't feel funny about it; it was the custom. I also learned it was customary that women who had their periods were isolated because menstrual bleeding was considered very powerful and suspicious. So a bleeding woman slept alone and didn't touch anything in the house; only when her period was finished and she had a bath and cleansed herself, could she enter the kitchen again.

Once a young woman started her periods, she became more valued and protected because she was then ready to conceive and potentially had great power to ruin the name of the family. So like other young women who had periods, I was rarely allowed to go alone anywhere anymore. Not that we understood it. There wasn't much overt importance attached to sex or mating when I was growing up. My introduction to mating was watching a group of monkeys out of my bedroom window. There was one male monkey that was the king of the group and it was obvious he could sexually mate with any of the female monkeys. I was always curious about what the king monkey was doing and asked one of my sisters about it once. She told me not to worry myself. I didn't, as I had many other interests at the time to occupy me. Needless to say, I had a very protected life concerning the opposite sex. If someone asked me, "How would you feel if some boy kissed you?" I would ask, "Why should he kiss me?" I didn't think I needed it!

In the 1920s in India, there was also no dating, only arranged marriages. My marriage and my daughters' were all arranged. Right after I graduated from college, and before I left for England to get a master's degree in education, we were betrothed. My husband and I knew each other only through letters for nearly two years before we first met. Then he came to England, too, to go to medical school. That's when we really began our relationship. Out of Indian traditions and the watchful eye of our parents, we went to the movies and dinners and stole a few kisses. We were very happy with each other. But we never had intercourse before we married. There was no sex phobia or pressure to do so at the time. I didn't even know sex was to be enjoyed! I became quite independent during my stay in England and, in some ways, did not relish going back to India. But we returned home and got married in 1937.

My husband and I learned to make love together after marriage. My experience was if you love each other, you don't need books to enjoy making love. It all comes with time. We had a good relationship and were more than satisfied. Every time we met it was a new enjoyment. We would sleep on a terrace because it was so warm in India, and once a week we would enjoy each other quietly. We never closed our door to our children.

Unlike most of my contemporaries, I worked. My husband was a doctor and very enlightened about my working. Most men would have forbidden their wives to do so. But he knew when we married that I had been educated for a purpose. I started teaching after my first child was born.

I also was unlike my peers because I planned my family. After I had my first daughter in 1941, my cousin, a doctor, said to me, "Now don't get pregnant every year; it's not healthy. Take this diaphragm and jelly and use it before you make love." I said okay and always used it. My second child was born in 1943 and the last in 1946. I really enjoyed being a mother. When each of my girls were born I thought, "What a gorgeous gift this is!" There is a tradition in India that boys are better than girls, and so every time I delivered a girl, my husband was disappointed but he never made me feel bad. I was pleased with my girls. But friends would say, "Who will take care of you when you're old? It's an economic necessity to have a son. Your husband's name won't be continued." I didn't believe all this. All these poor women that kept trying to have a son after so many daughters—it was crazy!

Planning a family was an unusual and forward idea in the 1930s. There were very few birth control devices available at the time. I felt strongly about family planning because I had visited a friend's health center and saw mothers, frail and emaciated, walking around with malnourished children. The women were almost dying from having too many children. All their illnesses were related to childbirth. I felt I was doing something sinful if I didn't do anything for these women. The only birth control alternative for these women at the time was taking a vow of celibacy and that didn't work.

After working for a few years as a principal at a secondary school for girls, I thought it would be a good idea to educate the girls about family planning. It was soon obvious that I was like a round peg in a square hole. The school said, "No, you can't do that." I said, "Okay, good-bye," and did family planning work the rest of my career. A few years later, with a $5,000 check from the Indian Family Planning Board, I was involved with starting a family planning clinic in my district. Family planning was not a popular concept then, particularly because Gandhi opposed it. He warned women that if they used birth control they would be immoral and likely to end up on the streets. So my clinic was more of an underground operation. Our practice was unusual because we went to the women; they didn't come to us.

I had two nurses who carried the birth control devices in their bags and went from house to house, talking to the women about family planning. Most women didn't want to have so many babies and liked the idea. Women liked diaphragms best because they could keep them secret from their in-laws and husbands. Of course, years later the state would give us money to do our work, though publicly they denounced family planning.

I was given a warning by the state authorities that I would be punished if I spoke about family planning and that I would never be given any posting or positions. But those early threats never stopped me from my work. It did cost me, though, because I never got a parliamentary seat nor was I ever elected to an office. I don't regret it. I did this work until I retired in my mid-fifties.

After I retired, I decided it had been a long time since I had learned anything new, so I enrolled in a Ph.D. program in education and got my degree. Another reason for going back to school was I had gone through menopause and was feeling older. I also noticed vaginal dryness when I made love with my husband. This made me a little sad but then I thought, "Now I have to go on to other things in my life." I felt a need for renewal. Then that phase of sadness passed.

My husband and I moved to the United States in the mid-1970s, because all our daughters had moved here and they wanted us to live closer to them. Since we were both retired, we thought why not? We had many grandchildren and wanted to see them grow up. We came for three months and then just decided to stay and are now American citizens. Leaving India was a very difficult thing and we still miss it and our social life. But we like American frankness. Of course, the standard of life is much better here than in India.

Right before my diagnosis, I was seventy-four years old and in good health, as was my husband. We were living a simple life in a small apartment in a retirement community in Santa Monica. We lived apart from our daughters, because we didn't want to disturb them and we wanted our independence too. All our daughters were happy, married with children, and having careers. I felt satisfied for their lives because they were all independent and getting along well.

I was spending my time helping one of my daughters, who was working and going to school, and needed someone to cook and care for her child. I'd stay for two or three hours each day and then return home so that my husband and I would have lunch together. Then we'd rest and read. It was a quiet and comfortable life. Over the years, we'd returned to India to visit, and in 1986, I had traveled by myself to visit relatives in India. I felt fine the whole trip.

When I returned from India, I went for a checkup and my doctor, Dr. Samson, found a lump in my breast. Though I didn't notice any changes or see any breast lumps, he suggested I have a mammogram. I had never had one before. I joked with him and said, "You always suggest these tests but I am fine; I don't have any breast cancer." But to satisfy him, I went for one. On the mammogram there was a suspicious lump about the size of a lemon. I am so glad Dr. Samson made me have this test because I might have been dead if he hadn't. He called me the next day and said, "We've found a suspicious lump and need to do a biopsy. Can you come in tomorrow for the procedure at the outpatient clinic?" I, of course, said yes.

The next day, Dr. Samson did the biopsy and also took out two lymph nodes. Soon after I learned the lump was cancerous, as were two of the lymph nodes. I decided to spend the night in the clinic because I felt a little depressed.

The next day my husband and I met with Dr. Samson. At that point I thought I would have to have a mastectomy and was game for it. Even my husband had said, "If you think taking the whole breast off is better, you do that. It makes no difference to me." My husband cooperated with me very well. But Dr. Samson said, "No, you can keep your breast. These days the treatment is different and we take out only the part we feel is cancerous, just the lump. Then we treat you with radiation and because your nodes are involved, chemotherapy." I told Dr. Samson, "I trust you to do whatever you think is best."

I never knew anything about breast cancer until I got it myself. I never knew anyone with the disease. It was not a common disease in India, certainly not in my circle of friends. It was one of the reasons I found it so hard to believe that I got it. I had been healthy my whole life and looked so hale and hearty. Everyone was so surprised to hear that I had cancer too.

But I wasn't that shocked about this bad thing happening to my body. My reaction to hearing the news was that my husband and I had such a full life together—over fifty years—and I was not afraid to die. I had done my duty and was ready to go. I have a different attitude about cancer than others here. As a Hindu, I don't consider that the body is everything. Hindus say that the body is made of a chemical combination of water, air, and fire, and it is a chemical mixture of a sperm and ovum by which another human body is created. But in the fifth month, the soul enters the body and then the moment of the child starts. So the body has a soul within itself, which is a part of God. That's why we are more interested in preserving the purity of the soul than preserving the body. So as a Hindu, I never so much cared for my body as for my soul. I believed in fate. So I wasn't that upset upon hearing the news that I had breast cancer. I was more surprised.

But in this country everybody was very curious about how I felt. "Oh my God, how are you?" they asked. "How do you feel? Do you need help?" I always said no. Everyone is very nice here but I think they are more afraid than I am. Even my daughters were very upset when they heard about this. I told them I was fine and to buck up. I think Dr. Samson understood my attitude because he wrote to my oncologist, "I am sending you a most pleasant and jovial patient."

When I met my oncologist, Dr. Stockton, he said, "I will be taking care of you." I said, "Only if you answer my questions. Then I may say yes to you." Though neither chemotherapy or radiation frightened me, I had many questions. I asked, "Supposing I don't feel well and don't take the chemo pills, what will happen?" He explained the importance of completing the whole cycle of treatment; otherwise it might be ineffective. After our discussions, I realized I wanted to be rid of the disease and decided to take the treatments.

My treatment plan included one cycle of chemotherapy, then radiation for eight weeks with an external beam booster, and then back to chemo again for a year. About two weeks after my biopsy, I had my first dose of chemo. Nothing much happened. Then I started radiation, which was simple. You stay still for five minutes on a table. There is no pain. When you hear and read about radiation side effects, you think you will have all of them but I was basically okay. I had some skin changes, like a sunburn, which didn't upset me much. But when they gave me the external booster for eight days, I had a severe skin reaction. My skin became charcoal-black but it was only temporary. Now my breast looks only a little different. After all, I took good care of my breast during this time.

After I finished radiation, I started chemotherapy again. In addition to the injections, I would take three chemo pills a day for fourteen days and then have fourteen days off. The second and third chemo treatments made my head feel as if it was on fire—as if my brain was burning up. To make the heat go away, I applied butter—cold clarified butter—to my head, which gave me a complete cooling. I rubbed it in my hair and massaged my head. When I had my next injection, the nurse said, "I smell something funny." I said, "It's butter." She asked me, "Why do you use it?" I told her, "The butter treats me well. It helps me sleep and keeps me cool. Whatever lotions you give me I have little faith in; I want to use my own lotion. It works for me." She said that was fine with her.

In addition to the burning feeling I had, each new chemo treatment made me more and more nauseous. Yesterday I had my sixth course of chemo and I felt awful. I don't know how I got through the whole night because my tummy was very upset and I got very sick. But with each treatment, I have learned how to deal with this better because I know my constitution. Throughout the night, about every three hours, I eat a little and then take a little to drink. If I drink first, I feel worse. By the morning, I feel better and then rest until about noon.

I have gained weight since starting chemotherapy. I didn't know gaining weight was a side effect. To lose the weight, I have tried to lessen my intake of food but it doesn't seem to change things. I have been fortunate in that I have only lost a small amount of my hair. I decided I wasn't going to wear a wig if I lost all my hair. I am glad that I have not needed to worry about it.

When I first started chemotherapy, the doctors said I had to have a year of treatment. But after five cycles, with my getting more and more sick, the doctors changed their minds. Now I only have one more month to go. I prayed to God that they would stop. I thank the Lord for listening to me. I feel the Lord is very powerful and that I can direct my life in the best possible way by surrendering to him.

One of my Indian friends who doesn't believe in taking medicines questioned me recently about why I was taking such toxic drugs. She thought I could cure myself. Though I do believe more in natural healing than scientific medicine, I told her, as long as I don't know the cause of the disease, I will submit to the scientific outlook. Because God gave us science and medicine also. I have faith that he will cure and heal me through these methods. Breast cancer is a dreadful disease and one that should be taken care of by medicines. It's no use bungling about with alternative treatments. If the treatments fail then I might think about these other ways. But I must be logical and thoughtful about treatment. I also told her that I don't want to suffer any stigma that I didn't treat myself properly. If I didn't take the drugs, I might also suffer more unnecessary pain in the future. I want to be treated and get rid of the disease, so *I* am allowing my body to be treated.

Before breast cancer, I was only sick once in my life when I was fifty. I had serious problems with menopausal bleeding. Although I had a D and C, the bleeding wouldn't stop. This is when I started taking some homeopathic pills and the bleeding stopped immediately. So over the last twenty-five years of my life, I have treated myself with homeopathic baths and pills. It is because of this natural treatment of my body that I believe I have been able to withstand chemotherapy, withstand any kind of medicine, because I am strong biochemically. Many older people cannot tolerate all these chemicals, but my seventy-five-year-old body is healthy and strong, no doubt about it.

Besides, it's not just the chemicals that work to help you; your attitude helps too, you know. I realize that how I feel about and look at this illness is determined by my own mental imagination. You have to be very strong as a soul to give your mind the power to withstand anything that comes your way. I have used both meditation and yoga to help me in radiation and chemo. They help me minimize the toxic effects of treatment.

It's a thought process. If you think of your house right now, you are in it. The space of thought is far more powerful than the space of the light of the sun. So as soon as I feel unwell from these chemicals, I think to myself,

"It is just for the time being and I will be positive. I won't suffer emotional pain from this treatment. Physical pain, yes; emotional pain, no."

When I got the diagnosis, I wondered why *I* got this disease. At first, I thought maybe I got cancer in my breast because I misused my breasts in some way. Another thing I considered was perhaps I had neglected the Lord and did not remember him as much as I should. Maybe I was thinking too much about the outside world, doing too much service to others, and not paying enough attention to myself. I thought this was a warning that I should sit down and pray quietly. But I realized worrying about this was not going to get me any better.

There is a belief both here and in India that you reap what you sow. You must have done something bad or had a bad attitude in your past life that gives you suffering now. But yoga philosophy, which I believe in, says that you shouldn't get stuck or continue to worry about the bad things in your life. You should be done with the bad and move on to new things. So I decided I would concentrate on getting better and not worry about the past.

I was fortunate in that I had no preconceptions about breast cancer; I didn't know what it meant or how to behave. Breast cancer didn't mean horror and death and loss of womanhood to me, so I was not fearful. Therefore, having this disease has not threatened my being a woman at all.

My sexual life hasn't changed, because before this all happened, my husband and I were abstaining from sexual relations for a number of years. We still are affectionate and close physically with one another, but we don't indulge in sex and don't mind it. There's nothing wrong with *not* doing it! After all, what is sex in life? Sex is only one item of life to be enjoyed, but it is a bodily pleasure and not to be revered too much. There is so much fuss about sex here in America. Too much importance is placed on the most natural of functions. To me, this is unnatural. Too much emphasis on the pleasures of the body can result in artificiality.

My sense of femininity remains the same. For most of my life, I have marched to my own drummer and never questioned my femininity. Femininity, to me, is not outside beauty; it's inner soul. We all have a feminine spirit within us that shines. It is for this reason I never needed makeup because I had my own natural glow and spirit. I always looked fresh and fine.

Losing a breast or having a diseased breast doesn't make me or anyone else less of a soul. It doesn't make me less than what I am. The body does not play such a crucial or important role in my femininity. It's also why I am unconcerned that my breast looks a little different now from radiation and chemotherapy. It doesn't change how I feel about myself.

I don't believe that being feminine is how you look. I am sad about all the attention paid to the outside body in America. It is too much. No wonder women are afraid of breast cancer. If a man loses his eye or hand or leg, is he looked upon as subhuman or less masculine? No. But what man has made of a woman's breast here! It's a pity that the Western world looks upon the body of a woman as a sex object only to be enjoyed by man. In one of Wordsworth's poems he wrote, "What man has made of man!" In the modern world, we women can say, "What man has made of woman!" I believe in this attitude grows the roots of human degradation. I am tired of this vision of a woman's body.

Femininity is also a spiritual characteristic that can only be defined in relation to others. Femininity doesn't stand alone. God has made two complementary parts, the feminine and masculine, to work together. Men and women have their own spheres, and that is why I don't believe in going out of my way to compete with men or undo what they can do better. To me, part of being feminine is going for balance and accommodation instead of getting into conflict. I believe by our nature that a woman is a caretaker. By our physical and emotional structure, we are designed for sacrifice and love, tolerance and taking care of others.

I don't mean that women should submit like slaves to men, but it is by cooperating and loving that a man and a woman complement one another and get more and more joy in life. Being feminine is what loving is all about. We need more femininity in this world.

I understand that breast cancer can recur and that I might die from this disease. But I am confident that I will not have a recurrence. I'm positive in my outlook and I am not living with the fear of dying. If someone told me today I was going to die tomorrow, I would say, "What a great fortune." I would face death any moment and not fight or resist it. When I was growing up, death was a natural part of life. It was not a calamity to die and it was not something to be feared because Hindus believe in reincarnation: The soul never dies; only the body dies.

I know lots of cancer patients worry about recurrence, but that kind of thinking doesn't help them. I believe whatever happens to you is in the plan of God. During radiation and chemotherapy treatments, I talked to other older breast cancer patients who were like me, not afraid of death or cancer. I think because I am old and have enjoyed my life that I have such an attitude. At my age I can afford to take things easier but it is harder for younger people. If I had been a younger woman with breast cancer, maybe I wouldn't be so positive in my outlook in facing the disease. I would have been worried about my children and who would care for them. I think about this, because the younger cancer patients I met during treatments, who were very attractive and well situated in life, were simply devastated with the fear of death and cancer.

I think they were most frightened of suffering and pain. It is difficult to be young and ill in this society, because of all its pressures and tensions and its preoccupation with sex, youth, and money. People seem more concerned with the superficiality of life rather than the deeper issues of living.

I befriended some of these younger cancer patients and told them that being afraid changes nothing. They must realize that they cannot let their fears control them. They have the power within to overcome their fears. Through their imagination, whether it be through prayer to God or positive thinking or meditation, they can learn to take care of themselves and make their lives livable. Don't fight or resist; accept it and move on. Sometimes they responded to me, "Yes, we agree with you, but it isn't as easy for us to think the way you do about this." I understand this.

My whole life I have been independent and happy, and breast cancer hasn't changed that. I have had a fortunate life, a wonderful family, a husband who has supported me in all my efforts, and a career in which I served others well. What I have done in life was God's grace; I was only an instrument for him. So I am thankful to God that I was given the opportunity to do service for women and children. But it was not my making. I would be sadly egotistic to believe otherwise.

My body has served me well too. I am feeling good now, because I have had strong faith in God that if I submitted to his will, he would take care of me and help me heal myself better. I believe the Lord has done everything he can for me. Also my positive view of life and my husband's support and his kind way of understanding things have helped me through this illness.

You get over the breast cancer treatment physically but some things change emotionally. For example, my relationship with my daughters has changed. They seem to love me more intensely because they think I will not be around four or five years from now. I say to them, "What are you talking about? I am always with you. God will take care of me and you too." Though they feel closer, I, on the other hand, have started to give up attachments and have become more distant. If I have to go, I can let go.

Another thing that has changed is my attitude toward others' suffering. Before having breast cancer, if someone told me he was in pain or something scared him, I would say, "What is this nonsense?" I even told my own daughter once when she was suffering from menopausal bleeding that she was too soft-minded. I suggested that she get up and do some work. I was flamboyant in my attitude, even with my own daughter's suffering. I realize now that pain and suffering are real and that one cannot discount a person's feelings. Having physically suffered from these cancer treatments, I have empathy now for others. I can no longer be immune to others' pain and suffering.

I believe I was egotistical before. I went through life like God's child— kicking, playing, and bumping into people. In many ways I took life and my health for granted and always thought it was God's grace. I was always in good health and had great energy. But when I got breast cancer, I realized I hadn't served God properly. This was God's way of teaching me to listen better, his way of making me humble. I have been humbled. In this respect, I realize now I am not different from everyone else. I am aware of how ordinary I am.

I am a better person now because I have had my eyes opened to see others in a more loving and supportive way. I am very proud of myself for accepting this challenge God has presented, and now I pray more for others than myself that they will not have recurrences. This sense of communion with others is very satisfying. We are all sailing in the same boat, cancer patients. We are more aware than others that today we are here but tomorrow we may not be here. Yes, this experience surprised me because you never stop learning about life. No matter what your age, you can always learn so many things.

MORE OF A WOMAN: DISPELLING THE MYTHS

Having breast cancer is a traumatic event. Throughout your diagnosis and treatment, cancer becomes the focus of your life, twenty-four hours a day, every day, for months, sometimes for years. Faced with the possibility of death, damage to or loss of your breast, and treatment that produces severe side effects for many, you are involuntarily placed on a roller coaster ride of emotional and physical changes that severely challenge your self-esteem. You wonder if you will ever feel good about yourself again. The diagnosis and treatment of cancer is only the first stage of this experience. Cancer patient and author Fitzhugh Mullan calls the time when you are solely involved with medical treatment and getting better the "acute survival period."[1] But when treatment ends, a new phase begins: You learn to live with the changes that have occurred and begin to readjust to the so-called healthy world. You move on as a survivor and start to pick up the pieces and reestablish who you are.

Each of the ten women in this book picked up the pieces in her own way and successfully learned how to adjust to the physical and emotional changes that occurred during breast cancer treatment. Not only did they weather the worst of the side effects but they emerged with their self-esteem intact, feeling good about themselves and their lives. You might ask, how could this happen? How can such a traumatic experience like breast cancer produce such positive outcomes? What accounted for these women's general satisfaction and emotional stability? Were there specific methods or skills they used that enabled them to cope and feel better? Knowing the answers to these questions may help you better mobilize your own resources and cope with your cancer experience.

As a counselor and breast cancer patient, I have come to the conclusion that the most helpful approach to answering these questions is to use the concept of self-esteem. Self-esteem is the sum total of all that a woman feels about herself, and it has four major and interrelated elements, any or all of which may be diminished by the diagnosis and treatment of breast cancer: (1) your interpersonal relationships, which comprise both your social as well as intimate interactions; (2) your body image, which has a functional component (What can I do?) and an esthetic component (How do I look?); (3) your achievements, which contain elements of work or competition in such areas as career, family life, athletics, or hobbies; and (4) your identity, which comprises those attitudes and behaviors that are related to your social, political, spiritual, ethical, or ethnic life.[2]

How your self-esteem is affected by breast cancer treatment depends largely on your individual strengths and weaknesses in each of the four interrelated categories. Though all aspects of your self-esteem may be adversely affected by treatment at one time or another, there are often several other components of your self-concept that provide sufficient support and rewards to offset the negative changes. For example, if you are a woman whose breasts play a critical role in her sexuality, having a mastectomy will be a terrible blow to your body image and may result in your having a lower self-esteem. However, you may use your confidence in other areas to compensate for your perceived inadequacy in your body image. Having a supportive partner and close friends or being successful in your career can do so much to reestablish your self-confidence.[3]

By examining the self-perceptions of the ten women in this book, I found that although each woman journeyed down a different path through her breast cancer experience, they all used some of the same coping mechanisms to help them adapt. In the following five chapters, I have identified and described the most common ideas and methods they employed, and the attitudes they embraced that helped them successfully manage their illness. Hopefully, some of these methods will be of value to you. I urge you to try them and also to assess yourself in terms of the four elements of self-esteem. By doing so, you will be helping yourself to cope more effectively with the changes that come from living with this life-threatening disease. This information should be a helpful and practical guide not only for you but also for the family members, friends, and health professionals who are concerned about your emotional and physical well-being.

13

The Interpersonal You

WILL I STILL BE LOVED?

One of the most frightening aspects of hearing a diagnosis of cancer is experiencing overwhelming feelings of aloneness. Cancer is a very lonely experience because no one can rescue you, kiss the hurt, and make it go away. From these feelings arise a great fear that you also may be left alone as well. This concern is not often shared or spoken, but it is there. It is not at all unusual for a cancer patient to worry about being abandoned or unloved. Since cancer in our culture is synonymous with pain and death, and death is something our society rejects, people with cancer may be avoided. You may feel that you represent mortality to others and worry that this will result in people withdrawing from you. Then you realize that you are somehow different from everybody else, not only on the outside but on the inside as well. You fear that you may no longer belong anywhere.

Your role as an independent adult woman, wife, or mother suddenly changes to that of playing the role of "sick person," who must now rely on others for your care. You're concerned not only about who will take care of you and who will *want* to but also who will take care of the kids and cook the meals. It's very difficult to be the primary caretaker in the family and then become the needy one. The fear of becoming a burden on your loved ones, and in many cases, for an unspecified time, is very scary.

IS THERE INTIMACY AFTER BREAST CANCER?

In addition, you may worry about the effect that treatment will have on your relationship with those who are intimate with you. Many questions arise: Will I be sexually unattractive, undesirable? Will I feel like making love again? Will my partner? Will my partner reject me? What will my sex life be like if I am single? Or, will I have a sex life as a single woman? Will there be such a thing as "normal" sexual relations again?

All these fears are understandable, because there are both emotional and physical problems that many breast cancer patients face that may affect their sexuality. In addition to the loss of a breast, there are many treatment-related problems that may affect a woman's sexual life: physical limitations from surgery, pain, limited arm movement, fatigue, and side effects such as loss of hair and weight gain from chemotherapy.

Therefore, there are numerous and legitimate reasons why cancer patients worry about both social and sexual rejection and abandonment. Healthy interpersonal relationships—both social and intimate—are crucial to your self-esteem. From the time of birth, it is human touching and emotional support that makes you thrive and grow. The networks of people and groups with whom you are connected—church, work, family, neighbors, or friends—are the lifeline of your existence. It is through these social networks with others that you can love *and* feel loved and accepted. Being closely involved with your loved ones is often the key to survival, and the fear of losing those who are important to you is very threatening.

WORKING THROUGH THE
EXPERIENCE

There is no doubt that the social and intimate relationships of the ten women you met in the book were significantly affected by surgery and treatment. Many of the changes were temporary in nature; others had more permanent effects. Yet, although every woman said that breast cancer changed her relationships with others, all the women felt the changes were overwhelmingly positive. Their connections to others were not severed; rather they were enriched by the experience. They felt neither rejected, unloved, nor unattractive. They resumed their sexual lives. For most, their worst unspoken fears did not materialize. What kinds of experiences and support did these women have that enabled them to feel this way?

*   *   *

They Told Their Family and Friends That
They Had Breast Cancer

Though they probably never thought about it, one of the most important steps these women took to help their emotional well-being was to tell their circle of family and friends that they had breast cancer. This disclosure sent a clear signal that not only could the situation be discussed but that they were willing to be recipients of care and love as well. Numerous studies have shown that the speed and quality of a woman's recovery is directly related to the strength of her social support system. People cannot offer help if they don't know you're in crisis. If you decide to keep your cancer diagnosis a secret, you may be denying yourself the love and support you need to get well and feel better about yourself. All these women were open about their cancer diagnosis and, as a result, benefited from their candor.

They Relied on a Wide Base
of Emotional Support

Valerie said, "When's there's a disaster in the family, all the garbage washes away and what's left is probably the most intense love and support." Most of these women shared Valerie's experience—their families came through with love and assistance. They were fortunate to have established support networks—partners, families, friends, and coworkers who provided them with love and emotional support, tangible resources, and information.

From the moment of diagnosis, visitors flocked to their hospital rooms bearing cards, books, flowers, and gifts of love and assistance. Mothers, fathers, sisters, brothers, and friends came and helped out at home during hospital stays and treatment periods. People provided information by researching health insurance plans or finding doctors to go to for second opinions. Valerie's friend took her to radiation treatments for a number of weeks. Upon her request, Barbara's friends formed a network of support services for her, making phone calls, taking her to chemotherapy, and helping her through long nights of sickness. Barbara, who said she was never alone when she threw up, said, "You know, it's more important who you throw up with than who you sleep with. Throwing up in front of somebody takes such trust and intimacy and dependency. It's easier to go to bed with somebody." The fear of being a burden was eased because of the way in which these women's friends and families responded. People stepped forward, not backward, when these women needed help. They listened and they touched.

The support they received was not only from people they knew. Some of the most touching moments of friendship came from strangers. A nurse's aide or a resident might hold a woman's hand on the way to surgery, or someone they didn't know would say, "You're going to be all right." Marcia told of receiving cards from many women in the community she did not know. Kate told of one night when, "I was totally wiped out and couldn't sleep, and a male nurse came to my room with tea and toast and talked with me. It was those small moments that meant so much to me and reinforced that I was okay."

These woman coped better because they knew they were loved. As Sarah said, "I wanted companionship and warmth more than anything else." It's important that you ask for assistance from your support network when you need it. Remember, everyone has different talents and skills to call upon; cast your net of potential support as wide as possible. People want to help and often don't know how or don't want to intrude. By asking for help, you are more likely to get what you need and make those giving to you feel good too.

They Learned to Screen Out Those Whose Support Was Not Helpful

As all cancer patients learn, though they are thankful for support, *all* the assistance they receive is not always welcome or helpful. All those well-intentioned, friendly people who tell you about the latest vitamin cures, about their friends who died from horrible cancers, and about their belief that one can cause one's cancer do not provide the kind of assistance you need. The women in this book had to learn to identify and screen out those people who seemed to bring their spirits down, rather than up. For example, Julia recalls that when she was in the hospital recuperating from her mastectomy, a family member called her and asked if she would call and cheer up a relative who had undergone surgery the week before and was depressed. She thought, "What is this? I'm in the hospital, and they still want me to console somebody?"

Although love and support may be plentiful, there sometimes can be too much of a good thing. Dealing with people, particularly trying to make *them* feel better, can be extremely tiring. In order to get well, each of these women had to conserve energy. When undergoing surgery and treatment, they found they had to protect themselves from situations that drained their emotional and physical energies. They were able to do so through a variety of ways: from getting telephone answering machines to recruiting a trusted friend or family member to act as their advocate or bodyguard, screening telephone calls, and limiting or declining visits. Terri's friends reacted to her saying, "Why can't I handle all this?" by saying, "Why don't you use this time for healing? Stop listening to everyone else." Terri realized, "I was given this gift of time to heal and rest, a time to go inward and I did." To get her peace and rest, she decided to go to her mother's for a week. It is therefore important to recognize that you can't do it all, and that relying on trusted others is not a sign of weakness but rather a path by which you can gain strength.

They Found Ways
to Get Additional Support

Though the support of family and friends was more than adequate for some of these women, there were others who felt a tremendous need to reach out and share with others who could really understand what they were experiencing. They joined cancer support groups, or found other cancer patients to talk with, or went into therapy. In her first group session, Valerie was told by another cancer patient, "By the way, you know you are going to be all right." She thought, "*Yeah*, that's right, yeah!" Hearing hope from other cancer patients gave her the peace of mind she was searching for. While waiting for treatment with other patients, Hemlotta, who would often counsel the younger cancer patients she sat with, found that "this sense of communion with others is very satisfying." Terri, who with other chemotherapy patients formed a phone support network, felt that "sharing was crucially important. I could not be the strong independent woman who could do everything for herself. I really needed people more than ever and they were there for me. Thank God, our society finds it acceptable for women to share their feelings and fears." Terri wanted acknowledgment not pity from others, and she felt that cancer patients understood that better than noncancer patients. All these women wanted to be treated as functioning adults, not invalids, and families and friends were often too emotionally involved to remember that. Cancer support groups or therapists also offered them the ability to talk about issues that were difficult to bring up with families—how to cope with the fear of dying, or the fear of being a burden, or with telling someone about the operation.

If you are interested in finding support resources, check the appendixes in this book, ask your doctor, other cancer patients, your local American Cancer Society, or your hospital oncology social worker. For most people, it is a worthwhile investment.

They Had an Ally in
Their Partner

While the support of these women's friends, family members, and groups was important, those women with partners found their partners' attitudes were perhaps most crucial to their recovery and sense of well-being. Many studies have shown that how spouses treat their partners during an illness has a profound impact on how well the ill partner adjusts to his or her situation. If the healthy partner or spouse refuses to talk about the illness, or complains about how the illness limits his or her activities, and is generally unsupportive, such attitudes often result in the cancer patient feeling like a burden, more helpless, and often hopeless.

Fortunately, and not atypically, all these women involved in intimate relationships, except one, received strong emotional support from their male and female partners. Only Nancy's husband withdrew from her, but in fact, his support had been withdrawn long before her diagnosis of breast cancer. This support came from men and women who, in spite of also being emotionally in crisis themselves, often feeling helpless, with deep fears about losing their partners, were still able to come through for their loved ones. Everyone expressed deep appreciation of the acceptance and love that her partner offered. Barbara spoke of the power of this acceptance: "I really felt it was not just me; it was us. That made me feel less alone." Susie said, "Our relationship didn't change at all. He was as affectionate and supportive after breast cancer as he was before." Valerie, who thought she would live a life alone after breast cancer and was asked by her boyfriend to live with him, said that his invitation made a "huge difference" to her.

The crisis brought many of the partners closer together, rather than moving them apart, enhancing and strengthening their relationships. Julia reported that her boyfriend "was accepting of me and so pleased I was living." Interestingly, it never occurred to many of the women that their partners would leave or reject them. Barbara said, "I was never concerned about the loss of my breast and my relationship with Sandy." Kate recalled, "I don't even remember thinking about my husband leaving me and we never talked about it. I knew it was okay. I would hope I hadn't married a man who would leave because of a lost breast."

They Had Partners Who Were
Involved in Their Care

The women in this book who experienced the least amount of stress in their relationships were those who had partners who not only gave them the opportunity to communicate their feelings and fears but also became involved with doctors, nurses, and treatments. Barbara said that Sandy "was really attentive to me all through the mastectomy experience. We looked at the scar together, we heard the news together about the number of lymph nodes involved, and she helped me drain the fluid from my hemovac and take showers and baths." Many partners took an active role in helping their spouses make decisions about treatment. For example, BJ, Julia's partner, asked her, "How do you feel about having your breast cut off? But before you answer, remember the loss of your breast is minor compared to your life. If this will save your life, do it and don't give it another thought. I'll be with you all the way through." That support meant a lot to her and gave her the confidence to go through with her mastectomy.

If at all possible, encourage your spouse, partner, or other close family member or friend to become involved in your treatment plans and care. Most will volunteer without your asking, but some need to know you want their participation. You will feel less alone and less anxious when you know that someone's by your side.

They Continued to
Have Intimate Relationships

Under ordinary circumstances, any *one* of the following things can have a negative effect on a person's sexual desire: depression, poor body image, fatigue, anger, anxiety, and fear. Cancer patients may be dramatically affected by *all* of these issues. As would be expected, because of the tremendous emotional and physical demands of surgery and treatment, a number of these women's sexual drive and interest declined. As Valerie said, "It wasn't life as usual. Sex wasn't an issue because I was very much a sick person trying to get better."

However, most of these women continued not only to have stable relationships but to maintain sexual intimacy with their partners as well. Sexual contact is broadly defined to include all touching behaviors, of which sexual intercourse is only one. It is important to note that throughout their experiences, *no one* totally abstained from sexual contact. The amount of sexual activity during and after treatment among the women varied. Although everyone reported having some problems adjusting sexually at first, over time many reported having satisfactory sexual lives. Why? A number of factors seemed to determine how well they adjusted.

They Were Held and Touched

Though their interest in an active sex life might be understandably lower, these women felt a tremendous need nonetheless for physical closeness—to be touched, held, and protected. Sarah described her boyfriend's holding her as the kind of sensual experience she needed at the time. "Sex" was the furthest thing from her mind. Kate found that touching was a life force that was not only a part of her healing but also of her grieving process.

Others spoke of the importance of hand-holding and of being comforted physically. The need for sensual touch, whether it was holding hands, hugging, cuddling, or kissing, was described as powerful and crucial to a sense of well-being. Almost every woman's partner provided these physical comforts, all of which contributed greatly to their healing process and the feeling of being wanted, accepted, and loved.

They Faced the Scar Together

Seeing the scar together, preferably in the hospital, was an important step for the individual woman and her relationship. It was not easy for either person to take that first look at the scar, but by doing so it enabled them to confront and deal with the fact that the breast was gone. The sooner the couple was able to look at the scar together, the better they were able to adjust. Doctors and nurses usually help initiate this process and encourage you to look as soon as you are able, and it sometimes helps to get the process started if your partner is willing to change the dressings. Barbara said Sandy made it "very clear to me through jokes and looking at the scar that she was extremely comfortable. She said things like, 'They are going to call us the three-breasted robin.' "

Going through this painful first step is crucial for you because it starts the process of grieving for the lost breast for both people. It's important to acknowledge that the loss of a breast is not only very sad for you but for your partner as well. Your breast may have provided a great deal of pleasure for you and your partner, and you will both miss it. It is totally appropriate for you *and* your partner to say, "I miss my/your breast." It promotes both your grieving *and* healing process.

It is clear that a number of the women's partners had a very high level of acceptance of the changed look of these women's bodies, because once the mastectomy or lumpectomy scars were healed, they touched the women's chest and scars, often incorporating this touching into their lovemaking routines. Barbara mentioned how sorry she felt for women whose lovers never touched or massaged their mastectomy scars. For some women the mastectomy scar even became an erotic area. Nancy experienced a "phantom nipple" that resurrected itself if she was touched in a particular area of her chest. For those who had lumpectomies, having their lovers touch *both* breasts in the same way was very important to them.

They Resumed Sexual Intimacy as
Soon as They Could

Following surgery and/or treatment, as soon as each woman and her partner (or others intimate with her) were able to resume sexual intimacy, they did so. The sooner this activity occurs, the better for both partners' emotional recoveries. Clearly, it took time, patience, and trying out new ways of feeling good before the women regained their sexual self-confidence.

Given all the possible negative effects of surgery and treatment on a breast cancer patient's intimate feelings, it is somewhat surprising to read how many women were engaged in active sexual relations following their surgery and during treatment. It has been said that issues of the flesh—sex and death—are closely aligned. They both involve intense body experiences of vulnerability, letting go, and surrender. It seems natural that some women, face to face with their mortality, may seek sexual experiences to reaffirm their connection to life, not death. It's a way of celebrating their *aliveness*.

For example, Nancy was in the arms of her new lover less than two weeks after her mastectomy. Marcia said that her sex life with her husband became more active and intense because she was so glad to be alive, able to love and be loved. During her radiation treatments, Susie continued relations with her husband and said, "Our sex life was the same as before. He never stayed away from me."

Interestingly, some of these women who were sickest from chemotherapy were sexually active. When they felt physically better between treatments, the women were interested, as were their partners. Sarah had an intimate relationship with a man while she was undergoing treatment. Throughout her two years of chemotherapy, Kate's sexual life included not only her husband but a number of men and a liaison with a woman. Kate said, "I don't know how I managed to sustain all that sexual activity."

Though resuming sexual intimacy after surgery and treatment is not often easy, the sooner it begins, the better you and your partner will feel emotionally. Remember that people's sexual intimacy needs vary greatly, so you should do only what is comfortable for you, both physically and emotionally. You may be tired, in pain, or physically unable to be close with someone else. At times like these, hand-holding is often the best medicine.

They Believed That Sexuality
Is a State of Mind

All of these women would agree that a crucial factor in their adjusting sexually to breast cancer, regardless of their marital status, was largely determined by how they viewed themselves. To start, through the love and touch of others, they received clear signs and signals that they were still attractive and sexual women.

They also carried a prior history of positive sexual intimacy with them into the breast cancer experience. Nancy said, "It never occurred to me that the loss of my breast would be a problem [sexually] and it hasn't been. It's been a matter of my self-concept and how I view myself." Valerie said, "I've always known sexuality resides in my head. It's really me that determines what happens sexually and breast cancer didn't change that. If you walk around worried about being disfigured and ugly, whether you are minus a breast or not, take it from me, everyone deals with you as if you're ugly." Sarah said, "Women with breast cancer who think 'I can't have a man' are focusing on the wrong issue. It's a woman's own self-perception and how much she cares about her looks that determine her value."

They Did Experience Some
Sexual Problems

Though many of the women in this book reported having few major sexual problems as a result of breast cancer, there were some who did. A recent study conducted by UCLA oncologist Pat Ganz[1] shows that many breast cancer patients experience some sexual problems for at least a year after treatment. It is not a surprising finding given the magnitude of a crisis such as breast cancer. Although at one point or another all the women suffered from anxieties, pain, fatigue, body-image changes, and depression, the changes experienced by the women who underwent chemotherapy were far greater than for those who only had radiation and/or surgical treatment. As would be expected, the severity and length of treatment has a great impact on a woman's sexual life.

The permanent side effects of chemotherapy in particular were devastating sexually for Kate, Barbara, Susie, and Terri, all of whom were young women. They all went through chemotherapy-induced menopause. As a result, most suffered from severe dryness of the vaginal walls, which makes sexual intercourse a dreaded, painful activity. Use of lubricants and other remedies do not seem to help this problem, which is a serious and chronic result of the treatment. For any woman, no matter what her sexual orientation is, to lose the ability to experience an important sexual pleasure is traumatic. Kate said, "I feel much more vulnerable about this than about the mastectomy. You can tell someone you don't have a breast but to tell them you have a problem with sexual intercourse is much more difficult." Barbara explained that her body doesn't or can't tell her when she's sexually excited and, as a result, she doesn't feel sexy very often. Although Susie resumed normal relations with her husband after her lumpectomy and radiation, she felt her sexual life changed drastically after the physical changes she underwent from her mastectomy and chemotherapy.

Some Had Difficulty Communicating Their Sexual Concerns

Susie had a number of sexual concerns that are not uncommon among breast cancer patients who undergo mastectomy and chemotherapy, whether married or single. Worried that her own sexuality had been diminished, she assumed her husband would feel that way too. She feared that in some way she would disappoint her husband and she had trouble communicating this fear. Her husband, not wanting to do anything wrong to make her feel worse, waited for signals from her to come forward and talk about it.

Sadly, Susie's embarrassment about communicating her feelings to her husband (and his not communicating with her) resulted in her doubting her sexuality and feeling isolated. But she is not alone in her feelings. Regardless of the kind of treatment they receive, many women have difficulty in talking with close friends or partners about their body image and treatment-related sexual problems or concerns. Judi Johnson and Linda Klein explain why in their book *I Can Cope* (DCI Publishing):

Several studies have concluded that 80 percent of all sexual activity is nonverbal. Almost all couples have ways of signaling their desires without speaking a word. One partner may wear a favorite negligee. Another may shower and use a particular aftershave lotion. Without words, the meaning is clear. We have communicated to one another our interest in making love without uttering a sound. But if people have never learned to verbally clarify their sexual needs in normal, relaxed situations, imagine how difficult it becomes when cancer imposes unusual stress. Now when people really must talk, many don't know how. For some people, suffering in silence is more comfortable than broaching the topic and risking embarrassment or rejection.[2]

Clearly, it's important for those of you who are having sexual difficulties to identify and verbalize your sexual needs to your partners. Communication is essential. Someone has to take the first step or both partners will begin to feel rejected and isolated. Like learning any new habit, it will take practice to talk comfortably about sexual feelings and desires, both positive and negative. Being able to say, "I need a hug," "I like when you do this," "I hurt here," "This is painful for me," or "I don't think I am ready to make love; could you please just hold me?" are appropriate ways to communicate feelings that will assist you in reestablishing satisfactory intimate relationships.

Some Found It Difficult to Seek and Get Help for Sexual Concerns

Like many women, Susie was too shy to ask for help, and yet there was no one reaching out to help her. Over a three-year period of being treated by surgeons, oncologists, radiation oncologists, and nurses, not one health professional offered sexual counseling to Susie. What is sad is that patients like Susie suffer alone. Even those who did ask for information were thwarted. Kate related her frustration at trying to learn about what she called "the emotional and sexual dynamics of breast cancer and breast loss," and she found no one capable of answering her questions.

Traditionally, breast cancer patients left the hospital following their surgery with no information about, or discussion of, possible sexual problems or concerns. It was and still is a difficult topic to discuss with a doctor: Most are not trained to ask about or discuss sexual matters. Clearly, the medical profession continues to fail in one important area of treating their breast cancer patients.

Fortunately, many health professionals are starting to recognize that sexual counseling should be an integral component of a treatment plan for the breast cancer patient. You can now find many enlightened health professionals (psychologists, social workers, and nurses) in the cancer field who can discuss the sexual impact of breast cancer with you, and advise you, if needed, on how to deal with your specific sexual problems. If you are having problems or concerns in this area, seeking counseling is not only appropriate but essential to your emotional and sexual health. Sometimes, unfortunately, the burden will be on you to ask for help, but the good news is that there *is* information, resources, and people available to help you with your concerns. There is no reason to suffer in silence anymore.

They Found Out That The Difficulties They Anticipated about Dating Did Not Materialize

Working out sexual-intimacy problems with an old partner presents one set of problems; trying to find a new partner is another sexual challenge. Of course, there are always concerns about starting a new relationship for the single woman with breast cancer. It's awkward enough for those who do not have breast cancer to begin dating someone new. Because breast cancer is a hidden handicap, you will worry about when and how to tell a new person about yourself. You may also wonder if and how the first sexual encounter will occur. Of course, you worry about rejection. Everyone deals with this in different ways: Some test the waters by plunging in; others only put their toes in the water, if at all. For example, Kate worried that she might be less attractive or desirable, and she actively pursued sexual relationships to calm her fears.

For those women in the book who were interested in pursuing new relationships, the problem of sexual rejection generally did not materialize. The women who were single (Sarah, Terri, Valerie), or who became divorced (Nancy and Kate), said they never experienced sexual rejections. Nancy, before and after her divorce, had numerous affairs and dates and never had a bad experience. She said, "I may have been missing parts, but I knew I was attractive because I got lots of reinforcement." Sarah said, "I have never had a problem attracting men since I had breast cancer." Valerie was surprised that even weight and breast cancer didn't get in the way of someone falling in love with her. Terri was the only woman not involved with anyone else before or after breast cancer but this was of her own choosing. Your own level of self-acceptance has a great deal to do with someone else finding you attractive. If you view yourself as unattractive, you may set yourself up for failure. Having a self-defeating attitude will certainly affect how others respond to you. Essentially, success comes to those who feel better about and accept themselves.

If fears about rejection worried them, these women found positive ways of dealing with the situation. Sarah said, "I knew off the top there would be a cross section of men who would not be interested in me. So I have an advantage. I find out right away if a guy is worth pursuing. If breast cancer gets in his way, I don't need him to begin with!" There will be people who do not want to be involved with you. If you are becoming interested in someone, tell them about your cancer; the sooner the better. It's better to find out their reactions before you are involved. If you think about it, why would you want to spend time with a person who can't accept you as you are?

If you are a single and/or divorced woman, there may be a greater concern that your survival is an issue in finding a new partner than the treatment for breast cancer, particularly if your prognosis may not be good. Barbara stated, "What kind of person is going to get involved with me if I only have five years to live?" As Sarah said, "Sure, there are some people who don't want to be involved with a cancer patient, but we all know of women who have beautiful romances and marriages after breast cancer."

Julia's experience supports this: "For those women who worry they'll never be involved again, remember me—a fifty-six-year-old woman who remarried after she had breast cancer."

Their Partners Did Not Leave Them

Regardless of the kind of treatment she received, every woman was understandably concerned about what impact breast cancer would have on her relationship with her partner. Couples cannot go through such a life-threatening crisis together and not undergo some level of change in their relationships. In fact, all of these women felt that their partnerships did change, both emotionally and physically. But those women involved in stable relationships said the changes were, on the whole, positive. They felt that the experience of breast cancer had brought them closer emotionally to their partners than ever before.

That is not to say that emotional or sexual problems did not exist in these relationships—they did for some of the women. Though no one suffered any major or long-term sexual problems as a result of having a mastectomy, it is clear that chemotherapy had a major long-term negative impact on some of the young women's sexuality. These problems, however, did not cause the end of relationships, nor did the women experience social or sexual rejection because of them—there were problems they had to learn to live with and accept.

At the time of diagnosis, eight of these women were involved in serious and/or married relationships, and two were single and not dating anyone seriously. Following treatment for breast cancer, five of the women remained with the same partner, two eventually became divorced, and one broke up with her live-in boyfriend and immediately became involved with someone else. Of the two single women, one had a significant relationship during her breast cancer treatment and the other remained uninvolved.

Lost breasts were certainly not the cause of the two divorces. The two marriages that ended in divorce a few years after breast cancer—Nancy's and Kate's—were troubled before the breast cancer. The intense crisis only widened the already existing marital cracks. As Valerie commented, "A woman may divorce after breast cancer not because of the cancer but because she can't get away with not dealing with the problems anymore. You can't pretend anymore; it's too hard." When faced with life and death issues, the women evaluated themselves and their lives honestly.

Breast cancer very likely was the catalyst, but was not the cause, of the breakups. In spite of the eventual breakups, both husbands stayed with their wives through surgery and treatment. And Kate and Nancy were instrumental in seeking their divorces. They were not victims.

You may worry about these interpersonal problems because there is a cultural expectation that they *will* occur. Part of these concerns are fueled by the myths about the woman with breast cancer who is deformed, less sexually attractive (and less lovable), and rejected by suitors and partners. These myths are based on the belief that breasts are somehow central to sexual conduct and a woman's identity. Without breasts, a woman may be perceived as losing some of her value as a sexual being. Though intimate sexual relations include a wide range of sexual behaviors—kissing, hugging, holding hands, cuddling, stroking—to most people in this country, sex is narrowly defined to include only the breasts and sexual intercourse. Women have adopted and internalized these societal standards and can accept them as long as they are healthy.

Not only is the sexual code of behavior narrowly defined but there is also a deep-seated belief, promoted heavily by advertising, that the only people who can have sex are those who are young and physically perfect. The aging, the physically unattractive, the handicapped, and those who are ill are excluded from the "club." When a woman no longer fits the mold—such as when she loses a breast—she may feel she is "damaged goods." And so, by societal standards, women with breast cancer are no longer allowed to, or supposed to, play the "sex" game. It is no wonder that women have concerns about getting breast cancer. "How can we be lovable and attractive if we aren't perfect?" Sarah said. "This culture doesn't teach you how not to be perfect."

Fortunately for these women, the reality was that it did not matter if they were perfect or not. Well aware of the cultural standards on beauty and sex, the women in this book learned that the myths were only myths and, in the main, not grounded in reality. Prior to breast cancer, all of these women had a history of satisfactory or positive sexual experiences. Following their breast cancer, most had positive sexual experiences, felt sexually attractive, and obviously others felt so too. Though the individual woman's sexual lifestyle may have been altered, sexual involvement was not over. By rejecting cultural notions about what and how much is sexually good, they could move on to their own comfort levels. Susie, after listening to an Oprah Winfrey program, was relieved to hear that just because she only wanted sex once a month, she was not a sexual deviant. Sex is often viewed as somehow crucial to the survival of a relationship, yet as Marcia said, "Sex is only a small part of a total relationship." Hemlotta expressed it well: "There is too much fuss about sex here in America. There's nothing wrong with not doing it! After all, what is sex in life? Sex is only one item of life to be enjoyed, but it is a bodily pleasure and not to be revered too much."

In your own way, you have to confront both your own and cultural beliefs about what relationships and sex mean to you as an individual. Like the women in this book, you should be comfortable establishing your own standards based on a balanced perspective on the value of sex and love in your life and relationships.

They Reaped the Rewards of
Giving Something Back

When Valerie first got her diagnosis of breast cancer, she thought, "I pictured myself living a life alone and thought I would be a completely unsexual being." Her response is not uncommon: The possibility of losing contact both socially and sexually with others is very threatening to anyone. However, for the women in the book these fears were unfounded. They did not end up living alone in isolation, nor did they become unsexual beings. Friends, family, lovers, partners, support groups, strangers, doctors, and nurses all responded with care, emotional support, and love. And when the women did not get what they needed, most of them were able to ask for help. All of this support was crucial to the women feeling acceptable and loved.

As a result of these positive relationships, all these women wanted to give something back and repay the enormous sense of gratitude they felt. The women were almost embarrassed by the emotional riches offered to them throughout their experience and were most grateful. They were in awe of the love people expressed and that so much was given for nothing in return. When they felt better, every one of the women made themselves available to counsel other women who were going through the breast cancer experience. Kate said, "I can never repay those people who helped me so much, but I can pass on the love they gave me to somebody else who really needs it." Susie said, "I get lots of phone calls from women who are about to have biopsies or breast cancer operations, and I feel good about myself as a woman because I can reach out and share with them." This situation was not temporary, as even now, at least six of the ten women are still actively involved with breast cancer patients, through counseling, writing articles, or working with the American Cancer Society's Reach to Recovery program. They also felt a responsibility to be a role model for their friends and others. Barbara, like many of the younger women, was the first of her peers to have breast cancer: "This injected me with a sense of purpose in the way I handled having this disease. I wanted to be a role model and have tried to conduct myself in a way that others can follow."

Your lifeline during the breast cancer experience is tied to your support network—those who know you and love you. Based on the ten women's experiences in this book, the factors that seemed to have the greatest influence on their coping effectively with the important people in their lives was their ability to do the following: being open about their disease, asking for assistance, involving and relying on their support networks, communicating both social and sexual concerns, resuming sexual intimacy with those close to them, and giving something back to others. If you are able to incorporate some of these behaviors, what you get in return is emotional and sensual support given to you by your family, partners, and friends, which may increase your ability to cope better and enable you to emerge with a stronger sense of self and well-being.

14

Your Body Image

WHAT WILL HAPPEN TO MY BODY?

For more than a century, women have believed that breast cancer is synonymous with disfigurement, disability, and death. Although this broadly held perception rests on exceptional results of the disease rather than on the outcomes, it is easy to understand why you expect the worst when you are first diagnosed with the disease. Almost reflexively you ask: "Will I die?" "Will I lose my breasts and become disfigured?" "What effects will treatment have on me?" These are the kinds of questions that cut to the very quick of your existence, not only your survival but the ongoing viability of your physical self.

Because it threatens your life and is sometimes treated by the removal of your breast, breast cancer makes you extremely body-conscious. Scared and uncertain about your future, soon all you can think about, twenty-four hours a day, is what is going to happen to your body. And you are not alone. Your breasts become the focus of everyone else's attention too; they become a part of the public domain. During diagnosis, you feel that you have been involuntarily thrust stark naked on a stage, with the audience free to question, examine, x-ray, inject, and cut you. Throughout treatment, you continue to feel "on stage" and exposed. You become increasingly vulnerable, desexualized, and dehumanized. You worry about the impact surgery will have on your body as well. What will the scars look like? Should I have breast reconstruction? Do I want to wear a prosthesis? What kind of clothes can I wear? If you undergo chemotherapy, you are plagued with such thoughts as: How sick will I be? Will I lose my hair? Will I look normal to the outside world? Will I ever look normal to me? You wonder, "Why did my body do this to me?" and "Can I ever trust it again?" Going through the breast cancer experience may make you feel like a stranger in your own body—it no longer feels like home. It may take time before you can move in again and become comfortable with it.

The condition and treatment of breast cancer constitutes a major assault on your body image, which is often understood as your own appraisal and perception of how your body functions and looks: What can my body do and how physically attractive am I? But it is more than this, for body image is part of a broader concept—body integrity—which includes biological, emotional, psychological, and interpersonal dimensions. The status of your health, your sense of body wholeness, and the perception others have of you affect your body image. This image is a part of your identity, for your feelings about your body are commensurate with the way you see yourself generally.

Each of the women interviewed for this book experienced a change in her body image as a result of being treated for breast cancer. There were physical changes that affected her appearance and biological changes that, in turn, affected how her body functioned. How much change each woman experienced depended on a variety of factors, the most important being the nature and intensity of the treatment she received. Not surprisingly, the women who had lumpectomies and radiation saw the fewest alterations and had the least number of problems with their body images. Those who were able to keep their breasts and had good cosmetic results from surgery and radiation were able to regain their confidence in their appearance quickly. On the other hand, the mastectomy and chemotherapy patients faced a far more difficult road in trying to restore balance and a sense of wholeness to their physical selves. After losing their breasts and enduring toxic drugs, they underwent biological and physical changes that naturally produced significant negative effects on their body images, which took longer to overcome.

A NEW IMAGE

Remarkably, despite all the painful losses and changes their bodies underwent, over time—and it did take time—most of these women were able to reestablish a body image with which they were comfortable. Their bodies still functioned well, although sometimes in new and different ways, and they were able to get on with their lives. They did not feel disabled or disfigured. They adjusted to their new appearance and developed a renewed affection for their bodies. What did the women do throughout their breast cancer experience that enabled them to adjust successfully to the significant changes in their physical selves and build confidence again in their body image?

They Confronted Their Scars

One of the critical first steps these women took to reestablish their body image was to confront their surgical scars visually. By doing so, they began the process of learning how to adjust to and deal with their changed body image. All of them had to cope with scars in some form or another, whether from a lymph node operation, a biopsy, lumpectomy, mastectomy, or breast reconstruction.

It was an awkward and uncomfortable process; the first look was never easy, but most viewed their incisions *soon* after their operations. The lumpectomy patients had minimal scarring of their breasts and consequently did not have a difficult time accepting their appearance. In time, these scars healed and all were satisfied with the cosmetic results of their surgery.

For most of the women who had mastectomies, the worst scar scenarios they had imagined did not materialize. These women harbored unrealistic anxieties regarding their postoperative appearance. *None* of them had any idea what a mastectomy scar looked like, nor were many of them even informed about what the operation entailed. Kate expected "to see a big hole in my chest." Fortunately, instead of the huge scar they anticipated seeing, the women who had modified radicals (removal of breast tissue and underarm lymph nodes) were all pleasantly surprised to see only a thin pencil line of stitches on their chest. Although initially upset by their appearance, the common reaction on viewing their scar was, "It wasn't that bad," or "It wasn't ugly." Susie reported, "I was expecting this huge scar but instead it was very much like my C-section scar." Kate thought her scar was "quite beautiful" and showed her friends who were surprised at how small it was.

Because they did not feel as disfigured as they had expected, most of these women were able to accept their scars more quickly. But it is still better for your peace of mind to ask your doctor *before* your operation what he or she is going to do and how it will look. Some women have said they felt more prepared when they were able to look at other women's scars or pictures of mastectomy scars.

On the other hand, those who had radical mastectomies, Marcia and Nancy, were understandably more upset at first by the physical results of their extensive surgery. Not only had they lost the breast and the underarm lymph nodes but part of their chest muscles as well. (It should be noted that at the time of their treatment, the radical was the only surgical option for breast cancer and now is very rare.) Nancy was horrified "by this huge red slash across my chest." Though told hers was a "beautiful operation," Marcia, too, upon her first viewing, was immediately repulsed. Over time, however, both Marcia and Nancy grew accustomed to and comfortable with their scars.

As has been mentioned in the previous section, numerous studies have shown that early acceptance of the mastectomy scar by a woman (and her partner or others close to her) speeds her emotional recovery.[1] The sooner you look at and accept these changes, the better for you and for others close to you. The experiences of the women in this book support these studies. It is notable that many of them showed their scars not only to their partners but to mothers, sisters, and close friends. With the support of others, these women learned that they still looked okay.

Recent studies also show that the trauma of surgery can be greatly assuaged by psychological preparation of patients through information and counseling.[2] All of these women said they would have preferred to have more accurate and detailed information about the physical and emotional impact of the operations prior to their surgery. It would have enabled them to adjust more quickly and be far less fearful.

Fortunately, many forward-thinking hospitals and physicians now offer presurgical consultations in which your concerns about surgery and its impact are addressed. Having prior knowledge about the physical and psychological impact that surgery and treatment will have on you makes you less anxious and better able to adjust to the changes in your body image. If this kind of presurgical consultation is not offered to you, insist on seeing someone who can provide you with this information. Remember, too, that being knowledgeable makes you feel more in control.

Mastectomy Patients Mourned the Loss of Their Breasts

While going through the process of incorporating their scars into their new body image, these women also undertook an equally important task: grieving for their old, and now lost, physical self. Letting go of their breasts, and the accompanying body image, though painful and sad, enabled them to move toward acceptance of their changed bodies and the development of a body image that would feel "normal" once again.

Actually, the process of releasing the old image had begun for a number of the women before their surgery. With the exception of Marcia, all of these women had the advantage of going through a two-step diagnosis procedure: They had a biopsy and other tests first, and then decisions were made about what kind of surgery and treatment would be performed.

When you go through a two-step process, it allows you time to adjust emotionally and to prepare for the possible loss of your breast. It also gives you time to collect information, ask questions, get second opinions, talk to others, and investigate treatment options. Traditionally, the one-step procedure, which Marcia had, whereby a patient underwent anesthesia not knowing if she would wake up with her breasts intact, did not afford the time needed to prepare psychologically for possible breast loss, which is so crucial for a woman's complete recovery. Most doctors now use a two-step process in diagnosis and treatment, and it is recommended by the American Cancer Society. When undergoing this two-step procedure, you first will be asked to sign a release form for a breast biopsy; make sure you give permission *only* for the biopsy, not a mastectomy.

Everyone finds it very hard to imagine how she will look and feel without her breast. Some of these women tried to prepare for the change by standing in front of a mirror and flattening their breasts. Others made a point of saying good-bye to their breasts, recalling all the pleasures their breasts had provided them. Terri said good-bye to her breast a whole week before her surgery. The night before her mastectomy, Susie felt great sadness as she said good-bye and thought as she looked in the mirror, "This is the last time I am going to see both of them together."

Those women who had mastectomies all grieved about the loss of their breasts. The intensity and duration of those feelings varied, but the first few months were definitely the most difficult for everyone. Nancy said, "I had just begun to love my breasts when I lost mine." In her profound sadness, weeks after her mastectomy, Kate felt a strong need to know what happened to her removed breast and likened the feeling to a mother yearning to hold the dead baby she had lost.

This loss is more traumatic for some women than others and depends on how you feel about your breasts and the role they play in your body image and sexual life. For some of these women, little value was placed on their breasts; others considered their breasts an integral part of their appearance but not important sexually; still others found them central to their sexuality but not to their appearance. Studies show that women with breast cancer whose breasts play a significant role in their appearance or sexual life may suffer a greater loss and have a more difficult time dealing with their new body image than women who view their breasts as functional and generally unimportant.[3]

For example, Barbara explained that her breast loss wasn't that major because, "my breasts were never that sexual to begin with"; whereas Susie's breasts were central in her sexual life. As might be expected, Susie had a more difficult time adjusting to her loss than did Barbara. Julia and Marcia never felt that their breast loss greatly damaged their body image. For these two women, the fear of getting cancer again had a greater influence on their body image than the loss of their breasts. Julia explained, "It's easier to deal with the mastectomy because it is real. Cancer, on the other hand, is something nebulous that you can't see or feel and it represents mortality."

Preparing for the loss of your breast and assessing how you feel about your breasts and the role they play in your body image will help you cope better with your loss. Before you have your surgery, ask to see a Reach to Recovery volunteer who has had a mastectomy, talk with a close friend, or have a health professional speak with you about your feelings and concerns.

Lumpectomy Patients Needed Time to Adjust to Their New Body Image

Although the women who were treated with lumpectomies and radiation kept their breasts, there was still a period of adjustment to the changes they had undergone. The lumpectomy patients were sad that their breasts would never be quite the same again and experienced some uncertainty about their attractiveness. Acutely aware of the possibility that they *could* lose their breasts, they reported feeling very protective of them. As Susie said, "For a while after treatment, I felt very protective of my breast and didn't want to be touched there for a time." Some said they had taken their breasts for granted but were thankful they were able to save them. Valerie said, "I didn't think about my breasts a whole lot before, but now I talk to them and pat them and am so pleased I have two."

However, it should be noted that, just because there are fewer appearance problems for those women treated with lumpectomy and radiation, it does not mean that they have fewer emotional concerns about their changing body image. Keeping your breast does not eliminate the trauma of breast cancer. The whole body is still highly vulnerable to the risk of recurrence; this vulnerability has a considerable effect on how *all* breast cancer patients view their body image from a functional standpoint. Valerie commented: "The physical side of cancer (lumpectomy and radiation) was a piece of cake, though dealing with my emotions was another matter."

Mourning for what used to be is a painful but necessary process for everyone, regardless of the kind of surgery they have. You *will* get through it, by yourself and with the support of family, friends, therapists, and fellow patients. By acknowledging your loss, grieving in your own way, you can then begin to move forward.

They Began the Process of Rebuilding
Their Body Image

By facing their scars and mourning their losses, these women were able to start the process of rebuilding their body image. Throughout treatment, each woman developed ways of trying to look better and trying to create a sense of wholeness.

Lumpectomy Patients Had the Least Difficulty
Integrating the Changes

The lumpectomy patients made a relatively smooth transition. Within six months of finishing treatment, they believed they had created a positive body image. They looked well, thought they were attractive, and were physically able to return to their normal routines. Initially worried about the cosmetic changes their breasts would undergo after biopsy and radiation, their concerns proved unfounded: Their scars were minimal and radiation produced few permanent physical changes to their breasts. Though going through radiation treatments was tiring, both physically and emotionally, the most common side effects—sunburn, soreness, and swelling to varying degrees—all proved temporary and disappeared within months. Although some women treated with lumpectomy and radiation do not get the best cosmetic results, these women did. As Valerie said, "My body looks fine!" Their experiences support recent studies that compare the psychological outcomes of lumpectomy versus mastectomy, and show that lumpectomy patients report less of a loss of feelings of attractiveness and are less self-conscious about their appearance than mastectomy patients.[4] If having a lumpectomy is an option for you, you may want to consider this information when you are making your decision.

Mastectomy Patients Chose a Variety of Means to Recreate
Their Sense of Physical Wholeness

The mastectomy patients began the process of rebuilding their body image by choosing from a variety of methods that would help them feel whole again: wearing a prosthesis, *not* wearing a prosthesis, or having breast reconstruction It did not matter which method they chose: What was important was that their choice helped them to recreate a normal body image. It is important to remember this point and do what is most comfortable for you.

Some Chose to Wear a Prosthesis

For some of these women, buying and wearing a prosthesis was a satisfactory way of restoring their normal appearance. The prosthesis made them look balanced and complete in their clothes and, particularly for women with larger breasts, helped prevent the posture, neck, and shoulder strains that can arise due to body asymmetry. Their introduction to a prosthesis was while they were still in the hospital. Many of these women were visited by a volunteer of the American Cancer Society's Reach to Recovery program, who gave them a temporary lightweight soft breast form, which could be used while the mastectomy wound was healing. It was important for them to see another breast cancer patient who had successfully managed to survive and felt good about herself and how she looked. Susie's volunteer was "an inspiration to me. She was an attractive forty-year-old woman who was very comfortable with her one breast, and her sexuality. I didn't look at her as a one-breasted lady. I looked at her as a pleasant, warm, witty woman whose style was feminine."

After their wounds healed, the women shopped for permanent prostheses. Many went to their local American Cancer Society to see and feel the different breast forms and then, often with a friend, visited specialty stores to buy a prosthesis that fit properly. It was an emotional experience for everyone, and difficult for some, like Nancy, who, after living for a year without a prosthesis, couldn't find a breast form that fit correctly. "All the salesladies did was make me look like a Sherman tank," she complained. Fortunately, there are now a number of companies that produce well-fitting and natural-looking breast forms. You can contact your local American Cancer Society, other breast cancer patients, and lingerie stores for further information about how to find a prosthesis. Be prepared to try on a number of different forms before you find the kind that is most comfortable for you. It's worth your time.

Most of those women who chose to wear a prosthesis have continued to do so comfortably for many years. Marcia, Nancy, and Julia liked wearing prostheses and felt they helped them look attractive in their clothing. But it's important to note that these women also accepted how their bodies looked without any kind of breast forms. As Nancy said, "I feel fine with my clothes on and without my clothes on."

Others Chose Not to Wear a Prosthesis

Like many breast cancer patients, Marcia felt strongly that it was essential for mastectomees to use a prosthesis. She said she did not want to attract attention to her loss and understandably wanted to have a normal-looking appearance. Kate, however, felt otherwise. She wore a prosthesis for three months and then decided to throw it away. She thought the prosthesis would make her feel like her "old self" but realized she didn't need it, "because it didn't change how I felt and I liked my new body."

There are many women like Kate who are comfortable and proud of being one-breasted. Audre Lorde, in her book *The Cancer Journals* (Spinsters, Ink.), recalls being scolded by a nurse for refusing to wear a prosthesis after her mastectomy. Ms. Lorde, like Kate, didn't care if someone else didn't think she looked "right," because she was not ashamed about how she looked and strongly rejected societal notions of how a woman should look. These women feel more comfortable with their own definitions of what their bodies should look like. What matters most is that you feel good about how you look, with or without a prosthesis.

Some Chose to Have Breast Reconstruction

Like some other breast cancer patients, Susie found wearing a prosthesis an encumbrance, a constant reminder of her loss. Though she wore her prosthesis, she was always self-conscious about it and never felt it was an acceptable part of her self-image. Consequently, she had problems in reestablishing a positive body image. After two years of struggling emotionally, Susie decided to have breast reconstruction. Her chances of feeling better about her appearance were greatly improved because studies have shown that women who choose to have reconstruction report a sense of enhanced attractiveness and more comfort with their bodies following the operation.[5]

Like Susie, Terri decided she, too, wanted to have breast reconstruction. But she chose immediate reconstruction at the time of her mastectomy. Terri reported that she never felt she was missing something and was able to "adopt" her new breast as her own. "I never had to deal with something foreign outside my body." In fact, according to one study, a reconstructed breast is more easily integrated into body image than a prosthesis.[6] As a result of her surgery, Terri had few problems because she was not "worried about being deformed, didn't have to change how I dressed, and never had to wear a prosthesis." Her experience supports recent studies of women who have had immediate reconstruction and show far fewer feelings of deformity, depression, and self-consciousness than those women who have only mastectomies or delayed reconstruction.[7]

They Explored the Cultural and Medical Biases
about Reconstruction

Before making their decisions to have breast reconstruction, both Terri and Susie struggled with the emotional issues about the procedure. Terri found herself justifying her choice to others who questioned her "need" for the surgery. Terri didn't have her breast reconstructed to look pretty or sexy; she felt it had to do with her sense of wholeness. She said, "Our cultural attitudes create a crazy-making situation for women. On the one hand, they tell you it's vain to want to look good, and on the other hand, they tell you that without a breast and being whole, you are not attractive and sexually good. Whatever makes a woman feel better about herself is okay. We shouldn't be judgmental."

This cultural attitude about women's vanity is one of the reasons a number of breast cancer patients have chosen not to have reconstruction. Of course, for at least three of these women, breast reconstruction was not a viable option at the time of their surgeries. Though Nancy never considered reconstruction in 1973, she said, "If I were forty-eight years old now, I would do it. But I am accustomed to what I am."

Choosing reconstruction also depends on your background—how important your breasts are to your self-esteem and sexual functioning—and your concerns about recurrence. For example, because she was more concerned about her survival, Barbara said she was less interested in reconstruction and breast loss. Three of the women had not considered reconstruction because they wanted to avoid additional surgery. Moreover, they became used to how they looked and liked it. Marcia said, "I don't need it for my ego or self-esteem or looks. I don't need it to make me feel better. I am comfortable."

Almost every woman treated now for breast cancer is a candidate for breast reconstruction. Unfortunately, many breast cancer patients are still not offered the option at the time of diagnosis or are advised by their doctors to delay reconstruction. Physicians still believe, incorrectly, that you must mourn the loss of your breast before you can have reconstruction. Findings of all the recent breast reconstruction studies refute this commonly held belief.[8]

Selecting reconstructive surgery is not a function of your age as much as how you feel about yourself and the availability of the treatment. There are as many older breast cancer patients as there are young seeking this option. For the first time, breast reconstruction offers a way to lessen the emotional and physical trauma of your breast cancer surgery. There is no longer any reason why you have to live with being one-breasted if you don't want to. Most insurance compaines now pay for this surgery. If you're considering this option, it will help you if *prior* to your surgery, you educate yourself thoroughly. Assess how you feel, discuss different options with both your surgeon and a plastic surgeon, look at pictures of the plastic surgeon's work, talk to other women who have had reconstruction, and read books on the topic (see appendixes).

They Realized They Could Look Good
With or Without Breasts

It did not matter *what* method the mastectomy patients used to help themselves feel better about how they looked. Any choice—wearing a prosthesis, not wearing one, or having breast reconstruction—was acceptable if it helped them regain confidence in their body image. All of these women made decisions that enhanced their body image, which resulted in their feeling more whole, complete, and comfortable. More important, the women learned from their experiences that they could function effectively and feel confident about their appearance with or without breasts.

They Got Through Chemotherapy by Not
Giving Up on Their Bodies

When these women went through the process of choosing to wear or not to wear a prosthesis, or having breast reconstruction, they were dealing with those body-image issues that were attendant to their physical appearance. However, the loss of or damage to their breasts had interfered little with their ability to function normally. Chemotherapy treatments, on the other hand, had a tremendous impact on how they lived their everyday lives. The seven women (of whom five had mastectomies) who were treated with chemotherapy said that the toxic drugs caused a far more protracted hardship on their body image than any surgical treatment they received. Marcia said, "I was never sick before or after the mastectomy. It had been very mechanical and my life marched on. Not chemo: Chemo was hell. Chemo produced illness." Not everyone experiences these side effects; it depends on the kind of treatment you receive. But the women in this book did undergo major changes as a result of chemotherapy treatments.

For at least six months, and up to two years for some, chemotherapy disrupted the women's home life, work, and social and sexual relations. The treatments mostly produced temporary side effects but some were permanent and often traumatic. All experienced terrible nausea that resulted in exhaustion for up to a week after treatment. Many gained weight, some lost all or part of their hair, and most were depressed. Many were concerned about what their bodies would be like after they had finished their treatment. Barbara, like many of the others, wondered, "if my body would do the same things as it did before chemo." Each woman's self-esteem and body image were sorely taxed during chemotherapy treatment.

Yet, these women found ways to live with and through these hard times. They constantly reminded themselves that the long-term benefits outweighed the short-term side effects. They always had to look forward to their end goal: *They* had chosen chemo treatments, and knew they had to be sick to get better. This was *never* easy. Every one of them, at one time or another, struggled with an overwhelming desire to quit treatments, as do thousands of other women. Yet they were able to remind themselves that it was *their* fight, and to stop meant giving up on their bodies. Giving up meant choosing death. They did not give up.

Fortunately, most of chemotherapy's side effects were temporary. The nausea, vomiting, hair loss, and weight gain stopped at the end of treatments. Their hair grew back, they lost weight, and they regained their energy. But it was some time before they felt they could reclaim their bodies as their own.

They Found Ways to Look and Feel
Better During Chemotherapy

Even though they felt unwell, and on occasion unattractive, during chemotherapy, they realized there were *some* things they could do to feel and look better. Learning how to get through the nausea was the biggest obstacle, but they found small ways to cope. Kate felt more in control when her doctor changed the sequence of drugs she was taking, which aided her in managing her nausea episodes. Barbara's spirits were lifted when her friends took turns helping her back and forth to the bathroom. Susie and Hemlotta found eating crackers or other small meals at certain times before and after treatments helped them feel better. On the other hand, Terri learned how to deal with her nausea by keeping a lot of food in her stomach. After a few treatments all of the women could anticipate how their bodies would respond and were able to develop routines around the times when they knew they would feel ill. Marcia scheduled her treatments for Thursdays so she could be sick on the weekends and get back to work on Mondays. Terri scheduled her multiple breast reconstruction operations in between chemotherapy treatments so she could have something positive to look forward to. For those women who experienced anticipatory nausea, learning self-hypnosis or doing relaxation and biofeedback exercises were some of the ways they tried to reduce the anxiety of waiting. Although you cannot eliminate chemo's side effects, you can perform these small tasks that will help you function a little better. Much of your learning will be through experimentation—trial and error—so be patient with yourself.

Gaining weight was another common side effect of chemotherapy and perhaps hardest on these women's body images. Unlike the mastectomy, which can be hidden from everyone, and the hair loss, which wigs can disguise, you cannot hide the weight gain. And because it is induced by drugs, the weight is very hard to lose. It was terribly frustrating for Terri, whose doctors claimed it wasn't the chemo that made her gain weight. Terri said, "I gained 25 pounds. I felt I looked horrible. The weight gain affected me more seriously than the breast loss." After doing some research on her own, Terri realized that it *was* largely the chemo: "It wasn't *me* that was causing the weight gain." This made her feel better and reinstated a sense of control. Barbara was frustrated about her additional weight but decided the way to handle it was to accept the situation and buy and wear bigger clothes until she could lose the extras pounds. Though weight gain is not easy to live with, remember it is a *temporary* condition, and you must learn not to be too hard on yourself. Wear loose clothing; do not attempt to get into your size eight jeans and keep reminding yourself that this weight gain is a part of the treatment that will help you get better.

Everyone knows before her first chemotherapy treatment that she stands a good chance of losing her body and head hair. Most of these women did. Some, like Terri, were surprised that they did not lose *all* their head hair, but may have lost their eyelashes. Each woman responded to this loss in different ways. For example, Marcia, whose breast loss had not been terrible for her, found her hair loss devastating. And when it grew back in, it was gray. She was initially very sad about this loss, because for years her hair had been a crucial part of her attractiveness. Susie, who viewed her mastectomy as a major loss, thought losing her hair, after the initial shock, was a small problem. "For the most part," she said, "I just kept telling myself, this is only temporary. It will grow back. I didn't really ever get into an ugly period with my baldness."

Regardless of their feelings, most of the women bought wigs prior to their hair loss, although there was a difference in how the wigs fit before and after hair loss. Nobody loved wearing the wigs, but at least the women were prepared and had arranged for something to cover their heads. Sarah cut her hair very short, "like an English punk crew cut," *before* her hair loss began so it would be less upsetting when clumps of hair began to fall out. Some found the wigs more of a burden than helpful—they were too hot and itchy—and they took to wearing hats and scarves instead. Many of the women even received compliments on how well the scarves made them look. If you have been told that you might lose your hair (you always think you will be the one who doesn't), plan on buying wigs, scarves, and hats before treatment begins, and consider getting your hair cut. Talk with other cancer patients and see what has worked for them. It will make the transition easier for you.

They Decorated Their Bodies More

When Susie lost her hair she "wanted to compensate for the hair loss, and so I relied on using a scarf and wearing makeup to highlight my face." She had rarely used makeup before but found during treatment it really made her look and feel better. Like many of the women, Susie also realized that looking good seemed to improve her attitude toward chemotherapy. Marcia's statement, "I wanted to look better after breast cancer, not worse," echoed the feelings of others. Actually, all of the women in this book, regardless of their treatment, began to pay more attention to, as Barbara said, "decorating" their bodies. They began buying new clothes, wearing more makeup and jewelry, routinely visiting hairdressers, and having manicures and massages. They felt they deserved to pamper themselves after all they had been through. It built their body confidence because there were so many times when they felt unattractive and never thought they could look well again.

There are now numerous courses offered to cancer patients through hospitals, breast centers, the American Cancer Society, department stores, and consulting groups that provide valuable information on how to improve your appearance during and after cancer treatment. Tips on everything from choosing a prosthesis to reconstructing eyebrows are included. As more and more women are now going through chemotherapy for the treatment of breast cancer, you need to know there is help available and that you *can* improve how you look and *feel* during treatment (see appendixes).

They Took Better Physical Care
of Their Bodies

You cannot go through a life-threatening illness without recognizing and understanding the true value of a healthy body. Prior to having breast cancer, many of these women said they took their health as a given. After being diagnosed and treated, their attitudes changed radically. "I treat my body more carefully and don't take it for granted," Sarah said. Terri explained that before her breast cancer, "I didn't really take good care of myself. I worked too hard, I drank too much, and I found all the ways I couldn't put myself first." Many of the women said that before their diagnosis they would care for others at the expense of themselves. After breast cancer they put themselves first. They became better caretakers of their bodies: more possessive, protective, and concerned about their health. Valerie said, "The breast cancer experience makes you quite assertive about your body. I feel strongly it's *my* body and will never ever consent for it to be treated with a lack of respect."

Having made it through treatment, and fully aware of the threat of recurrence, they knew how important it was to take good care of their insides, as well as their outsides. As a result, the women nurtured their bodies more than ever before, during, and after treatment through exercising, eating nutritious meals, resting, and trying to minimize the stress in their lives. Learning how to take good care of your body will result in your feeling better both physically and psychologically.

They Put Their Physical Losses
in Perspective

Like many cancer patients, these women adapted successfully to their physical losses by thinking how much worse things could be. Having experienced so many losses, they prioritized what really constituted a loss. For example, the women with mastectomies, though saddened, felt that breast loss was less important when compared to saving their lives. They knew that cancer is a systemic disease and one that is not just limited to the breast. "I was worried about my life—my breast doesn't count that much," Barbara said. They were thankful for being able to continue their lives, to go back to work, and to take care of their families. Marcia thought the loss of her breast was nothing compared to her daughter's mental illness. Terri was far more concerned about losing her mind than her breast. Valerie felt better because she didn't lose her breast. Julia's attitude was, "You can function fine without a breast but you can't get around very well with one leg."

For those who experienced permanent physical problems as a result of chemotherapy, it was a time of coming to terms with losses over which they had no control. The women who went through early menopause talked about not being psychologically prepared to be "physically older." Kate said, "I sure wasn't ready to be put ten years ahead of my biological schedule." Becoming prematurely menopausal also represented a significant loss to the younger women, particularly those who had not had children.

Though both Barbara and Terri had chosen not to have children, they had been interested in the possibility, and now they were forever deprived of that choice. Sarah and Valerie also knew that their health might be compromised if they decided to have children. Not being able to reproduce both challenged the biological side of their femaleness and represented a deprivation of an important choice. This was a particular hardship to the younger women who had not yet experienced the limitations of age on the body. But they considered ways in which they could become involved with children if they could not have their own: spending time with nieces or nephews, or adopting a child, or working with children in some form.

They Took Pride in Their Bodies' Ability
to Withstand Trauma

Though they emerged from the battle having suffered significant physical changes, their individual successes in overcoming these hurdles made these women feel strong and accomplished. They developed a newfound respect for the human body and its ability to withstand considerable trauma. The tremendous sense of pride they felt in the *physical* power of their bodies had a potent and positive impact on their body image. Traditionally, most women have not been physically active and do not know what their bodies are capable of doing; they have been more focused on the superficial aspects of their body image. Learning what their bodies could achieve, particularly when so severely challenged, was exhilarating. Susie said, "When I look back at the lumpectomy, lymph node operation, radiation, mastectomy, and chemo, I feel like Wonder Woman." Barbara was proud because her body tolerated the treatments. Valerie said, "I am very proud of my breast and me, scars and all." Hemlotta attributed her physical strength to the homeopathic medicines she'd been taking for years: "My body has served me well," she said. Kate described herself as a woman warrior, proud of her scars and her ability to fight and survive in the battle. She explained, "A man's scar is a sign of virility, proof that he has been through something that has made him stronger. A man can be proud of his scars. I look at my mastectomy scar that way instead of thinking of it as something ugly."

With Time and Patience, They Understood That Loving
Their Bodies Was Again Possible

The healing of your body image takes love and support, but most important, it takes time. How much time depends on you—your individual circumstances and your treatment plan. This process is not easy, but as can be clearly seen from the interviews, these women adjusted to the changes and came to love and value their bodies in new and different ways. The further away from treatment they were, the better they felt about the new body image they had created.

Nancy, a thirteen-year survivor, spoke for many of the mastectomy patients when she said, "I really feel confident about my body. I feel attractive with one breast." Marcia said, "I now accept and live with the physical changes I have undergone." Kate felt: "It was important after surgery to be attractive and still be considered desirable and to prove it. Now I am more interested in getting on with my life, rather than checking myself out in the mirror all the time. I feel attractive and think one looks how one feels."

Sometimes, regardless of their treatments, there are breast cancer patients who, because of their beliefs, feel their body image has not been threatened very much. Hemlotta, as a Hindu, believed: "The preservation of the purity of the soul is more important than preserving the body. I never so much cared for my body as for my soul. I don't consider that the body is everything." Though her chemotherapy treatment made her physically uncomfortable at times and concerned for her health, she was less concerned about her appearance than some of the other women.

Some of these women were still in the process of adapting to their losses, but were working toward acceptance. Susie decided to have breast reconstruction to alleviate her distress, and Barbara, dealing with her discomfort about her weight gain, struggled to accept her situation. "Some time in my life when my cancer is very advanced," she observed, "I am going to be in a hospital weighing 85 pounds, and in view of that, this weight gain doesn't mean that much. But you can't avoid society's notions about being overweight and the value of thinness. I wish I could be my normal weight, which is a little plump and chunky. . . . I am learning to live with all this." Adjusting to changes in your body image takes a willingness to be accepting of yourself, and the knowledge that it will take time. As you can tell from these women's experiences, you can and will feel better about how you look and function.

They Received Confirmation from Others That They Looked Okay

There is another significant factor that has an important bearing on your acceptance of the changes to your body. Strong support and reassurances about how you look from your families, friends, or new lovers throughout your breast cancer experience serve to help speed your newly minted image. Barbara talked about how much Sandy helped her accept her "differentness": "Sandy has been fine about my weight, joking around, saying how I look Rubenesque and how she loves chunky women." Receiving confirmation that they were still considered lovable and acceptable-looking was key. These women said that their partners, family members, friends, Reach to Recovery volunteers, therapists, support group members, dates, and physicians all were helpful in assisting them to live with the changed appearance of their bodies. It does not seem to matter who offers the support, or whether they are male or female—only that this kind of support is available and extended in a loving and accepting way.

Terri and Susie discussed the important role their physicians had played in enhancing their body images. Throughout treatment, their doctors continually told them how attractive they were. During chemotherapy,

Susie's doctor told her "how sunny and beautiful I looked. That meant so much to me when I was feeling low." This acceptance was particularly important because the physicians really knew what they looked like with and without clothes. This kind of affirmation was very powerful. For some, it was the first time they really knew that they were loved far more for who they were and less for how they looked.

They Decided for Themselves How Important Their Appearance Was for Them

Living in a country that values your appearance over your substance makes it difficult to love and accept your body, for few fit the idealized version of "woman" that repeatedly flashes across our TV screens. When you are treated for breast cancer, it makes this process of acceptance even harder. Getting through surgery, learning to live with one breast or damaged breasts, wearing a prosthesis, undergoing breast reconstruction, losing your hair, becoming violently ill, gaining weight, losing your ability to bear children, facing death—all of these events challenge every ounce of confidence you may have in your body and its attractiveness. Many find it difficult to believe that a woman could go through so many devastating changes and still feel good about her body. Yet despite these repeated bodily assaults, these ten women left the battlefield proud of how their bodies had performed under fire. They may have looked different from other women, but they felt good about how their bodies appeared and what they had accomplished.

Their attitudes were shaped by the way they coped with the changes in their body image. By confronting their scars, grieving for their losses, finding ways to cope with the side effects of chemotherapy, using a prosthesis or having breast reconstruction, pampering themselves, taking good care of their bodies, and putting their losses in perspective, they were able to rebuild their body images.

Because having breast cancer involves such a high level of breast and body consciousness, all of these women had to confront directly how important their appearance really was in evaluating their self-worth. There is no doubt that there is a definite association between how a woman feels about her body and how she feels about herself as a person. Women traditionally have relied on their appearance and body image to bolster their self-esteem. It is what they have been taught, and most never question the societal standards of what "looks good." As a result of having breast cancer, these ten women were forced to reevaluate the convention. Most would agree with Sarah, who commented, "My sense of myself was strengthened because I had to rely more on my inner strengths than on the 'goods' to make it. Now I groom my insides as well as my outsides. I am a whole package."

On balance, how they felt about themselves became a more critical factor in taking stock of their self-esteem than their body image. Certainly they still cared about their appearance, but they felt that how they looked mattered far less than *who* they were, and how they were living their lives. Because their perspectives changed, these women also developed their own standards of beauty and health: They were comfortably able to create a new woman in their *own* image. It is because they *owned* their bodies, and were more secure and comfortable with who they were and how they looked. Their priorities were very clear: "The fight isn't 'Am I too fat or ugly?' " as Valerie said. "The fight is for living." They understood that looking well is an important part of self-esteem, but having a healthy, functioning body takes precedence over all.

15

Your Achievements

THE OBSTACLE COURSE

From the first day of your diagnosis, it is clear that having breast cancer will challenge your ability to accomplish both physical and emotional tasks. You realize immediately that your life will be disrupted for a number of months, possibly years, as you undergo surgical procedures, radiation and chemotherapy treatments, and periods of recuperation. At first, all you can think of is death and dying, the possible loss of your breast, and what kind of treatment you will have to undergo. But soon you begin worrying about what impact breast cancer will have on your ability to work, and how much of you there will be left to give to your family and friends.

The critical issue for you will be *whether* you can manage this crisis successfully. How much help will you need at home and at work, and who will provide it? Can you still care for your children and carry out other family and work-related activities? Will you be temporarily or permanently removed from your full-time daily roles of worker, partner, mother, volunteer, or tennis player? Do you have the resources and skills to cope? What will you be able to accomplish while going through this crisis?

Moreover, some of your dreams and plans may be temporarily side-tracked because you do not know how long you might be alive. Not uncommon initially are feelings of resignation—what is the point of doing anything if you only have a short time to live? The uncertainty of the future can be very threatening, particularly to younger women, some of whom have not yet accomplished their goals and may be sad and angry about the possible loss of such opportunities in both their personal and professional lives. They worry about their chances for a meaningful relationship, marriage, children, and career. For some, cancer represents failure and an inability to do, to live.

Breast cancer challenges your ability to achieve, and achievement is a crucial component of your self-esteem. You feel a sense of accomplishment when you are able to succeed through overcoming obstacles, mastering an activity, hard work, skill, practice, and perseverance. Having a sense of self-determination—being able to make your own choices in life—is another important element of feeling successful. You also feel pride and a heightened sense of self-worth when you have a purpose in life and believe that what you do has value. Breast cancer disrupts and inhibits your ability to carry out these meaningful activities successfully and may result in feelings of depression, inadequacy, or failure.

AFFIRMATION OF ACCOMPLISHMENT

All of the women in this book were concerned about the extent to which their ability to achieve would be impaired by having breast cancer. Although there were many times when they certainly felt their lives were out of control, and they were unable to do very much, they ultimately were proud of themselves for what they were able to achieve during and after their breast cancer crisis. They felt they successfully had made it through the obstacle course. Not one of the women felt she had failed. What steps did these women take to help them feel accomplished?

They Chose to Survive

Even though they felt overwhelmed during the first week after their diagnosis, these women answered a critical question that gave them a sense of direction and control: Am I going to fight for my life? Each of the ten women, within days after her diagnosis, made a conscious and critical decision to *survive* her breast cancer crisis with, as Terri said, "as much courage and dignity as I can."

No matter how scared and alone they may have felt, they were glad to be alive and decided they wanted to stay that way. Like all the others, Kate felt "a tremendous zest and hunger for life," and was hopeful about her future. These women wanted to get better and made a choice to "make it through" the breast cancer crisis with as much energy as they could muster, fully aware of the tremendous emotional and physical challenges they would face.

Each woman approached her goal of survival as suited her own personal style. Some chose terms of battle to express their attitude toward their cancer: They were going to "beat" the disease, "fight it," or "lick it." Marcia's and Julia's attitude was that nothing could stop them because they were fighters. Although Sarah's first thoughts were, "Will what happened to my mother happen to me?" she, too, decided she was going to make it through and "be one hell of a lady."

Others were quieter in their approach but faced the crisis with no less resolve. Barbara believed that in her crisis there was an opportunity for growth and exploration: "I decided to live with this disease by deciding who I was and how I would face these ultimate questions of life." Terri felt it was important not to put her body at war with itself, but rather, wanted to have her body and mind working together to get well. Interestingly, at the time of her diagnosis, Terri had begun to move toward accomplishing this goal by eliminating alcohol from her life. While your own personal style will dictate the approach you take to cope with the issue of survival, what matters is that you decide you would like to live, with hope.

They Realized They Would Have to Rely on Themselves

One of the more terrifying feelings most cancer patients experience is the knowledge that they are suddenly completely alone. No matter how much love and support you might receive from others, you realize that the road ahead will be lonely. Nobody else but you is going to take the treatments and suffer the pain and losses. You are going to have to rely entirely on yourself. All of the women in this book were acutely aware that the *only* way they would succeed was through their own efforts. Their inner strength would take them through the experience. Nancy expressed this feeling well: "I would be climbing this mountain all by myself." She told herself early on, "It's up to you; you are on your own now." By making the decision to survive, on your own, with as much hope as you can muster, you immediately gain a small but significant sense of control in what still seems like an uncontrollable situation. Feeling in control leads you to a sense of accomplishment.

They Did Not Relinquish Their Power

There were innumerable decisions, both minor and major, that needed to be made throughout these women's breast cancer experiences. Time often was of the essence: They had to start reorganizing their family and work lives, select the surgery and treatment they would have, and choose the way they were going to cope and live with a life-threatening illness. Each woman had the option to make those decisions herself, or let someone else take over and make them for her. None relinquished her power to others; each ultimately made her own decisions. Though they did not realize it at the time, each decision they made from that moment on was an achievement, a way of mastering their world. Being an active participant in decision making is one important way of maintaining your control.

They Found a Doctor They Trusted

Like most cancer patients, you want a doctor who is competent, trustworthy, willing to include you in treatment decisions, and sympathetic to your needs. Some of these women were fortunate to have physicians whom they trusted. Those who were uncomfortable with their physicians found new doctors, often by seeking second opinions. They asked friends, other cancer patients, or called the local medical associations for recommendations.

Barbara, whose cancer had been misdiagnosed for over eleven months, left her HMO plan, and following discussions with a number of physicians, hired a whole new team of doctors whom she said made a substantial difference in her peace of mind. Valerie changed doctors because she was given no choice but mastectomy in treating her early stage cancer. Not until Terri met a plastic surgeon that she trusted was she able to make her decision to have a mastectomy and immediate reconstruction. Having a doctor who provides information and support, and who suggests getting a second opinion where appropriate, strengthens your self-confidence in decision making and enhances your sense of accomplishment.

While each woman wanted to be involved in her treatment plan, there was also a strong need among the women to know they were going to be well taken care of by their doctors. Trusting that their doctors were doing the right thing enabled them to feel safe, anchored. When Valerie realized she was in "capable hands," she felt more in control and relaxed. She felt that trusting her physician meant that she didn't have to spend all her time questioning whether her treatment was correct. This confidence in her doctor enabled Valerie to spend her energy on getting better.

You do not have to *like* your doctor, or always agree with everything he or she says, but being able to *trust* your physician's ability to provide quality care plays a key role in your well-being. Choose your physicians—surgeon, oncologist, radiation oncologist—with care. It's acceptable to interview a number of doctors before you make any decisions.

*   *   *

They Participated
in Their Treatment Decisions

Most of these women chose to be involved in their treatment decisions. Unfortunately, for Marcia and Nancy, there was never really an opportunity to "choose" their treatment, because during the early 1970s, there was only one way to manage breast cancer—with a radical mastectomy. They also went under anesthesia not knowing whether they would wake up with one breast or two. Nancy recalls, "I asked about options before the biopsy but was told there were none. I felt trapped and forced to make a decision quickly. I really didn't give myself much time to have second thoughts."

By the 1980s, when the other eight women were diagnosed, they had choices that Marcia and Nancy had not had: a variety of treatments from which to choose, including having only a biopsy, and then having the opportunity to take time to make their treatment decisions. Each woman had a different set of treatment decisions to make, depending on her diagnosis and her family situation, but they all felt like Julia, who said, "I wanted to go home and make my own decision." Though some of the physicians did not encourage the women to explore their options, each, in her own way, chose to be involved actively in making decisions about her surgery and treatment. Their response was not uncommon. A National Cancer Institute survey of women's attitudes toward breast cancer found that seven out of ten women said they would want to be involved in their treatment decisions.[1] Remember when it comes to your life and your body that it's in your best interest to be involved in those decisions because *you* are the one who will live with the consequences.

They Sought Information

Not uncommonly, most of these women knew very little about the disease when they were diagnosed. Valerie said, "I was amazed how ignorant I was about breast cancer. I didn't even know there was something other than a mastectomy to treat the disease." And thus began the breast cancer education of all these women. Their goal was to learn as much as they could to help them make decisions with which they could live. Some needed to know only the basics of breast cancer treatment; others wanted more. Because there are so many different treatment protocols and options available now that are constantly changing, it is clear that as a breast cancer patient you cannot afford to remain uninformed. You must learn about the disease.

Most of these women educated themselves—they were information seekers: reading books, calling friends and cancer patients, talking to oncology nurses, seeking second opinions, and shopping for doctors. Valerie, like many others, said, "I read everything that was not nailed down on the topic." Sometimes finding this information was not an easy task. There were few materials available on the topic in the 1970s, when Nancy desperately searched for information, found almost nothing, and wondered if she had done the right thing. Even the women diagnosed in the 1980s were astounded as to the amount of research they had to do on their own, locating books, finding the right people to talk to, and so on. They all expected the medical profession to provide resources and information, and yet, in many cases, this assistance was not forthcoming. Terri, like Kate and others, was frustrated: "I was railing against the lack of information given to me about this experience from the medical profession."

In spite of the difficulties in finding information, what stands out about these women is that they learned how to access medical information and resources in the community to get what they needed. Some women were persistent and even aggressive questioners in their search for information that would enable them to make a treatment decision. Psychologist Wendy Schain would call these women, who accept the fact that there is a problem and seek medical advice quickly, "acceptors" or "monitors." Those women who deny their symptoms and wait weeks or months to see a physician are "deniers" or "blunters." Clearly, by not acknowledging their symptoms or seeking information, the "blunters" put their lives at greater risk. None of the women in this book were "deniers."[2]

Unfortunately, there are many breast cancer patients who never receive the information they need to make informed choices about their treatment; perhaps they don't have the skills, knowledge, or the wherewithal to locate it. Or they may be the "blunters," women who minimize the seriousness of their diagnosis and do not want to know much. Regardless of the reason they don't receive information, breast cancer patients who make uninformed treatment choices often become resentful and angry later and have more difficulty coping with the changes in their lives.

It is clearly the responsibility of health professionals to help you become informed. In particular, your physician should not only discuss treatment alternatives with you but he or she should also have on hand or be able to direct you quickly to the resources you need to help you make your decisions. Unfortunately, this is not always the case. Thus, more than sixteen states have now passed breast cancer disclosure laws, stipulating that physicians provide explanations and information on treatment options to patients. This is a first step in helping you to become involved in what is a complex decision-making process in which you have a right to be an integral part.

Although at present there are numerous books, agencies, and groups that can provide you with breast cancer information and resources, these women's experiences demonstrate that it is *your* responsibility to seek this information; the medical profession cannot always be expected to provide you with the data and the answers. (See appendixes for further information.)

They Made Informed Decisions

As a result of obtaining and analyzing information, and getting competent medical advice, most of these women made informed treatment decisions based on statistics, facts, doctors' recommendations, and of course, their own judgments. Though she hardly became a medical expert in the field of breast cancer, each woman tried to learn enough to feel comfortable about the decision she made. Though these treatment choices often resulted in loss, pain, and sadness, the decision had been hers to make and resulted in her having a sense of self-determination. Studies have shown that women who are given choices in their breast cancer treatment adjust better over the long term than those who are not offered options.[3]

They Reorganized Their Activities

Once you know what kind of surgery and treatment you are going to have, you are better able to reorganize your personal and professional life. It is a time of adjusting to losing touch with the normal world and everyday responsibilities. Most of these women cut back their personal and professional activities and commitments in order to focus their energies on getting through surgery and treatment. As Kate said: "It was like making preparations for a long journey. It was really a time of paring down and only keeping up what was manageable. I even gave the family dog away because I knew I couldn't care for him and no one else would."

Susie and Kate, as mothers of small children, spent considerable time making arrangements for their care. Everyone's friends and family members were called upon or volunteered to assist at home and financially. Some of the women felt embarrassed to have to ask for help when previously they had been perfectly capable of doing everything themselves. Valerie, like others, had to rely financially on her parents: "It's hard to be a young adult dependent on your folks when you're trying to be independent."

It was frustrating not being able to fulfill commitments. At times, some of the women felt guilty and angry for being unable to pull their own weight anymore. They reported that the worst times were after chemotherapy when they were sick and could do very little. It was particularly difficult for the mothers with young children. There was often a strong longing to have a "normal" routine again. In the circumstances, it is important to remind yourself that this situation is temporary, and you will be able to do more in the future. It is okay to ask for help when you are undergoing treatment. This is your time for rest and recuperation.

Most of these women continued to be involved with their families and jobs, although less so, because of their treatments. Some of the women chose to take time out to rest and heal, while others coped by being active and involved. Some went back to work full-time, others, part-time; they cooked dinners, played tennis, went swimming, and visited with families and friends. Since Marcia couldn't go to her office, she brought her office to her hospital room while still recuperating from her mastectomy.

In fact, over the past thirty years, the proportion of women returning to their pretreatment activities within three months of surgery has risen from 57 percent in the late 1940s to 84 percent in the early 1970s.[4] With even less extensive surgical procedures for breast cancer now prevalent, one would expect the percentage to be even higher in the future. Being able to participate in everyday activities, even in small ways, helps you feel more useful and less dependent. But remember that it is better to err on the side of doing a little less while you are undergoing treatment.

Through Trial and Error, They Found Their Own Coping Styles

Though the decision to "get through" the breast cancer treatment was made early on, learning *how* to do that was not easy. There are no guidelines or roadmaps on how to cope with having breast cancer. Throughout treatment, the main issue for these women was how to live with a high degree of uncertainty and feel a semblance of control at the same time. The fact was that each woman had to learn through her own efforts of trial and error how to acquire the skills to be "successful" at coping with this life-threatening disease.

Barbara addressed the issue of "getting through this assault" by saying a woman "needs to know her own coping strategies, look at her past, and see how she has coped with other problems and that is probably a very good predictor of how she might cope with this disease. She should think about how functional these coping strategies are for her, and if they limit or help her."

Though all of these women had been functioning well in the "normal" world before they were diagnosed, breast cancer sorely tested their repertoire of coping skills and sometimes they required more help to get their needs met. In response to the crisis, they learned to utilize a variety of new coping methods to alleviate both their physical and emotional problems: learning new ways to communicate and share, finding creative ways to live with treatment side effects, and creating rewards and pleasurable activities for themselves. When asked how she coped with difficult times in her life, Eleanor Roosevelt is reported to have said, "I did what I had to do." These women did what they had to do to manage, too: learning how to be flexible enough to live with their now upside-down world.

Julia commented that the breast cancer patients she knew who had the most difficult time adjusting were those who were not flexible: "If they have a routine and nothing sways them from it, they won't change . . . they can't deal with it—breast cancer doesn't fit in their schedule." Most of the women made room, though somewhat reluctantly, for breast cancer early in their diagnosis and treatment. Given the uncertainty of her future, each woman had to find methods that provided a comfort level from which she could function on a day-to-day basis. For example, to give themselves a sense of control, Susie and Valerie investigated macrobiotic diets that they believed might prevent recurrences. Susie embarked on the diet, stayed with it for a year, and then gave it up when she had a recurrence. But for the time she was on it, the diet provided her with a mainstay, something to hold on to, to help make it through. Hemlotta's and Julia's religious faith played an important role in providing them comfort. Sarah used her journal to help her think more clearly, Valerie and Kate wrote poetry and stories, and Hemlotta went to a homeopathic doctor for lotions and pills.

Everyone developed techniques to manage, as best as she could, with the side effects of chemotherapy, learning when or what she could drink, eat, or rest. Hemlotta creatively concocted her own unconventional remedies to alleviate some of the side effects from chemotherapy. Other methods that proved helpful in getting through treatment were yoga, meditation, praying, visualization techniques, reading inspirational books, writing, taking photographs, playing music, and walking. Though often depressed and sad, many of these women kept telling themselves that the treatment was only temporary; things *would* get better. "I realize that how I feel about and look at this illness is determined by my own mental imagination," Hemlotta said. "As soon as I feel unwell from these chemicals, I think to myself, it is just for the time being and I will be positive. I won't suffer emotional pain from this treatment." It's important that you learn what coping strategies work for you, and then use them. It will enable you to get through your experience feeling more in control and accomplished.

They Reached Out for Support

As has been mentioned before, one of the most common and important coping strategies these women employed at one point or another during their treatment was to reach out and find other cancer patients to talk to, either individually or in support groups. Some also found it helpful to go into therapy. The need to talk about their experience was great, because depression, anger, and tears would inevitably occur, and made, according to Terri, "sharing crucially important." Being able to share with therapists or other cancer patients made some of the women feel less alone and gave them more confidence that they could succeed.

They also learned tools of the trade from others, ranging from how to talk to family members to hints on how to find wigs or wear scarves creatively. Valerie, who joined a group, believed, "People who end up in group by definition are probably better or at least searching for better ways to cope with cancer. They ended up with skills that got them through." They also attended seminars, developed telephone networks, went into individual therapy, and talked with friends and families. Nancy missed being able to share her grief following her mastectomy. Soon after her surgery, she moved to another country, and without old friends and other avenues of support, spent a difficult, lonely, and "cold" year trying to adjust to her radical mastectomy. Clearly, talking about their breast cancer experience, whether in groups or in therapy, had a significant positive effect on the quality of these women's lives. If you are able to express your feelings, fears, and concerns to someone, you will be better able to cope than the woman who is unable to discuss her feelings. (See appendixes for resources.)

They Planned Pleasurable Activities

Another way you can manage is by planning pleasurable activities. Although there were often times following surgery or chemotherapy when a number of the ten women did not have the energy to do anything, much less enjoy it, most were able to plan outings. As they became more familiar with their treatment routines, they knew when they would feel better or worse: It became easier to plan the best time for activities. For example, in between her chemotherapy treatments, Kate had massages, mudbaths, and hiked. Besides going out with their families or friends, many of the women visited beauty salons, had manicures, pedicures, or facials; some took vacations, went to movies, played sports, read, or just put aside a quiet time for themselves each day. Many went clothes shopping. It is crucial to do something that makes you feel good. You're entitled. Treat yourself.

They Laughed

Being able to laugh at your situation and yourself will play an important role in providing relief from the many serious and strange situations in which you will find yourself. Following her surgery, Marcia, who had limited arm mobility and had to resort to a dog paddle to swim, was teased by her colleagues: "You could never swim the crawl that well anyway." Valerie recalls that everyone in the waiting room laughed when the radiation machines broke down, probably because it was easier to laugh than to cry. Kate, after trying to hide her one-breasted condition in a bathing suit, laughed and threw her prosthesis in the bushes a few months after her mastectomy. Julia was able to laugh at her "teenage thinking" when trying to decide how to approach her partner with her nightgown on or off.

Through all the sickness and sadness, these women could still laugh at themselves. Many cancer patients see humor in things that are not funny to those in the noncancer world. This humor is sometimes seen by noncancer patients as morbid and sick; however, frank humor was a survival tool that helped these women move one step closer to getting through treatment and living normally again. Laughing will make you feel better too.

They Made Plans for the Future

Another critical coping strategy these women employed was to make plans for their future. What were they going to do when they were through treatment? Though each woman had different goals or aspirations, Sarah posed the question they all asked themselves: "How am I going to take this situation and deal with it creatively?" There was a strong need to do something worthwhile, and their plans usually involved "giving something back" to others in one form or another. During her chemotherapy treatments, Terri identified a number of problems of cancer patients and started support groups and new programs to meet her needs and theirs. Others, too, like Sarah and Julia, became involved actively with cancer groups and community advocacy. From the moment Julia met her Reach to Recovery volunteer, she decided that the American Cancer Society needed help and she was the one to give it to them. When your energy returns, you may want to consider volunteering your time for your church, a favorite group, other cancer patients, or a social agency.

A number of women used their breast cancer experience to enhance their already established professional lives as photographers, writers, or teachers. And some, like Susie, started anew. After her recurrence and during treatment, she began thinking about her future: "I thought of my assets and what I did best. I always loved cutting people's hair . . . so I decided to become a hairdresser." Even with fears of recurrence, you can begin to develop the foundations for your future with hope and an intense desire to achieve something important for yourself.

They Kept Moving Forward,
One Day at a Time

Paradoxically, from the moment of diagnosis, breast cancer had a significant and positive impact on these women's sense of achievement. There was a tremendous sense of accomplishment and pride because they had made it through the breast cancer crisis, overcoming sometimes overwhelming emotional and physical challenges. For some, there was almost a sense of disbelief that they had achieved their goal because there had been times when they had suffered setbacks, lost hope, and wanted to give up. But they had kept pushing, one day at a time. Barbara said, "I have been extremely proud of myself about my mental strength and attitude to tolerate chemo."

It had been a major accomplishment every time they voluntarily submitted to chemo injections, knowing full well they would be violently ill as a result. It had been a major accomplishment for the women to have said, yes, remove my breast. Sometimes, it had been a major accomplishment to get through one more day. Susie said: "I have accomplished this great feat, overcoming very tough times. I have been to the lowest point in my life and brought myself back to a high level of functioning. I am proud that I survived all this." These women succeeded in overcoming a series of life-threatening obstacles on their own two feet.

They Did the Best That They Could

There was a sense of pride and accomplishment in mastering the best ways they individually could deal with a life-threatening illness. There was no one right way to go through the experience of diagnosis and treatment; each woman had to find her own path. As Valerie said: "Everyone seems to think there is only one way to handle this disease and that is to fight and lick it. But everyone is different and uses his or her own unique strengths to muddle through. I used my book learning and my writing." Marcia used to spend many nights waking up at 3 A.M., facing all her worst fears, overwhelmed with the losses and feelings, but she'd "get up the next morning and get on with my life. You have no other choice. You get back into circulation. I have my own chop suey recipe of coping styles. I have learned to do this through experience, reading, education, support groups, and therapy." Each woman felt she had learned successfully to add to her own list of coping strategies. Terri said, "I felt if I got graded on my cancer experience, I would have gotten an A." They felt they had performed the best they could, and had not failed.

They Owned Their Illness

Some women were proud of accepting the responsibility to "own" their illness. That is, they accepted the fact that the cancer was *their* problem, and therefore took the responsibility to do something about it. Kate remembers thinking, "This is my cancer now . . . I am a cancer patient." At different stages, most realized that denying that cancer was now a part of their lives would result in their working against themselves in their bid to get well. Although they had not chosen to have this disease, and were not responsible for it, they alone had to be a part of the solution. Valerie's attitude about her radiation was, "I tried not to fight the idea of treatment; rather I accepted the fact that this was going to make me well." When Terri was having a difficult time with her chemo treatments, she was told, "Just don't put the body at war with itself; rather, see chemo as helping you to get well. It's part of you coming in to help you." Terri said, "After that I didn't look at chemo as this horrible thing I had to put up with."

Because they did a good job of nurturing themselves, both physically and emotionally, something many of them always had done well for everyone else, these women felt a sense of pride and accomplishment. By accepting responsibility for taking care of yourself, you too will feel a great sense of achievement.

They Set Priorities

As a result of having breast cancer, these women became far more goal- and achievement-directed than they had ever been before. Nancy said: "I have a whole second chance; now what am I going to do with it? I knew I was going to get through it all and get on with my life." Though most had achieved goals, and felt they had had successes in their lives, nothing propelled them to set and pursue their goals like breast cancer. There were a number of factors responsible for this. Faced with a life-threatening illness, and the possibility of a recurrence, these women realized that time was finite and therefore extremely valuable. Julia, like many others, felt, "I am really concentrating on *me* and what I want to be and do." Marcia said, "You know damn well you are more vulnerable than other folks. Suddenly your priorities are much clearer." They asked themselves repeatedly, "What is the best and most worthwhile way I can spend my time?" In the process of answering this question, they all reviewed and reevaluated their lives and emerged with a clearer sense of direction and a set of goals *they* wanted to accomplish.

They Pursued Their Goals

Once their priorities were clear, the women felt an urgent need to accomplish their goals. They had to do what was important for them *now* and were determined not to "audit" life anymore. As Susie said, "I am not waiting anymore for anything. I'm going to make the most of my life now." Like these women, you may feel this sense of urgency too, and realize how important it is to seek your goals and dreams now, not later.

They Were Ready to Change

Interestingly, at the time of their diagnoses, many of the women did not feel they had been making the most of their life. Prior to breast cancer, like many people, there had been a lack of direction and dissatisfaction in a number of the women's lives. They had mixed feelings about their self-worth and accomplishments in life. Sarah, Valerie, Susie, Kate, Terri, Marcia, Nancy, and Julia all had been in transitional stages either personally and/or professionally, and were searching for new directions. Sarah reported: "I felt I was a twenty-seven-year-old going nowhere. I was searching for something that I could do to put meaning to my life. I really wanted to accomplish something in my life." Valerie had just gone through a divorce and was unemployed. Susie was self-conscious about her lack of schooling and what she saw as her lack of intelligence, and worried about what she was going to do with her life: "I was getting ready to do something different with my life." Terri was an alcoholic, searching for meaning in her life and burned out from her work. Kate had been unable to focus on her photography and felt she was drifting away from her spouse; Marcia had been coping with a mentally ill child; Nancy's marriage was faltering; and Julia, who had been divorced, wasn't overly satisfied with her new job.

They Became Risk Takers

In a very strange but positive way, having breast cancer provided these women with the sense of direction and self-worth they had been searching for, and forced them to make life decisions they might have been avoiding. Valerie said: "Having breast cancer made me confront what scared me about being a self-employed full-time writer. What have I got to lose by trying? I am now determined to be a good writer and make a living from it." Near the end of her chemotherapy, Susie decided to become a hairdresser, took out a loan to attend beauty school, and started within a month after chemo finished. After graduating and becoming a successful hairdresser, Susie said, "Do you know what this does to my self-esteem? I thrive on it. It's made my life." Sarah saw her volunteer work with cancer patients "as a forward step in applying meaning to my experience. It was my way of coping and confronting breast cancer." She decided to pursue a degree in social work, saying, "Breast cancer has shaped my future and is continuing to shape it in a very positive fashion."

Terri, who in addition to getting through chemotherapy and reconstruction, also successfully stopped drinking, felt: "The crucial lesson I learned was to do what was most important to me. Out of my counseling breast cancer patients has come a full-time career. These programs are my babies. To stop this now would be like stopping in the middle of labor." Marcia decided her work was far less important than her family life, and made a point of planning her days to include the "joys of her life" as much as she could. Julia retired from her job and began volunteer work with cancer patients, which she loved: "It plays a huge role in my life from which I get fulfillment and great satisfaction. There's no prestige or money in it for me; it's just close to my heart." Assessing where you have been and where you are going is an important exercise that will make you feel more directed and accomplished.

All of these women overcame numerous obstacles that faced them during their breast cancer crisis. They learned how to rely on and trust themselves, becoming active participants and decision makers in their treatment plans, persistently seeking and utilizing information and resources, finding doctors they trusted, mastering new coping skills, laughing, reorganizing their activities, and making plans for the future. Early on, they decided they wanted to live. As a result of having learned to live with this life-threatening disease, they emerged with a significant sense of achievement, self-reliance, and personal power.

Valerie said: "I survived one battle, didn't I? I am very proud of how I was during this whole experience. It makes me so much more sure of who I am in other areas." Believing strongly that their lives had direction, meaning, and purpose, these women passionately pursued the goals they had set for themselves. They found they had the self-confidence to follow their inner voices, and they were much less afraid of failing and far more willing to take risks in living their lives. Success and failure had been placed in a new perspective because they knew the answer to the question: "What have I got to lose?" It was their life. Terri believed, "Having confronted the possibility of my own death from cancer, I learned how to live." Perhaps learning how to live was what gave rise to these women's greatest sense of accomplishment.

16

Your Identity

WHO WILL I BE?

When you become a breast cancer patient, you step outside the boundaries of everyday life. You are bound to ask yourself, "Why did I get cancer? What will my life be like and what kind of person will I be? Will my perceptions and beliefs about myself and the world change? What does it mean to be a person with cancer? How is a breast cancer patient supposed to behave and to cope? What kinds of beliefs and values will assist me in getting through this experience?"

Moreover, you know you are not just a person with cancer; you are a person with a *woman's* disease—a disease that more than any other poses a major challenge to your female identity because it centers on a symbolic and visible part of your body: your breasts. Therefore, as a cancer patient, you not only confront your mortality but also who you are as a woman: "What does it mean to be a woman with breast cancer—perhaps without a breast?" At some point you will face the cultural myths attached to breast cancer patients: A woman with breast cancer is somehow "less" a woman, less attractive, and less accepted both socially and sexually. On some level you may ask, "Will these things happen to me?" and then you will learn from your own personal experiences whether the myths are true or false.

From the beginning, the experience of breast cancer sorely tests your beliefs about living. Suddenly there are many more questions than answers.

"What is really important to me? What are my priorities? How do I want to spend my time?" Many of the assumptions you have accepted about life are tossed aside now because your world is proving not to be rational and orderly, and the only way to survive may be to adopt new ways of thinking. From this perspective, the breast cancer crisis can be viewed as the possible end of a former identity and the beginning of a new one.

REESTABLISHING A SENSE OF SELF

Having breast cancer is very much like experiencing a psychological earthquake—the foundations of your identity are shaken to the core. This threat to your identity, an important component of your self-esteem, may alter your own perceptions of yourself and your family. Your attitudes and beliefs about social, spiritual, psychological, and even political matters may change, and may alter the way you live your life as a result of these changed perceptions. Though the ground was shaky for all the women in this book for a period of time, and the process of rebuilding was often painful, they turned their crises into an opportunity for growth and change. It is clear that breast cancer had a significant and positive impact on the identities of these ten women. As a result, they valued themselves in new and different ways, felt good about who they were as women and how they were living their lives. What did these women do to reestablish the sense of who they were and what they believed?

They Asked: Why Me?

One question each woman asked when she heard she had breast cancer was, "Why did *I* get this?" In the beginning, the need to find an answer to this question seemed very important. How do you explain it, when one minute you are healthy and the next you have a life-threatening disease? For most, there had been no symptoms, no pain, no illness. Each of these women answered this question in different ways, depending on what she believed about the causes of breast cancer and who gets it.

They Searched for the Cause

There are a number of popular theories that seem to answer this unanswerable question, "Why me?" You may think that if you are a good person, unselfish and giving, you will not get sick, because bad things only happen to bad people. As Susie said, "Why me? I had been a good person."

Susie, like some others, also believed that stress might be the cause of her illness. After her diagnosis, she wondered if "maybe stress had caused it. I looked at the stressful times in my life." Sarah, who had lost her mother to cancer and felt that her "emotions were locked in my heart," did not find it surprising that she had developed cancer in the breast because "my breasts are over my heart. That's one of my theories about how I got breast cancer." Kate, who had a family history of breast cancer, viewed her cancer as "more like something unexpressed, trying to get out, like creativity that had not been given its free rein. I saw cancer as a negative side of creativity—something growing wild and out of control." Valerie felt that an unhappy life or perhaps her own personality might produce cancer: "Catastrophic illness was a personal beeper tone that says, 'something's wrong, something's wrong.' I don't know if you can be a totally happy being and do everything right for yourself and be thirty years old and get cancer. Yet, people go through horrible things all the time and never get cancer, so it has to be predisposition and other factors that go into this. I think I was predisposed to cancer because of my strong family history, and that certain environmental factors—poor diet, lack of exercise all my life, and severe depression—all may have contributed to my illness."

You may share Valerie's belief that the environment, that is, diet, air, toxins, and other elements, may be a contributing factor. Nancy said: "I also questioned why I got breast cancer—the classic 'Why me?' syndrome. I did not have a family history and was still young. I think it was partly environmental because when I was twelve I had a spot on my lungs and the doctors used to x-ray me all the time. . . . If it hadn't been the x-rays, then what? I wanted to know why."

Further, you may believe that cancer is a punishment, like Marcia, who felt, "I was finally being punished and paying the price for being a bad mother. . . . Okay God, you've punished me." At first, Hemlotta wondered if she had misused her breasts, or perhaps she neglected the Lord. Julia, on the other hand, believed there were no good reasons why she or others got sick. When she asked herself, "Why did *I* get cancer?" she decided: "The one thing that stood out was that everybody gets sick—rich people, poor people, white, black, good, and mean people. Regardless of what they did, bad things happened to them, so I guess I wasn't unique. I was no better than anyone else, and living right had nothing to do with it."

All these comments remind us that we simply do not know what causes breast cancer. Whenever the causes of a life-threatening disease are unknown, theories are presented to explain it, which are then adopted as "truths" by society. Though Julia's comments are probably the most accurate in describing why women get breast cancer, most people will not accept the fact that life is not fair and that we experience the luck of the draw.

Every cancer patient speculates on what causes her illness. The explanations these women offered for their getting cancer reflect some of the more common social attitudes held in this country about people who get this disease: that stress causes cancer, or that certain personality flaws predispose them to cancer, or that they must deserve it and are being punished for their bad deeds—a popular belief that today is often associated with homosexual AIDS victims.

Inherent in many of these attitudes is the dangerous and unsupported belief that the "victims" are in fact not only responsible for their illness but are responsible for getting well, and failing in this endeavor means they cause their own death. Blaming the victim is an irresponsible burden to place on cancer patients, and one that often produces tremendous guilt that does not enhance their emotional health. Susie's experience with her macrobiotic diet was a good example of this: With her recurrence she felt that *she* had somehow been responsible and had failed.

Susan Sontag wrote a book on this topic, *Illness as Metaphor* (Vintage Books), in which she compares the social attitudes about tuberculosis in the late nineteenth century to the twentieth-century's attitudes about cancer. Sontag writes, "Today, many believe that cancer is a disease of insufficient passion, afflicting those who are sexually repressed, inhibited, unspontaneous, incapable of expressing anger."[1] She goes on to say, "The hypothesis that distress can affect immunological responsiveness (and in some circumstances lower immunity to disease) is hardly the same as—or constitutes evidence for—the view that emotions cause diseases, much less for the belief that specific emotions can produce specific diseases."[2] Her main point is that we must "cease to think of cancer as a mark of doom, a punishment or a sign of a repressed personality, and recognize it for what it is: one disease among many and often receptive to treatment."[3]

They Asked: Why Not Me?

After having gone through the breast cancer experience, most of these women came to believe Ms. Sontag's main point. Many of them had been successfully treated. And as time passed, the women were far more likely to ask, "Why *not* me?" instead of "*Why* me?" and it also mattered less *why* they had developed the disease because the answer, if there is one, did not enable them to heal faster or survive better. They had it now and couldn't do anything about the past, but they could do something about the present. For example, following breast cancer, they all believed that it was crucial to take good care of their health, and as a result, they adopted new behaviors such as lowering stress in their lives, eating a balanced diet, resting, and exercising. Moreover, these women had met many other breast cancer patients during their treatment and often found there was no way to generalize about the disease. In the long run, each was far more likely to be empathic than to offer judgments and theories to others with cancer. If you find that you are measuring yourself or others by these theories, remember that we really do not know enough yet to pontificate, nor will doing so help you or anyone else to get well.

They Felt No Shame or Stigma

Until recently, our culture has not been kind to cancer patients, particularly breast cancer patients. It was commonly believed not too many years ago that cancer patients were contagious, that they should be isolated in hospital wards and left alone to die. As a result of such practices, patients naturally felt stigmatized, embarrassed, and experienced great shame. It was not socially acceptable to talk about their disease. As Marcia said about her mother's cancer, "In the 1930s, cancer was very hush-hush and something bad. I was told never to tell anyone my mother had died of cancer." It also was assumed that all cancer patients would soon die and therefore were not to be hired, or insured. Fortunately, many of these attitudes have changed in the past few years, although some still linger. Unfortunately, for example, all these old stereotypes have reemerged in full force with AIDS patients: Believed to be contagious, they are fired from their jobs, placed in isolation in hospitals, refused personal services, and denied their insurance. There is still a stigma attached to the disease and it will be years before the public is educated well enough to deal with this disease in an objective way.

Interestingly, unlike AIDS victims, or those who had breast cancer twenty years ago, none of these women felt any shame or stigma about having this disease. They did not feel that they were victims and they did not want to be pitied. Terri said, "I didn't want the 'Oh, poor Terri' routine. I wanted acknowledgment, not pity." Like many of the others, Marcia said, "It never occurred to me that no one would pay attention to me or not love me anymore because I had breast cancer." No one shunned them; rather, the women were overwhelmed with love and support. Perhaps we can all look forward to everyone sharing Hemlotta's attitude: "I was fortunate in that I had no preconceptions about breast cancer—I didn't know what it meant or how to behave. Breast cancer didn't mean horror and death and loss of womanhood to me, so I was not fearful."

The fact that most of these women openly discussed their disease with others demonstrates another shift in attitudes that has occurred in the past fifteen years. Julia explained that when she was growing up, "breast cancer was a secret and no one talked about it. Now it's easier. . . . It's so much more open. Breast cancer can be discussed just about anywhere now and at least women are beginning to realize there's life after breast cancer." From these women's experiences, it is clear that what other people, and patients themselves, believe about cancer has clearly changed in the past two decades, and these beliefs are still evolving. There is no reason for you to feel any shame or embarrassment about having cancer.

They Learned That They Couldn't Have a Positive Attitude All the Time and to Let Go of the "Shoulds"

Although you may be accepted by others, you still may discern subtle expectations and attitudes about how cancer patients should cope and behave. For example, a cancer patient should have a positive attitude, not be depressed or angry, do what the doctor says, and above all try to be "normal." Each of these ten woman was subjected to these cultural expectations. Many found, however, that it was unrealistic, if not impossible, to live by them. It was often difficult to feel normal or "the same" as before, much less feel positive about having breast cancer.

Like these women, you will probably feel a constant pressure to be "positive." All cancer patients believe this is important, and wrestle with it every day. You struggle with the feeling because there is a commonly held belief, not necessarily accurate, that a positive attitude increases your chances of survival. Though it is clear that living with hope is important, and that a positive attitude feels better than a negative one, you simply cannot be "up" all the time. Most mental health professionals would say that being depressed, sad, or angry are all natural reactions to a major crisis such as breast cancer, and they would recommend that you not suppress your feelings. Yet, the pressure to "keep a stiff upper lip" took an emotional toll on a number of the women. They often found themselves saying "I'm fine" when they weren't. Terri said, "A few times I responded, 'I am not okay.' But I noticed people had a low tolerance for that." The message she and others heard was that no one wants to see a sad, depressed, and angry cancer patient. You may feel it is not permissible to talk about your negative feelings.

"One of the problems I had in dealing with my feelings," Valerie said, "was our culture's obsession with being positive. You have to think positive to get well. Because of this I cut off the bad feelings I had by telling myself, 'You cannot allow fear, Valerie, you can't focus on death, you must focus on life!' . . . One day I stopped doing that and let my worst fears play out in my head. Then I couldn't get over how good I felt!

Come on! We're talking about a life-threatening illness and I have every reason to be fearful and depressed. I don't think it's a matter of being positive; rather it's a question of being open."

After months of trial and error, most of these women realized the importance of expressing not only their joys and happiness but their rage, anger, sadness, and disappointments too. The importance of being able to openly express the wide range of feelings you have, particularly the negative feelings, cannot be understated. You need to let go of the "shoulds," stop listening to everyone else, begin to trust your feelings, and do what feels best for *you*. There are many cancer support groups available that provide a forum for these expressions. In this environment you don't have to live up to cultural expectations.

They Accepted That They Had
Become "Different"

Another recurring theme in these women's breast cancer experiences was attempting to keep one foot in the land of the healthy while the other one was firmly planted in the world of serious illness. Each woman continually had to question who she was and where she fit. Though each woman would have loved nothing more than to be "normal and fine," the plain fact was she was not. You are living an abnormal life and as a result your concerns are different and the way you live your life changes. At first, being "different" increases your sense of isolation. Barbara observed, "What bothered me a lot were the things that nobody else can really see. It is said sometimes that when you have an invisible, hidden kind of disability like a mastectomy, it's harder on the individual because she appears normal to the outside world, but inside she knows she's different." Valerie described her awareness of this tension when she walked home after her radiation treatments: "No one would know I was a breast cancer patient. Only minutes before, technicians were hiding behind two tons of steel while I was being blasted, and then, nothing. What would people on the street think if I wore a sign saying, 'I am having radiation therapy.' It made me start looking at people differently because they may look normal, but they aren't normal." However, after a while of not being "normal," you may feel there are hidden gifts in your experience. For example, some of these women felt more humble, and had a much greater tendency to be sensitive to and accepting of other people who were "different" too.

*   *   *

They Asked What It Means to
Have Breast Cancer

Throughout your breast cancer experience, you not only deal with your beliefs about cancer and your perceptions of yourself as a cancer patient but you also deal with the fact that you are a woman with a woman's disease. "You can't help but think about your femaleness, your womanhood, with this disease," Barbara said. "Breast cancer, more than any other life-threatening illness, challenges a woman's femaleness. It's a female-hormone-related disease and it takes place in a part of the body that is associated with sex, sex drive, appearance, and cleavage." Valerie agreed: "Breast cancer forces you to confront the basic elements of being a woman."

As a result of having this disease, each woman examined and explored many issues relating to her womanhood and her femininity. What does it mean to be a woman with breast cancer? What does it mean to be one-breasted? What kind of woman do you want to be? For example, Barbara thought: "Breast cancer opened up areas of my life as a woman that I maybe wouldn't have explored. It's a sense that I am many things, I am many parts, that are all part of me. That includes various aspects of both my femininity and my masculinity, whether it is dressing up, being sexual, powerful, assertive, soft, independent, or dependent. So now I am exploring different ways of being a woman, coming to terms with my total womanhood."

They Discovered Their Femininity
Was Not Lost

Society presents some conventional wisdom about breast cancer patients that you will sooner or later be forced to confront. It boils down to this: The woman with breast cancer is less a woman, deformed, unattractive, unfeminine, rejected by suitors, and abandoned by partners. Some of the women in this book were concerned about these stereotypes; others considered them unimportant and irrelevant.

None of these women felt they had lost their femininity or were "less a woman." Did breast cancer have an impact on how they felt about themselves as women? Yes—they felt better about themselves. All would agree that the issue of "losing one's femininity" is an absurd concept to begin with, as Françoise Giraud, the well-known Swiss-French journalist and politician, was quoted as saying: "As though femininity is something you lose the way you lose a pocketbook: Hmmmm, where in the world did I put my femininity?"[4]

The question of breast cancer and "lost femininity" is based on an outdated societal attitude that equates a woman's femininity almost exclusively with her breasts. It arose from a male worldview that a woman's breasts and appearance are crucial to attracting men, and that nothing is more important to a woman than attracting a man. Susan Brownmiller discusses this point in her book *Femininity:*

> It is they [the men] who invent and refine the myths, who discuss breasts publicly, who criticize their failings as they extoll their wonders, and who claim to have more need and intimate knowledge of them than a woman herself. . . . But the otherness of breasts, their service in the scheme of male erotic satisfaction long ago promoted the myth that a flat-chested women is nonsexual and ungiving.[5]

Given these definitions, therefore, a woman who is flat-chested or loses a breast to cancer is sexually unattractive and less feminine. Brownmiller argues:

> To fail at the feminine difference is to appear not to care about men and to risk the loss of their attention and approval. To be insufficiently feminine is viewed as a failure in core sexual identity, or as a failure to care sufficiently about oneself, for a woman found wanting will be appraised (and will appraise herself) as mannish or neutered or simply unattractive, as men have defined those terms.[6]

A woman with "damaged" breasts would qualify as lacking in femininity, although the failure is regarded as more of a loss to the man than to the woman herself. Barbara agreed with Brownmiller: "I think women's fear of losing their femininity is culturally induced. Many women are acting out the culture's commercial notion of what it means to be feminine. With nothing better to do than shave our legs, put on makeup, and do our hair, no wonder women [with breast cancer] fear that they are now damaged goods and that nobody will ever pay attention to them."

They Believed That Femininity Is Not Defined by Breasts

No matter what their definition of femininity, all these women would agree with Sarah when she said, "I didn't worry about my femaleness through the experience of breast cancer because I always knew that my femininity did not rest in my breasts."

If you choose to define your femininity solely by your breasts, then losing a breast to breast cancer will make you feel less feminine and less of a woman. Barbara made an important point when she stated that "perhaps femininity is not the real issue at hand when it comes to breast cancer." She pointed out that "sometimes femininity can be a disguise or defense against dealing with the deeper issues in facing your life. Many women want to limit breast cancer to their breasts alone because they are invested in having a conception of the disease as local, rather than systemic. Many women have to go through their concerns with femininity and their breasts first . . . resolve that issue . .. and then maybe they will get to the deeper questions about life." Valerie remembers that her first attitude about breast cancer was, "Thank you for saving my breast. . . . Isn't it wonderful?" But then during her radiation treatments, she realized, as she sat each day in a room full of people, many of whom were dying, that though it was important to have her breast, balanced against her life, it meant little.

Most of these women felt their femininity had not been compromised by their breast surgeries. Hemlotta said: "My sense of femininity remains the same. The body does not play such a crucial or important role in my femininity. For most of my life I have marched to my own drummer and never questioned my femininity. . . . Therefore, having this disease has not threatened my being a woman at all." Nancy always thought, "I was feminine and still feel very much a feminine woman." Marcia felt, "After two bouts with cancer and a hysterectomy, I still believe that I am a feminine woman. My looks may have changed but the other qualities I associate with my femininity haven't."

Even Susie, who from time to time felt "this little pang of self-consciousness," also thought, "maybe I am less than a whole woman, but it doesn't have to do with my feminine qualities. I have never felt that I was less desirable or less feminine because of breast cancer, except perhaps when I lost my hair. Now I think I project femininity and have a good attitude about myself." Julia perhaps summed up the feelings of the women best: "To me, being a woman has more to do with your heart than your breasts."

They Developed Personal Definitions
of Femininity

Caroline Bird wrote, "Femininity appears to be one of those pivotal qualities that is so important no one can define it."[7] However difficult femininity may be to define, it includes a *wide* range of both biological and social characteristics, of which sexual attractiveness is only one. Though there may be popular cultural standards by which to judge a woman's femininity, it was clearly these women's *own* definitions, all of which were different, that determined whether they felt feminine or womanly. Julia said it well: "I don't like the word *feminine,* because it restricts the definition of a woman." Susie felt, "Being feminine is being gentle, soft, nurturing, poised, and nonaggressive. I also believe a feminine woman pays attention to looking and dressing well and is not sloppy." She didn't believe feminine women could be assertive. A different definition was offered by Marcia: "I was never the delicate flower type. Though I was the 'supermom' type, I don't suspect I would have been considered your traditional feminine woman because I have always been a mover, shaker, and a fighter. I have never felt my outspokenness and my femininity were mutually exclusive because I believe you can be a feminine person and be assertive." Nancy thought, "I like being a woman and I wouldn't rather be a man. I like being attractive to men. I am feminine in my concern for and sensitivity to people's feelings. That's a strong part of being feminine. I am not aggressive, but I don't back off."

Hemlotta felt, "Femininity to me is not outside beauty; it's inner soul. We all have a feminine spirit within us that shines. To me, part of being feminine is going for balance and accommodation instead of getting into conflict. Being feminine is what loving is all about. We need more femininity in this world."

Some Refused to Accept Traditional Labels

Some of these women did not think of themselves as feminine because of the negative qualities they associated with the word, and preferred to think of themselves as womanly. For Valerie, femininity wasn't an issue because she had "never characterized myself as feminine and wasn't overly concerned that I wasn't." Femininity to her meant "having no substance, being pink, wearing frills and painted nails." Barbara felt there were "three things I most associate with being a woman: her sexuality, her being a powerful person in her own life, and finally a cultural way of being traditionally female by dressing in a feminine style, wearing makeup." Julia drew, as did others, a clear distinction between being feminine and being a woman: "I never considered myself a feminine woman to begin with, so it doesn't bother me. To me, feminine women are quiet, passive, fragile, and break easily. I have never been that way, never been fragile. But I have been a woman, a good woman, and *womanly* all my life." All of these women's perceptions of femininity demonstrate that your femininity is determined by how *you* define the term and how you feel about yourself. It really doesn't matter what others think. Trust your own feminine spirit instead.

*   *   *

They Believed Their Femininity Had Been Enhanced
by the Cancer Experience

Interestingly, some of these women felt they were *more* feminine after breast cancer than before. Barbara said: "I was not brought up to believe that femininity was very important. Since having breast cancer I feel I am not more or less a woman, I am a woman in a different way. In terms of femininity, I think I have gone down on the sexual dimension and up on the dressing conventional dimensions. I have gotten more feminine in the conventional sense of paying attention to my body and breasts." Valerie said: "What surprised me was that having breast cancer affected my sense of femininity. Now, in a funny way, it matters more. I've allowed more femininity into my life. Being feminine is not life or death, but it is nice. I wear more dresses, jewelry, and makeup." Terri, too, felt: "I am a far more feminine person now. I define femininity as feeling at home with being a woman, a female person, inside and outside. It's being comfortable with who I am as a human being. I am softer and more gentle now. I never let myself be that way before. The nurturing, giving part of me has been freed up." Sarah thought that "having breast cancer actually enhanced the essence of my femininity because I confronted some very basic questions on who I was as a woman. I had to work hard as a woman to get back to my pure state. There is something that I know about life now that I didn't know before, which makes me feel more of a woman and worldly."

They Felt Stronger and More Human

Eda J. LeShan, an American educator, once wrote, "We are learning that there are no longer any simple patterns or easy definitions. Each of us has to discover who and what we are, and our own special qualities; what makes us feel womanly."[8] Clearly, living with breast cancer, these women found new strengths and meaning in their womanhood and femininity. They would agree with Sarah who said, "It is overwhelming to think about adapting to a new definition of oneself. But basically, I think most breast cancer patients adjust pretty well." Julia's comment represents how all the women perceived themselves: "I am stronger than ever before now. Would you say that makes me less of a woman? I am more of a woman now than I ever was before." Kate felt similarly when she said: "Through all this, I feel more in touch at a very deep level with my femaleness and my womanness. . . . Even though I have deepened feelings about my identity as a woman, I feel more *human*, because going through an experience like this transcends gender. In some ways you could say I feel more of a man for having gone through this. Breast cancer put me in touch with the androgynous side of me." Terri believed that feeling good about who they were as women was "all a part of women learning how to care for themselves: taking back and owning their bodies again." You can be strong, in charge of your life, *and* feminine too.

They Learned to Face and Live with the Fear of Recurrence

For these women, coming to terms with their femininity was a major achievement, and yet the greatest challenge facing them was learning to live with the threat of possible recurrence. You cannot avoid thinking about it. Every one of the women was well aware that it didn't matter if her doctor had said, "We got it all," or "You've passed the five-year mark—you're scot-free," because she knew she would *always* be at risk of getting breast cancer again. Valerie believed: "The woman with breast cancer faces an additional challenge in that she must get comfortable with the possibility that she may die from breast cancer. The fear of recurrence is strong, and you must learn to live with that fear. Cancer is not about two months of treatment and a couple of minor surgeries. This is what cancer is about to me, living with possible recurrence. Am I really going to be okay?"

You have to consider how you are going to live with this threat, deciding what kind of attitude you will adopt to make you more comfortable with facing your mortality. In the first year or so, it is difficult to deal with those thoughts, because you are generally very worried about recurrence. Every lump found, each cold or sign of any illness, raises great fears about a recurrence and possible death. Even completing chemotherapy, in spite of its devastating side effects, is very frightening, because as Terri said, "I was afraid there were no drugs in me to fight the cancer anymore. All I could think was, 'Oh my God, now my estrogen will start producing and then the cancer cells will find the estrogen receptors and it's boom! A recurrence.' " Every checkup is nerve-racking. The sense of vulnerability is ever present, as Nancy described: "I felt vulnerable in a way that I have never felt before; I still do. Once you've had breast cancer, you learn to live with the unpredictability of life. It doesn't matter how many years you've survived."

They Mourned the Loss of Their Immortality and Reembraced Living

Recurrence was, and is, a very real fear for all of these women, particularly for Barbara, Marcia and Susie, who had already experienced it. But the longer they lived without recurrence, the more they moved the fear aside.

Kate said, "All of a sudden, cancer became a small part of my consciousness, which is really amazing, because somehow I thought it would never go away." Though these women acknowledged and accepted the possibility of getting cancer again, they believed it was more important to focus on their living and not on their dying. Worrying about recurrence and death was not going to help.

Their attitudes were best expressed by Julia, who felt: "Though recurrence is in the back of my mind—I know it's there—I don't worry about it. You realize the five-year survival mark doesn't mean much. But it's that knowledge—living with your mortality—that's going to make a woman's life be even better after breast cancer . . . because she is going to care more about herself than she ever did before and do what she wants and enjoy what she has—because we all want to survive and make each day count." Hemlotta expressed it this way: "I understand that I can die from this disease but I am confident that I will not have a recurrence. I am positive in my outlook and I am not living with the fear of dying. . . . We are all sailing in the same boat, cancer patients. We are more aware that today we are here but tomorrow we may not be here." Paradoxically, facing your mortality makes you fear death less and enjoy life more.

They Believed Every Day Is a Gift of Time

Barbara believed "there were some hidden gifts in having a life-threatening illness." She explained: "I would say, when you face your death, you begin to live. Then you deserve everything and can laugh deeper, cry louder, spend more, eat richer, and goof off more. You can be depressed better! It all becomes more; it's an edge. It make me feel more alive." Terri thought that by facing her mortality she had "shaken off that ridiculous veil of immortality. We live in a culture that believes we will be young forever. Everyone is betting on tomorrow. But putting things off in life is not cool. People faced with cancer get this gift of knowing we must live every day to its fullest. All I have is now, today." All of these women basically shared this attitude, perhaps best described by Susie: "I am only living day to day here on earth. By God, I am going to enjoy life, and my family? Life is short and you can't put anything on hold; you just go for it. I'm not waiting anymore for anything. I am going to make the most of my life now."

*   *   *

They Discovered Meaning and
Purpose in Life

Living with possible recurrence and making the most of life also can produce major changes in the way you live your life. Valerie believed: "Cancer doesn't necessarily change your life and cancer doesn't make you a different person and cancer doesn't solve your problems, but it gives you an experience so intense, so frightening, so energy-creating, that it's almost like being launched from a pad. You must, must change. . . . Having cancer creates a situation in which there is suddenly a shining spotlight on your whole life and nothing can be hidden anymore. You can't pretend. It's a hard time to pretend. Whatever is wrong in your life when you get sick floats right to the top and cannot be avoided anymore."

These women were suddenly questioning everything in their lives; as Valerie said, "I suddenly wanted everything to change, where I lived, who I lived with, and who I worked for. Everything felt old and finished." They found that many things that had always been acceptable in their lives were no longer okay. Their questioning and search for meaning and purpose led these women to alter their priorities and change the way they conducted their lives. Kate believed, "Cancer changed the circumstances of my life so much. Though I gained much from this, I also lost some very important things—my marriage and my breast. I got back part of my soul."

They Valued Their Self-Worth and
Pursued Personal Nurturing

All of these women believed that what was critically important in their lives was to take care of themselves first, an item that for many had been low on their priority list before having breast cancer. Nancy found that "breast cancer made me aware of how valuable my life is and taught me that I am in charge and not to be trifled with. I am much less frivolous now. I let myself be used and let things happen to me because I didn't have enough respect for myself. That doesn't happen now. My life is not to be taken lightly." Like many of the others, Julia said: "Perhaps the biggest change for me was that I started thinking about me first and others second. For most of my life I thought I was a strong woman, and I was, for other people, but not for myself. Now I am very assertive. Now *I* am in charge. I wasn't before. Now I really am concentrating on me and what I want to do and be."

"I think women have been very good about denying themselves their wants and needs," Terri said. For example, Susie felt that before, she would "do for others" at her own expense: "Now I care less what others think and do what I want to do. Now I take care of me and have more to give to everybody else." Terri shared Susie's opinion: "Before breast cancer, I didn't ever take good care of myself [but] now the challenge always seems to be learning how to take better care of myself. I think this is a very human thing to do. It's also a feminist thing to do, bringing energy inward instead of putting the energy out all the time. It's very womanly of me to nurture myself." Marcia would agree: "Women traditionally have felt that they are responsible for everything, particularly when things go wrong. They take it on themselves to try and solve others' problems. It comes from being a wife and a mother and all those years of protecting and nurturing. Having breast cancer points out quite clearly that you are only responsible for yourself. You can only control yourself, and whatever will be, will be."

They Believed in Themselves

The cancer experience transformed each woman's perspective about herself in many ways, and she learned valuable lessons about who she was and where she was going. Terri thought: "Throughout my whole cancer experience I felt there were teachings for me. I never would have chosen to be taught this way but I like the changes in me. . . . I am now more honest and open about how I feel. I accept myself as I am. I always had to contribute and it wasn't okay to just be a person. I needed an identity with a label of 'worker' or 'student.' Learning that it was okay to just be, with no labels, was one of the major things that came out of my having cancer." Valerie learned, "Who the hell I am and what I want and don't want has all been a result of having cancer and not beating myself over it. Having cancer helped me keep in perspective what matters in life and what doesn't."

As a born-again Christian, Julia thought: "I have more faith in myself to express what I feel and have the confidence to know I am saying the right thing. Having breast cancer really changed me. It changed my whole life. I became a different person and a different woman. I feel more secure and better about myself. It's like when you're born again; you're still the same person, you're just doing things differently afterward."

Breast cancer had a significant impact on the identities of these ten women. Although they came from a variety of backgrounds and had different breast cancer experiences, there was a remarkable similarity in the women they became. They all shared a willingness to learn, grow, and change. They searched for answers and learned there were few. They realized they could have a positive identity as cancer patients and learned that societal expectations about how they should behave would not dictate their behaviors. They rediscovered their femininity and redefined for themselves what it meant to be a woman and a person. They integrated the positive lessons from their experiences, and learned from, and let go of, the negative ones. They accepted their mortality and learned that every day is a gift of time.

As a result, they valued themselves in new and different ways; they felt good about who they were as women and how they were living their lives. Although these women felt more autonomous and self-directed, and were proud of their individual strengths, they also emerged with a powerful, almost global, sense of connection to others, particularly with those who suffer or who are in pain. Having cancer, or any life-threatening disease, makes you acutely aware that we are *all* at risk, no matter how special or different we may think we are. Once you've been diagnosed, you can no longer distance yourself from others by saying, "It can't happen to me." Hemlotta expressed simply but eloquently these feelings: "I have empathy now for others. I can no longer be immune to other's pain and suffering. I have been humbled. In this respect I realize now that I am not different from everyone else. I am aware of how ordinary I am."

17

Crisis, Courage, Change

When they were first diagnosed with breast cancer, few of these women would have believed that the crisis would do anything but threaten and possibly destroy their self-esteem. During and following their breast cancer treatment, these women experienced severe psychological and physical distress that sorely tested their well-being. And yet, from a seemingly uncontrollable, frightening, and life-threatening set of circumstances, they emerged with their self-esteem very much intact: obviously rearranged and changed, but restored.

No matter how different their backgrounds or ages were, or how traumatic their experiences were, each woman eventually was able to turn her breast cancer crisis into an opportunity for growth and change. Each one explored different and sometimes underdeveloped aspects of herself. Though women traditionally have garnered more of their self-worth from their interpersonal relationships and appearance, these women gained their greatest sense of self-esteem from their feelings of achievement and belief and confidence in themselves. As a result, they emerged as self-directed, more autonomous women, who were proud of their accomplishments and had a newfound self-respect. Barbara said, "You know, a life is like a trajectory that can be quite narrow. Breast cancer has deepened, broadened, and opened up my life. That's the way I decided to live with this disease, by deciding who I was and how I would face these ultimate questions."

Like Barbara, each woman made a decision to take charge of her life, to master her world to the best of her ability. As Marcia said, "*Many* women live through the experience of breast cancer and are no less people or women. They are functioning in the world, feeling good about themselves, and *living*."

The fact that they could do this successfully, along with so many other women, demonstrates that women are far stronger and more capable of coping than society would have us believe. For example, a recent study published in *Cancer* indicates that psychologically healthy women who lose their breasts undergo short-term psychological trauma but have no more difficulty coping than women who have gallbladder operations or even simple biopsies.[1] Perhaps society eventually will stop perpetuating the pervasive myths and misconceptions and broaden its view, as these women did, about what it truly means to be a woman. Barbara would agree: "Many women internalize other people's way of looking at themselves. Breast cancer challenges that by making you deal more with your personhood: what kind of person and woman you are and what your ultimate values are. With breast cancer, a woman starts owning her own life."

More than two million women will develop breast cancer in the next fifteen years. Chances are that you or someone close to you will be affected directly by this disease. It's important to know that a diagnosis of breast cancer no longer has to mean death, disability, disfigurement, or loss of love and self-esteem, and that the chances for successful treatment and long-term survival are increased significantly by the detection of breast cancer in its earliest, most treatable stages. The earlier this disease is found, the greater number of options and choices a woman will have for her treatment. But at this time, the *only* way this disease can be detected early is for each woman to take an active role in her breast health by becoming educated about the disease, having mammograms, seeing a doctor for checkups regularly, and practicing breast self-examination monthly. When a woman becomes informed about breast cancer, and chooses to care about and take responsibility for her health and life, she demonstrates that she values herself. She will have made a crucial decision that could save her life and her breast(s). She will be a better woman for it.

Finally, everyone needs to know that the breast cancer crisis is one that can be mastered, and though having this disease almost certainly produces enduring changes in a woman's life, those changes can be surprisingly positive. As the ten women's stories in this book clearly demonstrate, the quality of life after breast cancer treatment, in many respects, can be enhanced. They represent the many women who have learned that breast cancer can mean hope, survival, growth, and living life to its fullest.

Recommended Reading

General Readings on Breast Cancer Diagnosis and Treatment Options

Alternatives: New Developments in the War on Breast Cancer, by Rose Kushner, Warner Books, 1986 edition (formerly entitled, *Why Me? What Every Woman Should Know About Breast Cancer to Save Her Life,* New American Library, New York, 1977). Written by a breast cancer patient who became nationally known for her pioneer work in breast cancer, this book provides a general overview on breast cancer, its diagnosis and treatment, in-depth information on all treatment options and issues, and some of the latest research available in the field.

Breast Cancer: The Complete Guide, by Yashar Hirshaut, M.D., and Peter Pressman, M.D., Bantam Books, New York, 1992. An excellent handbook by two noted specialists who have written a comprehensive guide to diagnosis, treatment, breast reconstruction, follow-up care, and ways to live with cancer.

The Breast Cancer Digest: A Guide to Medical Care, Emotional Support, Educational Programs and Resources, NIH Publication No. 84-1691, second edition, National Cancer Institute, Bethesda, MD, April 1984. (Third edition now available.) Excellent in-depth background information on all aspects of breast cancer detection, diagnosis, treatment, rehabilitation, psychosocial impact, and the resources available to patients.

Choices: Realistic Alternatives in Cancer Treatment, by Marion Morra and Eve Potts, revised edition, Avon, 1987. An invaluable paperback handbook of down-to-earth questions and answers about every kind of cancer treatment. The book is designed to provide patients with the information they need to ask questions of

245

their doctors and make decisions about their treatment. Jane Brody of the *New York Times* said, "Perhaps the single most comprehensive and reliable source of information and guidance for cancer patients and their families." It includes a nationwide listing of treatment centers. This is a particularly helpful book at the time of diagnosis.

Confronting Breast Cancer: New Options in Detection and Treatment, by Sigmund Weitzman, M.D., Irene Kuter, M.D., and H. F. Pizer, PA-C, Vintage Books, New York, 1987. One of the most comprehensive and concise books on breast cancer. The authors emphasize the importance of each woman becoming a partner in her own health care, and discuss *all* aspects of breast cancer, from how to detect the disease early, to breast reconstruction, and coping with the process.

Dr. Susan Love's Breast Book, by Susan M. Love, M.D., with Karen Lindsey, Addison-Wesley, Menlo Park, CA, 1990. Dr. Love, a well-known and well-respected breast surgeon and feminist, discusses all conditions of the breast and presents a clear and balanced view of all breast cancer treatment options. Love also discusses treatment-related controversies. A user-friendly book that is a good general reference book for breast cancer patients.

How Cancer Is Diagnosed, Treated and Managed Day to Day, by Malin Dollinger, M.D., Ernest Rosenbaum, M.D., and Greg Cable, Andrews and McMeel, Kansas City, 1991. This is a valuable, comprehensive guide for cancer patients and their families. There are thorough sections on decision-making, working with health professionals, the latest developments in assessment, diagnosis and treatment, supportive care strategies, and information on forty-five different cancers and how they are treated.

If you've thought about breast cancer . . ., by Rose Kushner, Women's Breast Cancer Advisory Center, Inc., Kensington, MD 20895. A helpful booklet in question and answer form that describes breast cancer detection, diagnostic procedures, and treatment options; it provides a list of questions to ask the doctor and tells where to call for help.

The Race Is Run One Step at a Time: My Personal Struggle and Every Woman's Guide to Taking Charge of Breast Cancer, by Nancy Brinker, with Catherine McEvily Harris, Simon & Schuster, New York, 1990. An excellent guide that provides valuable resources and skills to any breast cancer patient interested in becoming an active participant in her treatment, written by a breast cancer survivor and activist whose outstanding work in the breast cancer field is recognized nationally.

General Readings
on Breast Reconstruction

Breast Implants: Everything You Need to Know, by Nancy Bruning, Hunter House, 1992. An up-to-date, thorough, and unbiased book that clearly explains the issues and controversies, addresses the fears, and answers questions women have about breast implants.

Breast Reconstruction: A Matter of Choice, NIH Publication No. 88-2151, National Cancer Institute, Bethesda, MD, 1987. This booklet describes all the different breast reconstructive procedures, the complications that may arise, and its impact on body image; it addresses basic questions that women may have about choosing a doctor and the surgery.

Breast Reconstruction Following Mastectomy, by the American Cancer Society, Publication No. 4630-PS. A useful guide for those considering reconstructive surgery that includes a description of the different kinds of surgery, drawings, and a glossary of terms.

An Informed Decision: Understanding Breast Reconstruction, by Marilyn Synder (M. Evans, New York, 1984), Little, Brown, 1989 edition. Informative mixture of one woman's experience of breast reconstruction; it includes illustrated information about breast reconstruction.

A Woman's Decision: Breast Care, Treatment and Reconstruction, by Karen Berger and John Bostwick, M.D., C.V. Mosby Company, St. Louis, 1984. Clearly presented and valuable information on the pros and cons of breast reconstruction, with illustrations. Followed by eight case studies on women who had breast reconstruction.

Coping with Treatment

Bone Marrow Transplants: A Book of Basics for Patients, by Susan K. Stewart, BMT Newsletter, Highland Park, IL, 1992. An excellent source of information on all aspects of bone marrow transplants, including chapters on insurance, and available resources. Order by calling (708) 831-1913.

BMT (Bone Marrow Transplant) *Newsletter,* by Susan Stewart, 1985 Spruce Avenue, Highland Park, IL 60035; (708) 831-1913. Published six times a year, this informative and helpful newsletter is written by a former BMT patient who discusses medical, psychological, physical, and insurance issues involved with bone marrow transplants. An excellent resource for breast cancer patients going through autologous bone marrow transplants.

Chemotherapy and You: A Guide to Self-Help During Treatment, NIH Publication No. 83-1136, National Cancer Institute, Bethesda, MD, 1987. This booklet describes what chemotherapy is, how the treatment is given, what the most common side effects are, and what drugs are most commonly used.

Coping with Chemotherapy, by Nancy Bruning, Ballantine Books, New York, revised edition, 1992. (First published by Dial Press in 1985.) An outstanding, objective, and comprehensive overview of the medical, physical, and emotional aspects of chemotherapy treatment by a breast cancer patient who went through the experience.

Managing the Side Effects of Chemotherapy and Radiation, by Marylin J. Dodd, Prentice Hall Press, New York, 1991. A practical resource guide for patients and families, which includes information on all chemotherapy agents, their potential side effects; and how to manage and minimize side effects of both chemotherapy and radiation therapies.

Radiation Therapy: A Treatment for Early Stage Breast Cancer, NIH Publication No. 84-659, National Cancer Institute, Bethesda, MD, 1987. This booklet explains lumpectomy, lymph node surgery, and radiation therapy procedures; it provides suggestions on how to manage treatment side effects and emotionally adjust to the diagnosis of breast cancer.

Radiation Therapy and You: A Guide to Self-Help During Treatment, NIH Publication No. 83-2227, National Cancer Institute, Bethesda, MD, 1987. This booklet describes what radiation therapy is, including external radiation and implant therapy, and how it works. Also included is how to manage side effects, nutritional advice, and follow-up care.

Winning the Chemo Battle, by Joyce Slayton Mitchell, W.W. Norton and Company, New York, 1988. One woman's account of her experience with chemotherapy; it includes drug information and glossary.

Coping with Breast Cancer

Affirmations, Meditations, and Encouragements for Women Living with Breast Cancer, by Linda Dackman, Lowell House, Los Angeles, 1991. This inspiring book is the next best thing to being in a support group. Each affirmation or meditation is preceded by an anecdote from the author's own experience or other breast cancer patients she interviewed.

Invisible Scars: A Guide to Coping with the Emotional Impact of Breast Cancer, by Mimi Greenberg, Ph.D., Walker and Company, New York, 1987. A helpful guide, written by a psychologist who had breast cancer, that provides honest information on how to make decisions regarding breast cancer treatment, how to choose a doctor, and how to build support systems. The author discusses, through question and answer format, how to deal with some of the major psychosocial issues involved with breast cancer, including coping with partners, dating, and work-related problems.

Man to Man: When the Woman You Love Has Breast Cancer, by Andy Murcia and Bob Stewart, St. Martin's Press, New York, 1988. The authors, both married to breast cancer patients, one of whom is the actress Ann Jillian, have written a warm, upbeat book that describes the impact of a woman's breast cancer on the man in her life. In combination with their own personal stories and practical tips, the authors present factual and useful information on breast cancer diagnosis and treatment, as well as how to deal with the range of emotions both partners feel when going through the breast cancer experience. Though this book is directed toward men, it is also an excellent resource book for any woman with breast cancer.

Spinning Straw into Gold: Your Emotional Recovery from Breast Cancer, by Ronnie Kaye, Simon & Schuster, New York, 1991. The author, both a therapist and breast cancer survivor, shares what she has learned from her many years of work with breast cancer patients and presents comprehensive, helpful, and practical information on how to cope with the breast cancer experience.

Living with Cancer

The American Cancer Society Cancer Book: Prevention, Detection, Diagnosis, Treatment, Rehabilitation, Cure, edited by Arthur I. Holleb, M.D., Doubleday, Garden City, New York, 1986. Written by numerous medical specialists, this comprehensive book offers a collection of thirty-five separate articles on everything from living with cancer to how to manage specific treatment-related problems. It also offers a good directory of resources and a glossary.

And a Time to Live: Toward Emotional Well-Being During the Crisis of Cancer, by Robert Chernin Cantor, Harper Colophon Books, New York, 1978. A psychologist presents strategies that will help any cancer patient to cope with the emotional stress of having cancer. An insightful and thoughtful book, the author writes about the importance of finding meaning in the cancer experience, and he describes the most common emotional reactions to the disease and how to deal with them.

At the Will of the Body: Reflections on Illness, by Arthur W. Frank, Houghton Mifflin, Boston, 1991. The author, a sociology professor, experienced a heart attack at age thirty-nine and cancer at age forty. In this profound and well-written book, he writes about the experience of illness, the role of the patient, doctors, and society, and discusses the value of going through the process of illness, rather than around it.

Cancervive: The Challenge of Life After Cancer, by Susan Nessim, Houghton Mifflin, Boston, 1991. A useful guidebook for cancer patients and their families, who as survivors must deal not only with the long-term effects of treatment but society's attitudes as well. The book also includes discussions on jobs, insurance problems, and how to live with cancer and fears of recurrence.

Charting the Journey: An Almanac of Practical Resources for Cancer Survivors, by the National Coalition for Cancer Survivorship, Consumer Reports Books, New York, 1990. An excellent and complete collection of practical resources, facts, personal experiences, and strategies on how to get through the cancer experience. Detailed appendixes are included.

I Can Cope: Staying Healthy with Cancer, by Judi Johnson and Linda Klein, DCI Publishing, Minneapolis, 1988. One of the cofounders of the American Cancer Society's national I Can Cope program and a professional writer have coauthored a valuable resource guide that helps cancer patients and their families identify the problems and obstacles that will be encountered. They outline how to cope with and get through the cancer experience. A solid and highly recommended book for any cancer patient.

Intimacy: Living as a Woman After Cancer, by Jacquelyn Johnson, New Canada Publications Limited, Toronto, 1987. A discussion of gynecological and breast cancers and their impact on women's emotional and sexual lives. A helpful guide that rejects the common myths that surround cancer; it gives suggestions on how to get through the cancer experience and live a full life.

The Road Back to Health: Coping with the Emotional Side of Cancer, by Neil Fiore, Ph.D., Celestial Arts, Berkeley, CA, 1990. A former cancer patient, Dr. Fiore writes about how patients can be active participants in their treatment and maintain control of their lives. He also discusses how to build emotional support systems with doctors, family, and friends. An excellent, insightful book for everyone.

Surviving!: A Cancer Patient Newsletter. Informative, touching, and helpful newsletters written and created by cancer patients, for the benefit of all cancer patients and their friends and families. Their goal is to share common experiences and to help recovering patients manage the challenges of their illness, treatment, and life after cancer. Write a $12 donation or subscription check payable to Surviving! and mail to: Stanford University Hospital, Department of Radiation Oncology, Division of Radiation Therapy, Room A035, 300 Pasteur Drive, Stanford, California 94305.

Surviving Cancer: A Practical Guide for Those Fighting to Win! by Danette G. Kauffman, Acropolis Books, Washington, DC, revised edition, 1989. A very upbeat, informative collection of resources, including books, tapes, helpful hints about cancer treatment, and a listing of cancer centers that assist the patient with everything from getting a second opinion to dealing with medical insurance. An excellent resource book.

Third Opinion: An International Directory to Alternative Therapy Centers for the Treatment and Prevention of Cancer and Other Degenerative Diseases, by John M. Fink, Avery Publishing Group, New York, 1992. In this second edition, the author presents a comprehensive guide to many alternative treatment centers, information services, and support groups located throughout the world. Everything from addresses, phone numbers, prices, and philosophical approaches and methods of treatment are included.

Coping with Loss

Coming Home: A Guide to Dying at Home with Dignity, by Deborah Duda, Aurora Press, Santa Fe, NM, 1987. For those terminally ill people who wish to die at home, this book is a sensitive and resourceful reference guide that identifies sources of help, discusses medical considerations, and answers patients' and families' questions about how to make the final months or weeks of life as comfortable and meaningful as possible.

A Consumer Guide to Hospice Care, by Barbara Coleman, National Consumers League, 815 15th Street, N.W., Suite 516, Washington, DC, 1985; (202) 554-1600. This booklet includes basic information about hospice care, the kinds of services that are offered, and a checklist of questions for families and patients to ask when evaluating these kinds of programs.

The Courage to Grieve, by Judy Tatelbaum, Harper Colophon Books, New York, 1984. A clearly written, wise, and helpful guide on the grief and recovery process.

Exploding into Life, by Dorothea Lynch, photographs by Eugene Richards, Aperture, New York, 1986. An emotionally powerful and graphic photoessay book about one woman's experience with breast cancer, who died before the publication of the book.

On Death and Dying, by Elizabeth Kubler-Ross, Macmillan Company, New York, 1972. The internationally known psychiatrist wrote this ground-breaking and valuable book about societal attitudes about death and dying, and identifies five basic emotional stages patients experience as they move toward their death. Through interviews and case studies, she shares how to help the terminally ill and their families move toward acceptance of their death.

To Live Until We Say Goodbye, by Elizabeth Kubler-Ross, Prentice Hall, Inc., Englewood Cliffs, NJ, 1978. Through photographs and commentary, Dr. Kubler-Ross demonstrates her counseling work with a number of terminally ill patients who come to terms with and accept their dying.

Personal Accounts of the Breast Cancer Experience

Cancer in Two Voices, by Sandra Butler and Barbara Rosenblum, Spinsters Book Company, San Francisco, 1991. Using essays, journal entries, and letters, the authors collaborated on writing a beautiful and painfully honest book about their love partnership, and how they sustained it throughout Barbara's breast cancer experience. This life-affirming book, published after Barbara died, is unique in that it deals with both perspectives of a patient and her partner.

Diary of a Pigeon Watcher, by Doris Schweirin, Paragon House Publishers, New York, 1987. An inspirational book in diary form about the author's radical mastectomy and the changes she undergoes. While recovering from the surgery, she identifies with the pigeons who nest on her window ledge, which rekindle her memories of her own family origins and ties.

First You Cry, by Betty Rollins, New American Library, New York, 1976. The first best-selling book to be written on a woman's personal experience with breast cancer, by a well-known TV broadcaster.

Getting Better: Conversations with Myself and Other Friends While Healing from Breast Cancer, by Anne Hargrove, CompCare Publishers, Minneapolis, 1988. The author writes twenty-five self-contained vignettes about her breast cancer experience.

Grace and Grit: Spirituality and Healing in the Life and Death of Treya Killam Wilber, by Ken Wilber, Shambhala Publications, Boston, 1991. This beautifully written and inspiring love story chronicles the five-year journey of Ken and Treya Wilber's dealing with Treya's living with and dying of breast cancer. The book uses Treya's journal entries and Ken's narrative to convey the inner experience of their ordeal.

Hanging in There: Living Well on Borrowed Time, by Natalie Davis Spingarn, Stein and Day, Briarcliff Manor, New York, 1982. A well-written account of a journalist's personal experience with breast cancer. She writes about all the major issues facing those who live with a serious illness.

Headstrong: A Story of Conquest and Celebrations . . . Living through Chemotherapy, by Rena Blumberg, Crown Books, New York, 1982. A midwestern broadcaster's account of her experience with breast cancer and chemotherapy.

Her Soul Beneath the Bone, edited by Leatrice Lifshitz, University of Illinois, Urbana and Chicago, 1988. A moving collection of more than two dozen women's poetry about their breast cancer experiences. Order from CUP Services, P.O. Box 6525, Ithaca, NY 14851, or call 800-666-2211.

Life Wish, by Jill Ireland, Little, Brown, Boston, 1987. The actress's account of her personal battle with breast cancer.

My Breast: One Woman's Cancer Story, by Joyce Wadler, Addison-Wesley, Reading, MA, 1992. With much courage and a sense of humor, a New York woman tells the story of her breast cancer experience.

Modified Radical and Other Cancer Poems, by Ann Davidson, Monday Press, Palo Alto, CA, 1990. A collection of poems about the author's breast cancer experience.

Of Tears and Triumphs: The Family Victory That Has Inspired Thousands of Cancer Patients, by Georgia and Bud Photopulos, Congdon & Weed, New York, 1988. This couple discusses how they dealt with Mrs. Photopulos's multiple cancer crisis over a twenty-year period. They write about what they learned and offer constructive and sensitive suggestions about how other cancer patients can help themselves and their families.

The Cancer Journals, by Audre Lorde, Spinsters, Ink., San Francisco, 1980. One black woman's experience with breast cancer and her thoughts and comments about the way women with breast cancer are perceived and treated in American society.

Tree, by Deena Metzger, Wingbow Press, 2929 Fifth Street, Berkeley, CA 94710; 1983 (published in one volume with *The Woman Who Slept with Men to Take the War Out of Them*). The author's experience with breast cancer, as taken from the journal she wrote from the time of her diagnosis through the postsurgery weeks at home. Not only a record of her experience, the author includes a "map of roads toward healing."

Upfront: Sex and the Postmastectomy Woman, by Linda Dackman, Viking Penguin, New York, 1990. The author writes about her own personal experience with breast cancer, and how as a single woman she coped with a number of psychosocial and sexual issues that confronted her during her treatment and recovery.

Other Helpful Personal
Accounts of Cancer

A Private Battle, by Cornelius Ryan and Kathryn Morgan Ryan, Fawcett Popular Library, New York, 1979. Cornelius Ryan kept a secret account of his battle against cancer for over four and a half years. His wife, also a writer, compiled and edited her husband's journals, and published a deeply moving book about one man's cancer experience.

Vital Signs: A Young Doctor's Struggle with Cancer, by Fitzhugh Mullan, M.D., Laurel Books, 1984. A very moving memoir of a young doctor's experience with cancer; he describes what it is like to be seriously ill, face death, and then journey back to recovery.

We the Victors: Inspiring Stories of People Who Conquered Cancer and How They Did It, by Curtis Bill Pepper, Doubleday, Garden City, New York, 1984. The author interviewed thirty-one people who had cancer and survived, and wrote a moving and authentic book that weaves the patients' stories with five significant factors that he believes contributed to their recovery.

General Information on Beauty and Cancer

Beauty and Cancer, by Diane Noyes and Peggy Mellody, Taylor Publishing, Dallas, TX, 1992. A helpful guide on how a woman can improve her appearance during and after cancer treatment. Helpful suggestions are offered on wigs, scarves, makeup, prostheses, and clothing. Can be ordered from Noyes Sales, Ltd., 12085 NE 107th Place, Kirkland, WA 98033.

Looking Up: The Complete Guide to Looking and Feeling Good for the Recovering Cancer Patient, by Suzy Kalter, McGraw Hill, New York, 1987. Written in a supportive and sensitive yet no-nonsense style, Katler provides a wealth of information and practical suggestions on hair care, wigs, makeup, fingernails, weight loss, diet, and postmastectomy exercises.

General Information on Breast Cancer
Risk Factors and Breast Health

If You Find a Lump in Your Breast, by Martha McClean, Bull Publishing, Palo Alto, CA, 1986 (revised). A short but helpful book that explains the methods of breast cancer detection, diagnosis, and treatment, and it outlines what steps to take if a lump is found.

The Informed Woman's Guide to Breast Health: Breast Changes That Are Not Cancer, by Kerry McGinn, Bull Publishing, Palo Alto, CA, 1992. (Formerly entitled, *Keeping Abreast: Breast Changes That Are Not Cancer.*) This revised and updated excellent guide clearly presents factual information on the anatomy of breasts, and the normal and abnormal changes they undergo through a lifetime. The author, an oncology nurse and breast cancer survivor, strongly emphasizes the importance of early detection of breast cancer.

Questions and Answers about Breast Lumps, NIH Publication No. 83-2401, National Cancer Institute, Bethesda, MD. This informative pamphlet explains what the most common breast benign lumps are and what can be done about them. Includes a glossary and other pertinent information about breast self-examination.

Relative Risk: Living with a Family History of Breast Cancer, by Nancy C. Baker, Viking, New York, 1991. A very good overview for women who have a family history of breast cancer. The author, whose mother had breast cancer, provides important information on the risk factors involved in being a relative of a breast cancer patient, and discusses how both patients and families are affected emotionally by the breast cancer experience.

Special Touch: A Personal Plan of Action for Breast Health, by the American Cancer Society, Publication No. 2095-LE, 1987. A brochure that talks about how

women can detect breast cancer early through mammography and clinical breast
exams; it provides instructions on how to perform a newly modified and more
effective breast self-examination technique.

Understanding Breast Cancer Risk, by Patricia T. Kelly, Temple University Press,
Philadelphia, 1991. An excellent book that provides women concerned about
breast cancer with an analysis of the latest scientific evidence, and factors that
contribute to breast cancer risk. Dr. Kelly also provides practical guidelines by
which women can develop a breast health plan.

General Information on Nutrition

The American Cancer Society Cookbook, by Anne Lindsay, Hearst Books, New York,
1988. More than two hundred recipes that reflect the newest research on the
simple nutritional guidelines that can reduce your risk of developing cancer.

Diet, Nutrition and Cancer Prevention: A Guide to Food Choices, NIH Publication No.
87-2878, National Cancer Institute, Bethesda, MD. A booklet that provides
current information about diet and its relationship to cancer. It shows the
consumer how to lessen the chances of cancer by providing nutritional information on foods.

The Diet the Doctors Won't Give You, by the National Women's Health Network,
1325 G Street, NW, Washington, DC, 1987; (202) 347-1140. This pamphlet
provides practical information on how women may lower their chances of
getting breast cancer by reducing the fat in their diets.

Eating Hints, Recipes and Tips for Better Nutrition During Cancer Treatment, NIH
Publication No. 84-2079. National Cancer Institute, Bethesda, MD, 1983. A
booklet that provides helpful information and advice on what to eat during
cancer treatment; it also offers nutritious recipes.

Jane Brody's Nutrition Book, by Jane Brody, W. W. Norton, New York, 1981
(revised, Bantam, 1988). An excellent, thorough guide to diet, nutrition, and
dispelling myths that surround weight control.

Nutrition and the Cancer Patient, by Joyce Daly Margie, M.S., Abby S. Bloch,
M.S., R.D., Chilton Books, Radnor, PA, 1983. Resources, references, and
recipes for coping with cancer. The authors discuss cancer and its treatment,
background information on nutrition and diet, and offer practical solutions to
nutritional problems associated with cancer treatment.

Nutrition for the Chemotherapy Patient, by Janet Ramstack and Ernest Rosenbaum, M.D.,
Bull Publishing, Palo Alto, CA, 1990. Informative and helpful guide for eating
well during treatment.

The Real Vitamin and Mineral Book, by Shari Lieberman, M.A., R.D., and Nancy
Bruning, Avery, Garden City Park, NY, 1990. A nutritionally sound, common-
sense book about how to create your own vitamin program to supplement a
balanced diet.

Simply Nutritious, by Sabine Artaud-Wild, R.D., Editor, American Cancer Society,
Oregon Division, 1986. Excellent recipes and recommendations on how to
reduce the risk of cancer, including a chapter on the food basics of healthful

eating. Order from American Cancer Society, California Division, 1710 Webster Street, Oakland, CA 94612.

Something's Got to Taste Good, by Joan Fishman, R.D., M.S., and Barbara Anrod, Signet Books, New American Library, New York, 1982. Developed as a result of a questionnaire answered by cancer patients, this book, filled with easy-to-prepare recipes, also offers good advice for common problems associated with nutrition and cancer treatments.

General Information on Sexuality

For Yourself: The Fulfillment of Female Sexuality, by Lonnie Garfield Barbach, Signet Books, New York, 1975. The author provides helpful down-to-earth information on female sexuality and a step-by-step program of exercises that may help a woman learn more about her own body and its needs, assist her in realizing her own sexual potential, and overcome sexual difficulties.

Midlife Love Life: How to Deal with the Physical and Emotional Changes of Midlife and Their Effect on Your Sex Life, (formerly entitled *Love and Sex After 40*) by Robert N. Butler, M.D., and Myrna I. Lewis, A.C.S.W., Perennial Library, New York, 1988. The authors present solid information on the normal physical changes in sexuality with age, including the effects of common medical problems on sex, and provide an excellent overview of the psychological issues related to sexual problems with partners, dating, and remarriage. They also offer sound advice about where to seek help when specific problems arise. The authors also have written a helpful book entitled *Sex after Sixty: A Guide for Men and Women for Their Later Years,* Perennial Library.

The New Our Bodies, Our Selves, by Boston Women's Health Book Collective, updated and expanded for the '90s, Simon & Schuster, New York, 1992. This invaluable book was written by a group of women for women to help them learn about their bodies and take control of their health care and how they live their lives. Everything a woman wants to know about being a woman is provided in this collection of chapters on body image, sex, health and healing, new reproductive technologies, plus other important women's social and political issues.

Sex: The Facts, the Acts, and Your Feelings, by Michael Carrera, Crown Books, New York, 1981. The author presents a thorough discussion of sexuality and makes helpful suggestions to those whose sexual lives have been affected by surgery.

Sexuality & Cancer: For the Woman Who Has Cancer and Her Partner, by Leslie R. Schover, Ph.D., edited by Michael Randers-Pehrson, American Cancer Society, Atlanta, GA, 1988. Excellent and comprehensive booklet that addresses the medical, physiological, and psychological aspects of cancer and sexuality, including the effect of cancer treatment on female sexual desire, strategies for dealing with sexual problems, how to cope with changes in appearance, and a helpful short resource guide. Contact your local American Cancer Society for copies.

Woman's Experience of Sex: The Facts and Feelings of Female Sexuality at Every Stage of Life, by Sheila Kitzinger, Penguin Books, New York, 1983. An outstanding comprehensive guide that explores the full range of female sexuality, including women's bodies, feelings about sex, sexual lifestyles, children, relationships, and growing older.

General Readings on Attitudinal Healing

Healers on Healing, edited by Richard Carlson, Ph.D., and Benjamin Shield, Jeremy Tarcher, Inc., Los Angeles, CA, 1989. Thirty-seven essays, written by some of the world's leaders in healing, including Ram Dass, Stephen Levine, Elizabeth Kubler-Ross, Gerald Jampolsky, Carl Simonton, and Bernie Siegal, provide the reader with a sampling of the wide range of approaches to the complex nature of healing.

The Healer Within, by Stephen Locke, M.D., and Douglas Colligan, Mentor Books, New American Library, New York, 1987. A Harvard Medical School professor and an *Omni* magazine editor provide a thorough study of the new science of psychoneuroimmunology that shows the ways in which emotions and attitudes can affect health and the treatment of illness.

The Healing Family: The Simonton Approach for Families Facing Illness, by Stephanie Matthews-Simonton, Bantam Books, 1984. The author offers a positive approach that enables families to work together as a healing team when they are confronted with a serious illness. She offers techniques that assist in learning how to improve communications, how to manage stress, and how to work with doctors.

The Healing Power of Humor: Techniques for Getting through Loss, Setbacks, Upsets, Disappointments, Difficulties, Trials, Tribulations, and All that Not-So Funny Stuff, by Allen Klein, Jeremy Tarcher, Inc., Los Angeles, 1989. A useful and entertaining guide for those times when all you feel like doing is crying. The author describes the psychological and physiological benefits of laughter, shares humorous anecdotes, and shows ways in which you can look for laughter in loss.

Minding the Body, Mending the Mind, by Joan Borysenko, Ph.D., Bantam Books, New York, 1988. Using methods based on psychoneuroimmunologic theories and cases from the Mind/Body Clinic at New England Deaconess Hospital, the author provides practical exercises to promote physical and emotional well-being. A useful guide to learn how to take an active role in healing.

Recommended are all of the following books by Stephen Levine. In all his books, the author, a poet, teacher of meditation, and counselor of the terminally ill, teaches how to focus on and live in the present moment, and live life in a state of mindfulness and awareness.

A Gradual Awakening, Anchor Books, Garden City, NY, 1979.
Healing into Life and Death, Doubleday, Garden City, NY, 1987.
Meetings at the Edge: Dialogues with the Grieving and the Dying, the Healing and the Healed, Anchor Press, Garden City, NY, 1984.
Who Dies? Anchor Press, Garden City, NY, 1982.

General Reading

Coming Back: Rebuilding Lives after Crisis and Loss, By Ann Kaiser Stearns, Ballantine, New York, 1989. The author, a noted professor of psychology, has written a helpful book that discusses people who have made comebacks after suffering great losses, and then identifies and describes the methods that helped them cope successfully with their experiences.

The Courage to Be Yourself: A Woman's Guide to Growing Beyond Emotional Dependence, by Sue Patton Thoele, Pyramid Press, Nevada City, CA, 1988. A hopeful and nurturing book written by a psychotherapist that addresses the common fears and emotional dependencies of women, and offers, through true stories and case studies, a road map by which a woman can create her own feelings of well-being.

Flying Without Wings: Personal Reflections on Being Disabled, by Arnold Beisser, M.D., Doubleday, New York, 1989. The author, now a psychiatrist, was left paralyzed from the neck down by polio when he was a young medical school graduate. In this beautifully written book, he describes his search to make a new life for himself, and provides ways in which anyone faced with loss, pain, disability, or a life-threatening disease can find meaning, peace, and humor in their lives.

From Fear to Freedom: Choosing High Self-Esteem, by Darlene Deer Truchses, Fulcrum Books, Inc., Golden, CO, 1989. The author, a psychotherapist, believes that improving self-image is the key to women's personal growth. She discusses a variety of ways in which a woman can examine her role behaviors and feelings, and offers models for improvement, including a five-step formula for change, and effective communication techniques that will enhance a woman's self-esteem.

The Healer's Art, by Eric J. Cassell, M.D., Penguin Books, New York, 1978. A physician writes a book about the problems between doctor and patient. Believing that a physician can play a vital part in a patient's physical and emotional recovery, Cassell offers insightful and humane suggestions on how doctors can improve their approach to their patients.

Healing the Wounds: A Physician Looks at His Work, by David Hilfiker, M.D., Pantheon Books, New York, 1985. One physician's honest and open account of what it is like to be a doctor in the 1980s. Dr. Hilfiker identifies some of the pressures and frustrations under which doctors must now practice medicine, which often result in burnout, depression, and loneliness.

If You Meet the Buddha on the Road, Kill Him, by Sheldon B. Kopp, Bantam Books, New York, 1988. The author, a psychotherapist, offers a different but realistic approach to those seeking to alter their destiny. Through the use of myths and epic tales, he shares revelations that help to shape Everyman's journey through life.

Illness as Metaphor, by Susan Sontag, Vintage Books, New York, 1979. The author examines and compares societal attitudes, from the late nineteenth century to the present about tuberculosis and cancer. She presents an insightful discussion about what kinds of foolish myths are developed about people who have diseases with unknown causes, and why we cling to them.

Lifeprints: New Patterns of Love and Work for Today's Women, by Grace Baruch, Rosalind Barnett, and Caryl Rivers, Plume Books, New American Library, New York, 1983. An outstanding book that addresses the major social, personal, and political issues affecting all women today, including career, motherhood, marriage, and divorce. Through numerous interviews, the authors debunk many myths about women, and reveal what women really want and need from life, and what makes them happy. It is an inspiring and helpful guide for those who are interested in finding ways to evaluate and enhance their self-esteem.

Living through Personal Crisis, by Ann Kaiser Stearns, Ballantine Books, New York, 1984. The author, through case histories and her own experiences, provides practical advice to those who have suffered a loss and are in pain. An easy-to-read and helpful book that includes a section on the most commonly asked questions on the subject of grief.

Necessary Losses: The Loves, Illusions, Dependencies and Impossible Expectations That All of Us Have to Give Up in Order to Grow, by Judith Viorst, Fawcett Gold Medal, New York, 1986. This perceptive book describes how we grow and change through the losses that are an inevitable and necessary part of life. The author has written a thoughtful and intelligent book about how we are shaped by loving, losing, leaving, and letting go.

We Are Not Alone: Learning to Live with Chronic Illness, by Sefra Korbin Pitzele, Workman Publishing, New York, 1986. A comprehensive and useful book that provides practical guidelines for patients who live with chronic illness. Drawing from her firsthand experiences, the author describes how to cope with the diagnosis, manage daily routines, and live better, not "just differently." She includes a detailed listing of special services, self-help organizations, books, and articles.

When Bad Things Happen to Good People, by Harold S. Kushner, Avon, New York, 1981. A clergyman, whose young son died, writes a compassionate book that provides some comforting answers to the question, "Why Me?"

Other Sources of Written Information

The American Cancer Society (ACS) offers many helpful pamphlets, booklets, brochures, and other resource materials on breast cancer and related topics that are free of charge, but are not listed here. Contact your local American Cancer Society for further information.

The National Cancer Institute (NCI) offers a variety of excellent patient education booklets, pamphlets, and brochures. They are free of charge and can be ordered by writing: Office of Cancer Communications, The National Cancer Institute, Building 31, Room 10 A 18, Bethesda, MD 20014; (301) 496-5583. Individual copies may also be available at your local ACS office. Of special interest to the breast cancer patient is the NCI's booklet series on breast cancer, some of which were included in this book list. Also available are "What You Need to Know about Breast Cancer," "Breast Biopsy: What You Should Know," "Breast Cancer: Understanding Treatment Options," "Mastectomy: A Treatment for Breast Cancer," "When Cancer Recurs: Meeting the Challenge Again," and "Advanced Cancer: Living Each Day."

Glossary

Adjuvant treatment. Secondary form of treatment that usually follows surgery and involves chemotherapy or radiation therapy.

Advanced breast cancer. Stage of cancer in which the disease has spread from the breast to other body systems by traveling through the lymphatic system or bloodstream.

Aspirate. Fluid withdrawn with a needle from a lump or mass for microscopic examination.

Autologous bone marrow treatment. An experimental treatment for advanced breast cancer which involves removing a patient's bone marrow (autologous means from the patient's own body), keeping it in cold storage, and then transplanting it back into the patient's body, following a course of high-dose chemotherapy and/or radiotherapy.

Axilla. The underarm, which contains the axillary lymph nodes.

Axillary dissection. Incision made under the armpit to remove lymph nodes to determine if breast cancer has spread to other parts of the body. *See also* Lymph node operation.

Baseline mammogram. A woman's first mammogram, usually done between the ages of thirty-five and forty, that doctors use as a diagnostic tool for evaluating changes in future mammograms.

Benign. Not cancerous.

Biopsy. Removal and microscopic examination of a piece of tissue from the body to determine whether it is benign or malignant. Excisional biopsy is the total surgical removal of the tissue to be examined. Incisional biopsy is the surgical removal of only a sample of the tissue to be examined. Needle localization biopsy is a method used when a breast abnormality can be seen on a mammogram but cannot be felt. Before a biopsy, the suspicious area is marked with needle(s) and sometimes dye. The surgeon is then able to locate and remove the marked area of tissue, which is then x-rayed to be sure all the suspicious areas have been removed. *See also* Needle aspiration.

Breast reconstruction. Rebuilding or creating of a new breast by plastic surgery, using tissue expanders, silicone implants, or tissue transplants. The surgery can be performed at any time, from immediately following the mastectomy to months or years later.

Breast self-examination (BSE). Monthly examination of the breast performed by a woman in which she becomes familiar with the normal look and feel of her breasts.

Cancer. General term used to describe over a hundred different diseases characterized by abnormal uncontrolled cell growth. Cancerous cells invade and destroy normal cells, and spread or metastasize to other areas of the body.

Chemotherapy. Treatment by powerful chemicals or drugs that have the ability to destroy cancer cells. Often used in conjunction with radiation and surgery. The most common drugs used to treat breast cancer are: Adriamycin, methotrexate, 5-fluorouracil, cyclophosphamide (Cytoxan), vincristine, and prednisone.

Early stage breast cancer. When cancer is limited to the breast and has not spread to the lymph nodes or other parts of the body. Also called in situ, or localized, breast cancer.

Edema. Presence of an abnormally large amount of fluid in the body, characterized by swelling or puffiness.

Hormone therapy. Manipulation of hormone levels in the body that can cause a tumor to stabilize or shrink. Tamoxifen is a common antiestrogen drug used in the treatment of breast cancer.

Informed consent. Legal standard that states how much a patient must know about the potential risks and benefits of a therapy before being able to undergo it knowledgeably. Many states have "Informed Consent" laws regarding breast cancer that require physicians to provide treatment options to patients before any medical treatment is given.

Lump. Mass of tissue found in the breast or other parts of the body; 80 percent of breast lumps are benign.

Lumpectomy. Surgical removal of a cancerous breast lump and a portion of the adjacent tissue.

Lymphedema. Chronic edema of the arm due to the accumulation of fluid as a result of breast surgery, such as axillary dissection and mastectomy. Characterized by swelling or puffiness to the arm.

Lymph node. Bean-size structures in the lymphatic system that filter cancer cells and harmful bacteria through the lymph fluid, keeping them from entering the blood stream. Their work helps the immune system fight off infection and disease.

Lymph node operation. Incision made under the armpit to remove lymph nodes to determine if breast cancer has spread to other parts of the body. Also referred to as an axillary dissection.

Malignant. Cancerous.

Mammogram. Image produced by an x-ray procedure that details the structure of the breast tissue.

Mammography. Process of taking breast low-dose x-ray pictures. Screening mammography is for women who are asymptomatic, and diagnostic mammography is for women who have suspected breast problems.

Mastectomy. Surgical removal of the breast, also known as a simple mastectomy.

Menopause. Cessation of menstruation, usually a result of aging. Also may occur temporarily or permanently as a result of chemotherapy or hormone treatment.

Metastasis. Spread of cancer from one part of the body to another. It can spread through the lymphatic system, the bloodstream, or across body cavities.

Modified radical mastectomy. Surgical removal of the breast and most of the axillary lymph nodes. It is the most common breast surgery done for the treatment of breast cancer.

Needle aspiration. Diagnostic method of removing fluid or tissue from a breast tumor or cyst by a fine needle for microscopic examination. Also, a special needle can be used to withdraw a piece of tissue or several cells from a solid lump.

Negative nodes. Lymph nodes that are free of cancer cells.

Oncologist. Doctor that specializes in cancer. (There are medical, surgical, and radiation oncologists.)

Oncology. The study of tumors.

One-step procedure (one stage). Surgery that involves performing both a breast biopsy and mastectomy in the same operation.

Positive nodes. Lymph nodes that have been invaded by cancer cells.

Prognosis. Forecast as to the probable outcome of a disease.

Prosthesis. Artificial substitute for a missing body part. After mastectomy, breast prostheses, which come in many shapes and forms, are often used to restore a sense of balance and completeness, and normal appearance in clothing.

Radiation therapy. Treatment of breast cancer by x-rays or high-dose radiation to reduce or eliminate malignant cells. Most often used following lumpectomy.

Radical mastectomy (Halstead radical mastectomy). Surgical removal of the breast, skin, underlying pectoral muscles, and all axillary lymph nodes. Once the standard treatment for breast cancer, this operation is rarely performed anymore.

Radiotherapist. Also known as radiation therapist or oncologist. A physician that specializes in treating cancer patients with radiation therapy.

Recurrence. Return of cancer at the same site (local), near the first site (regional), or in other areas of the body (metastases).

Side effects. Reactions to radiation treatments or chemotherapy that are usually temporary in nature, such as nausea, hair loss, vomiting, or weight gain.

Staging. System for classifying cancer to its stage of development and the extent of its spread, determined by diagnostic tests such as x-rays, blood tests, and body and bone scans. In breast cancer diagnosis, these tests are done after the biopsy or mastectomy to ascertain the level of malignancy beyond the breast. There are four stages: Stage T1 has the best prognosis. Early stage, in situ or localized, breast cancer (stage T1 or stage 1) means the cancer is confined to the primary site; regional breast cancer (most often stages 2 and 3) means the cancer has spread to nearby lymph nodes or other tissues; and distant (stage 4) means the cancer has spread to other parts of the body. The stage of the breast cancer will determine the treatment to be performed.

Tumor. Growth of cells in which the multiplication of cells is uncontrolled and progressive. Can be either benign or malignant.

Two-step procedure (two stage). Breast biopsy and breast surgery performed in two steps, allowing diagnosis and treatment to be separated by hours, days, or longer periods of time.

Appendix A:
Guide to Resources and Support

The American Cancer Society, National Office, 1599 Clifton Road NE, Atlanta, GA 30329; 800-ACS-2345; also (404) 320-3333. This national organization provides both the public and health professionals with information and services involving cancer. They have a variety of excellent programs for cancer patients and their families, such as I Can Cope, Cansurmount, Reach to Recovery, and Look Good, Feel Better. (For further information on this last program, call 1-800-558-5005.) Also call 800-ACS-2345 and your local ACS for further information on where you can obtain a low-cost mammogram and training for breast self-examination.

American College of Radiology, 1891 Preston White Drive, Reston, VA 22091. This association will provide names of certified radiologists for mammography in your local area.

American College of Surgeons, 55 East Erie Street, Chicago, IL 60611; (312) 664-4050. Names of certified surgeons specializing in breast surgery by geographical areas will be provided.

American Society of Plastic and Reconstructive Surgeons, 444 East Algonquin Road, Arlington Heights, IL 60025; (312) 228-9900. Written information will be provided as well as a list of certified physicians by geographical area.

Breast Cancer Advisory Center, Inc., Box 224, Kensington, MD 20895. A nonprofit, consumer-oriented organization, whose purpose is to give men and women information about all aspects of breast cancer.

Breast Implant Network (Command Trust Network), P.O. Box 17082, Covington, KY 41017; (606) 331-0055 or (310) 556-1738. A network established to provide assistance and information to women with, or considering, breast implants. Material packets and newsletters are available.

Cancer Care, Inc. and the National Cancer Care Foundation, 1180 Avenue of the Americas, New York, NY 10036; (212) 221-3300. A social service agency that helps patients and their families deal with the impact of cancer. Although they only serve the greater New York metropolitan area, individuals may call them and will be referred to similar assistance in their regional area.

Cancer Information Service, (CIS), National Cancer Institute, offers a toll-free information service at 800-4-CANCER. CIS will answer questions about all kinds of cancers and provide resource information, including second-opinion centers. Their PDQ service provides a patient and her doctor with all the latest treatment information on her particular cancer. In Hawaii, call 524-1234. (Neighbor Islands can call collect.) In Alaska, call 800-638-6070. Spanish-speaking staff are available to callers from California, Florida, Georgia, Illinois, New Jersey (area code 201), New York, and Texas.

Corporate Angels, White Plains, NY; (914) 328-1313. This group provides free long-distance air transportation on corporate and private jets for cancer patients who need to travel for their treatment. To inquire about the availability of flights, call at least five days before you need to travel.

FDA (Food and Drug Administration) *Breast Implant Information Hotline.* Answers both consumer and professional questions about breast implants, and will assist in registering complains. Call 800-532-4440.

The Komen Alliance, 3500 Gaston Avenue, Baylor University Medical Center, Dallas, TX 75246. A comprehensive program for the research and treatment of breast disease. Information is available by calling 1-800-IMA-AWARE, or The Susan G. Komen Foundation, 6820 LBJ Freeway, Suite 130, Dallas TX 75240, at (214) 450-1777.

"Look Good, Feel Better" is a public service program sponsored by the Cosmetic Toiletry and Fragrance Association, in partnership with the American Cancer Society (ACS) and the National Cosmetology Association. This program helps cancer patients manage changes in their appearance as a result of treatment. Both print and videotape materials are available, as well as instructional programs run by ACS. Call 800-395-LOOK.

Make Today Count, P.O. Box 22, Osage Beach, MO 65065. A nonprofit organization for cancer patients and their families. Contact your local chapter or write for further information.

Mammatech, Inc., 930 Northwest Eight Avenue, Gainesville, FL 32601. A for-profit group that has developed "Mammacare," an excellent program that teaches the latest and most effective method of breast self-examination. The company has trained specialists around the country that teach women how to do breast self-examination. Call 800-626-2273 for further information.

National Alliance of Breast Cancer Organizations (NABCO), 1180 Avenue of the Americas, Second Floor, New York, NY 10036; (212) 719-0154. This national association is a central information network for breast cancer interest groups, organizations, and individuals, it is also involved with research and legislative issues. Individuals and organizations who join NABCO receive the quarterly *NABCO News*, resource lists, and other important information such as *Breast Cancer: Your Best Protection . . . Early Detection and Partner's Guide*. Available free of charge upon written request. An excellent resource organization for any breast cancer patient. Membership fee to join.

National Breast Cancer Coalition, P.O. Box 66373, Washington, DC 20035; (202) 296-7477. A constituency-based national advocacy effort whose focus is to increase legislative and regulatory support for breast cancer policy issues and concerns. The Coalition is working to promote research into the causes of breast cancer, improve access to high-quality care for all women, and increase the involvement and influence of those living with beast cancer.

National Cancer Institute (NCI), Office of Cancer Communications, Bethesda, MD 20892. NCI is part of the Public Health Service under the U.S. Department of Health and Human Services. NCI supports treatment centers around the country (listed in Appendix B) and conducts research on the causes, prevention, diagnosis, and treatment of breast cancer. In addition to its Cancer Information Service, NCI also conducts clinical studies, in which you may be eligible to participate. If you want to learn more about participating in these clinical studies, speak with your physician, write NCI, or call the Cancer Information Service.

National Coalition for Cancer Survivorship (NCCS), 1010 Wayne Avenue, Fifth Floor, Silver Spring, MD 20910; (301) 585-2616. The primary goal of this national group is to generate a nationwide awareness of survivorship, showing that people live quality lives after cancer. The coalition serves as an information clearinghouse for cancer patients and their families and also promotes peer support. They publish a newsletter, the *Networker*, for members. Anyone who is interested is encouraged to join this group. Membership fee to join.

National Consortium of Breast Centers (NCBC), Johns Hopkins Oncology Center, 550 North Broadway, Suite 1003, Baltimore, MD 21205. A recently founded professional membership organization of comprehensive breast centers throughout the nation. To locate a comprehensive breast center near you, write for further information or check local phone listings. Comprehensive breast centers are full-service facilities that offer detection, diagnosis, and treatment services. Among many of the well-known centers throughout the country are The Breast Center in Van Nuys, California; Albert Einstein Medical Center's Breast Cancer Program in Philadelphia, Pennsylvania; the Comprehensive Breast Center at the Robert Wood Johnson Medical Center in New Brunswick, New Jersey; and the Long Beach Memorial Breast Center in Long Beach, California.

The National Hospice Organization, 1901 North Fort Meyer Drive, Suite 307, Arlington, VA 22209. For further information call (703) 243-5900. This national organization will provide information on the location of hospices and their services in your region, and it acts as a clearinghouse for more than a thousand hospices throughout the country.

National Lymphedema Network, 2211 Post Street, San Francisco, CA 94115; 800-541-3259. This not-for-profit organization was recently founded to meet the informational and treatment needs of people who suffer from lymphedema, a common complication from lymph node surgery.

National Self-Help Clearinghouse, (212) 642-2944. Any individual who is looking for a self-help group in their region can find it by calling this organization. Also check for listings of statewide self-help clearinghouses. Call 800-555-1212 for information.

National Women's Health Network, 1325 G Street, NW, Washington, DC 20005; (202) 347-1140. This group is the only public-interest organization devoted solely to women and health, and acts as a strong advocate for legislative and medical issues, including breast cancer. They have produced pamphlets on breast cancer and diet-related issues. They also write informative newsletters (*Network News*) with all the up-to-date information on a variety of women's health issues. Anyone may join this group. Membership fee to join.

Planetree Health Resource Center, 2040 Webster Street, San Francisco, CA 94115; (415) 923-3680. Planetree is a nonprofit organization that provides a health and medical library, bookstore, and research-by-mail service for those who live in northern California, although some of their services are available to everyone. The library collection consists of more than two thousand medical texts, consumer health books, and medical journals. The organization also provides a healthfinder information and reference service, which lists more than two thousand health agencies, clinics, practitioners, and support groups, that is available *only* on-site for use by the public. (No telephone referral service is available.) Its research-by-mail service provides personalized information by mail to individuals and organizations. Research requests may be placed by letter or telephone. For a fee, in-depth research on any health or medical topic is compiled through computer searches based on your personal questions and concerns.

Reach to Recovery, a nationwide program offered by the American Cancer Society to all breast cancer patients (including lumpectomy and mastectomy patients). A woman who has had breast cancer will visit and counsel newly diagnosed patients, and offer practical information and support. Contact your local American Cancer Society for further information.

RENU (Reconstructive Education for National Understanding), part of the Einstein Medical Center in Philadelphia that offers a hot-line counseling service for women considering breast reconstruction. Call (215) 456-7383.

Second Opinion Centers, a number of major hospitals throughout the country that offer second-opinion consultation services at varying costs. A multidisciplinary team of specialists will meet with the patient and the family to review the diagnosis and other diagnostic tests in order to provide the patient with a recommended second opinion for the course of treatment. Call the Cancer Information Service at 800-4-CANCER to locate the center nearest you.

Y-Me National Organization for Breast Cancer Information and Support, Inc., 18220 Harwood Avenue, Homewood, IL 60430. Started by breast cancer patients, this group provides support and counseling through a national toll-free hot line (800) 221-2141 (9 A.M. to 5 P.M. CST) or twenty-four hours at (312) 799-8228. Membership is open to all, and members receive the Y-Me Hotline newsletter, published four times a year. Membership fee to join. Y-Me also maintains a prosthesis bank for women with financial need. In exchange for a nominal donation, Y-Me will mail a breast prosthesis anywhere in the world, if one is available in the appropriate size.

The YWCA Encore Program, one of the first national support programs created for breast cancer patients, offers support and rehabilitation services for women with breast cancer. Contact your local YWCA for further information or the YWCA National Headquarters, 726 Broadway, New York, NY 10003; (212) 614-2827. Numerous YWCA's across the country also have breast cancer resource centers.

In addition to the previously listed organizations and groups, there are thousands of support and self-help groups around the country, and many communities offer cancer information telephone services that will provide information and resources on them. Many hospital and comprehensive breast care centers offer their own public education programs on breast cancer and hold regular support groups. Contact the Social Service Department for further information. Also many religious groups offer services to cancer patients; contact your clergy for further information.

For those interested in individual therapy, call your local hospitals to see if there is an oncology social worker on staff who is usually aware of local therapists who work with cancer patients. Also contact 800-4-CANCER, your local American Cancer Society, or write the National Alliance of Breast Cancer Organizations for help in finding a qualified therapist (social workers, marriage and family counselors, psychologists, psychiatrists, and some nurse practitioners).

National Association of Oncology Social Workers, 1233 York Avenue, Suite 4P, New York, NY 10021; (212) 734-8891. This national organization has more than six hundred members. They are not only well informed about available resources but are also well trained to deal with all the emotional concerns of cancer patients. They are some of the best informed and helpful health professionals available to people with cancer. Contact the social services department at your local hospital or any comprehensive cancer center.

Oncology Nursing Society, 1016 Greentread Road, Pittsburgh, PA 15220-3125; (412) 921-7373. The health professionals who have the most interaction with cancer patients are often oncology nurses. Well educated and trained to serve both cancer patients' medical and psychological needs, the oncology nurse can be a great source of support for cancer patients and their families. This national membership organization offers nurses professional education training and conferences, provides publications, and other support services.

For a list of qualified sex therapists in the United States, contact:

American Association of Marriage and Family Counselors, 225 Yale Avenue, Claremont, CA 91711.

American Association of Sex Educators, Counselors, and Therapists, 5010 Wisconsin Avenue, NW, Washington, DC 20016.

Sex Information and Education Council of the U.S. (SIECUS), New York University Resource Center and Library, 51 West 4th Street, New York, NY 10003. An excellent resource for lay people. Ask for their complete list of available topics.

Appendix B:
Cancer Centers

COMPREHENSIVE* AND CLINICAL** CANCER CENTERS
SUPPORTED BY THE NATIONAL CANCER INSTITUTE

The National Cancer Institute supports a number of cancer centers throughout the country that develop and investigate new methods of cancer diagnosis and treatment. Information about referral procedures, treatment costs, and services available to patients can be obtained from the individual cancer centers listed below.

Alabama

University of Alabama Comprehensive
Cancer Center*
1918 University Boulevard
Basic Health Science Building, Room
108
Birmingham, AL 35294
Telephone (205) 934-6612

Arizona

University of Arizona Cancer Center**
1501 North Campbell Avenue
Tucson, AZ 85724
Telephone (602) 626-6372

California

University of Southern California
Comprehensive Cancer Center*
Kenneth Norris Jr. Cancer Hospital and
Research Institute
1441 Eastlake Avenue
Los Angeles, CA 90033-0804
Telephone (213) 226-2370

Jonsson Comprehensive Cancer Center
(UCLA)*
10-247 Factor Building
10833 Le Conte Avenue
Los Angeles, CA 90024-1781
Telephone (213) 825-8727

Charles R. Drew University of
Medicine and Science (consortium)
12714 South Avalon Boulevard,
Suite 301
Los Angeles, CA 90061
Telephone (213) 603-3120

City of Hope National Medical Center**
Beckman Research Institute
1500 East Duarte Road
Duarte, CA 91010
Telephone (818) 359-8111, ext. 2292

University of California at San Diego
Cancer Center**
225 Dickinson Street
San Diego, CA 92103
Telephone (619) 543-6178

Northern California Cancer Center
(consortium)
1301 Shoreway Road
Belmont, CA 94002
Telephone (415) 591-4484

Colorado

University of Colorado Cancer Center**
4200 East Ninth Avenue, Box B190
Denver, CO 80262
Telephone (303) 270-3019

Connecticut

Yale University Comprehensive Cancer
Center*
333 Cedar Street
New Haven, CT 06510
Telephone (203) 785-6338

District of Columbia

Howard University Cancer Research
Center*
2041 Georgia Avenue, NW
Washington, DC 20060
Telephone (202) 636-7610 or 636-5665

Vincent T. Lombardi Cancer Research
Center*
Georgetown University Medical Center
3800 Reservoir Road, NW
Washington, DC 20007
Telephone (202) 687-2110

Florida

Papanicolaou Comprehensive Cancer
Center*
University of Miami Medical School
1475 Northwest Twelfth Avenue
Miami, FL 33136
Telephone (305) 548-4850

Illinois

Illinois Cancer Council* (includes insti-
tutions listed and several other
organizations)

Illinois Cancer Council
36 South Wabash Avenue
Chicago, IL 60603
Telephone (312) 226-2371

University of Chicago Cancer Research
Center
5841 South Maryland Avenue
Chicago, IL 60637
Telephone (312) 702-6180

Kentucky

Lucille Parker Markey Cancer Center**
University of Kentucky Medical Center
800 Rose Street
Lexington, KY 40536-0093
Telephone (606) 257-4447

Maryland

The Johns Hopkins Oncology Center*
600 North Wolfe Street
Baltimore, MD 21205
Telephone (301) 955-8638

Massachusetts

Dana-Farber Cancer Institute*
44 Binney Street
Boston, MA 02115
Telephone (617) 732-3214

Michigan

Meyer L. Prentis Comprehensive Cancer
   Center of Metropolitan Detroit*
110 East Warren Avenue
Detroit, MI 48201
Telephone (313) 833-0710, ext. 429

University of Michigan Cancer Center**
101 Simpson Drive
Ann Arbor, MI 48109-0752
Telephone (313) 936-2516

Minnesota

Mayo Comprehensive Cancer Center*
200 First Street Southwest
Rochester, MN 55905
Telephone (507) 284-3413

New Hampshire

Norris Cotton Cancer Center**
Dartmouth-Hitchcock Medical Center
2 Maynard Street
Hanover, NH 03756
Telephone (603) 646-5485

New York

Memorial Sloan-Kettering Cancer
   Center*
1275 York Avenue
New York, NY 10021
Telephone 1-800-525-2225

Columbia University Cancer Center*
College of Physicians and Surgeons
630 West 168th Street
New York, NY 10032
Telephone (212) 305-6730

Mt. Sinai School of Medicine**
One Gustave L. Levy Place
New York, NY 10029
Telephone (212) 241-8617

New York University Cancer Center**
462 First Avenue
New York, NY 10016-9103
Telephone (212) 340-6485

Albert Einstein College of Medicine**
1300 Morris Park Avenue
Bronx, NY 10461
Telephone (212) 920-4826

Roswell Park Memorial Institute*
666 Elm Street
Buffalo, NY 14263
Telephone (716) 845-4400

University of Rochester Cancer Center**
601 Elmwood Avenue, Box 704
Rochester, NY 14642
Telephone (716) 275-4911

North Carolina

Duke University Comprehensive Cancer
   Center**
P.O. Box 3843
Durham, NC 27710
Telephone (919) 684-6342 or
   (919) 286-5515

Lineberger Cancer Research Center**
University of North Carolina School of
   Medicine
Chapel Hill, NC 27599
Telephone (919) 966-4431

Bowman Gray School of Medicine**
Wake Forest University
300 South Hawthorne Road
Winston-Salem, NC 27103
Telephone (919) 748-4354

Ohio

Ohio State University Comprehensive
  Cancer Center*
410 West Twelfth Avenue
Columbus, OH 43210
Telephone (614) 293-8619

Case Western Reserve University**
University Hospitals of Cleveland
Ireland Cancer Center
2074 Abington Road
Cleveland, OH 44106
Telephone (216) 844-8453

Pennsylvania

Fox Chase Cancer Center*
7701 Burholme Avenue
Philadelphia, PA 19111
Telephone (215) 728-2570

University of Pennsylvania Cancer
  Center*
3400 Spruce Street
Philadelphia, PA 19104
Telephone (215) 662-6364

Pittsburgh Cancer Institute**
230 Lothrop Street
Pittsburgh, PA 15213-2592
Telephone 1-800-537-4063

Rhode Island

Roger Williams General Hospital**
825 Chalkstone Avenue
Providence, RI 02908
Telephone (401) 456-2070

Tennessee

St. Jude Children's Research Hospital**
332 North Lauderdale Street
Memphis, TN 38101
Telephone (901) 522-0694

Texas

The University of Texas
M.D. Anderson Cancer Center*
1515 Holcombe Boulevard
Houston, TX 77030
Telephone (713) 792-6161

Utah

Utah Regional Cancer Center**
University of Utah Medical Center
50 North Medical Drive, Room 2C10
Salt Lake City, UT 84132
Telephone (801) 581-4048

Vermont

Vermont Regional Cancer Center**
University of Vermont
1 South Prospect Street
Burlington, VT 05401
Telephone (802) 656-4580

Virginia

Massey Cancer Center**
Medical College of Virginia
Virginia Commonwealth University
1200 East Broad Street
Richmond, VA 23298
Telephone (804) 786-9641

University of Virginia Medical Center**
Box 334
Primary Care Center, Room 4520
Lee Street
Charlottesville, VA 22908
Telephone (804) 924-2562

Washington	*Wisconsin*
Fred Hutchinson Cancer Research Center*	Wisconsin Clinical Cancer Center*
1124 Columbia Street	University of Wisconsin
Seattle, WA 98104	600 Highland Avenue
Telephone (206) 467-4675	Madison, WI 53792
	Telephone (608) 263-6872

For additional information about cancer, write to the Office of Cancer Communications, National Cancer Institute, Bethesda, MD 20892, or call the toll-free number of the Cancer Information Service at 1-800-4-CANCER. In Hawaii, on Oahu, call 524-1234 (Neighbor Islands call collect). Spanish-speaking staff members are available to callers from the following areas (daytime hours only): California, Florida, Georgia, Illinois, New Jersey (area code 201), New York, and Texas.

Appendix C:
Mammography and Breast
Self-Examination

AMERICAN CANCER SOCIETY GUIDELINES FOR
BREAST CANCER DETECTION

TEST	AGE	FREQUENCY
Breast Self-Examination	20 and over	Monthly
Clinical Breast Examination	20 to 39	Every 3 years
	40 and over	Yearly
Mammography	35 to 40	Once
	40 to 49	Every 1 to 2 years
	50 and over	Yearly

A FACT SHEET ON MAMMOGRAPHY*

What is mammography? Mammography is an x-ray of the breast that creates an image of the breast tissue. It is used to find cancer in women without symptoms (screening breast x-rays) or to help study changes in the breast (diagnostic breast x-rays). The test is called a mammogram. Mammography can detect cancers too small to be felt by a doctor or nurse (clinical breast exams) or by the woman

*The following information was written and distributed by the California Division of the American Cancer Society.

herself, (breast self-exams or BSE). If cancers can be found when they are small, there is a higher cure rate and a better chance of saving the breast. Most breast changes are *not* cancerous.

Does mammography detect all breast cancers? Mammography is the best method to detect breast cancer early. But, even if done by an expert, breast x-rays miss at least 10 percent of all cancers. For this reason, the American Cancer Society suggests using mammography along with clinical breast exams and breast self-exams to screen for breast cancer.

At what age should a woman have a mammogram and how often should this test be done? The American Cancer Society suggests that women without symptoms have their first breast x-ray to compare with future breast x-rays between the ages of thirty-five and forty. Women age forty to forty-nine years should have breast x-rays every year or two depending on their risk factors. Women age fifty and over should have breast x-rays every year. Women who have had breast cancer or whose family members have had breast cancer may need more frequent breast x-rays and should consult their doctor for advice.

What about radiation risk? Modern x-ray machines use very small radiation doses. The potential benefits of finding breast cancer early far outweigh the slight radiation risk related to screening breast x-rays. No case of breast cancer has ever been traced to the use of screening mammography.

What machines and methods are used to take mammograms? X-ray machines—the machine of choice is an x-ray machine designed just for mammography (dedicated machine). This machine provides a sharper image and lower dose than an all-purpose x-ray machine. There are two types of x-rays—film-screen or xerox paper. For routine screening, two pictures are taken of each breast. Dosage— x-ray doses are measured in rads, which are units of absorbed radiation. The American Cancer Society suggests that each breast receive no more than one rad per complete breast x-ray exam. A modern low-dose breast x-ray exam exposes the breast to less than one rad. Positioning and breast compression—with the women sitting or standing, the x-ray technologist places the breast on a plastic plate. Each breast is briefly compressed during filming to produce a clear picture at low radiation doses. Squeezing the breasts may cause some brief soreness but is not harmful.

Who takes the mammograms? The x-ray technologist. This health professional has been trained to safely control the machine, position the patient, and develop the film. The technologist will explain how the breast x-ray is taken and answer questions.

Who interprets the mammograms? The radiologist. This doctor specializes in x-ray diagnosis and will study and interpret the breast x-ray. The radiologist consults with your doctor and will send a written report to the doctor who ordered the breast x-ray.

What is the cost of mammography? Prices for breast x-rays range from no cost (in a health maintenance organization) to $250 and may or may not be covered by health insurance. Some clinics may provide screening breast x-rays at reduced cost. Your local American Cancer Society may be able to provide you with a list of these facilities.

What if I have had mammograms before? Any prior mammograms are very helpful to compare with your new breast x-rays. They may help the doctor to detect subtle changes that might not have been found before. Bring the prior mammogram with you any time you have a new breast x-ray. If you cannot bring them, tell the technologist (x-ray staff) you have had mammograms in the past.

How can I find out how much a mammogram will cost and whether the facility (hospital, clinic, or doctor's office) has modern machines and skilled staff? Before you go for a screening mammogram, ask how much it will cost (with technical fee and radiologist fee), what kind of machine is used, and how skilled the staff is. A woman should choose a place that does at least five mammograms per day with a machine designed just for breast x-rays.

BREAST SELF-EXAMINATION (BSE)

The American Cancer Society recommends that all women over the age of twenty examine their breasts monthly. BSE is encouraged because breast cancer symptoms can develop and be noted between clinical breast exams and mammography. In fact, most lumps are found by women, themselves. Therefore BSE is an important part of the early detection of breast cancer. BSE is a method by which a woman becomes familiar with the normal look and feel of her breasts. It's important for you to be familiar with your own breasts, and by doing BSE each month, you can improve your skill at feeling different structures in your breast tissue. After you learn how your normal breast tissue looks and feels, you will be able to recognize a change if one occurs. If you do find a change such as a lump, thickening, dimpling, a change in the size or shape of the breast, see your doctor as soon as you can. Remember most breast changes are not cancer. The best time to perform BSE is approximately 3 to 5 days after the end of your regular menstrual cycle. If you do not have a menstrual period, BSE should be done on the same day of every month. Pregnant women should continue to examine their breasts throughout their entire pregnancy.

Briefly, there are seven important components of BSE: (1) *Regularity* (examine the same time each month), (2) *visual inspection* (four different positions in front of a mirror), (3) *palpation through a lying-down position* (with pillow under the breast to be examined, and arm to the side, not behind the head), (4) *complete coverage* (examine all of the breast, including underarms), (5) *consistent pattern* (use a vertical strip pattern), (6) *use of finger pads* (press with top third of fingers, making dime-sized circles), and (7) *adequate pressure* (make at least two circles and press firmly enough to feel the different breast textures).

It is important to allow sufficient time for a thorough breast self-examination. In general, it takes from 12 to 15 minutes to perform all the steps.

LEARNING HOW TO DO BSE

Because breast self-examination is a learned motor skill, like Braille, it is difficult to learn to do it confidently and proficiently by reading a brochure. Also in the past few years, new and more effective methods of performing BSE have been developed, specifically by Mammacare, Inc., and the California Division of the American Cancer Society. Therefore the best way to learn how to do BSE is to be trained by a health professional who is familiar with the most up-to-date techniques of BSE (ask about training at your doctor's office, your local American Cancer Society, or clinics) or by viewing one of the following excellent videotapes: Mammacare's Personal Learning System (call 1-800-MAM-CARE, includes breast model, 45-minute videotape, and a manual: $59.50, plus fifty cents for postage), Lange Production's "BSE: A New Approach" (call [213] 874-4730, $125, plus tax), or the American Cancer Society's "BSE: A Special Touch." Call your local American Cancer Society for further information. Some of the ACS units may have lending libraries for all of these videotapes.

Notes

Chapter 1

1. Interview with Fitzhugh Mullan. *Coping* 1(7):16–20 (May/June 1987).

Chapter 2

1. National Cancer Institute. National survey on breast cancer: A measure of progress in public understanding. U.S. Department of Health and Human Services. NIH Publication No. 81-2306, November 1980.
2. Ibid.

Part Three

1. Interview with Fitzhugh Mullan. *Coping.* 1(7):16–20 (May/June 1987).
2. Wendy Schain. Sexual functioning, self-esteem, and cancer care. *Frontiers of Radiation Therapy and Oncology* 14:12–19 (1980).
3. National Cancer Institute. *The Breast Cancer Digest: A Guide to Care, Emotional Support, Educational Programs and Resources,* 2nd ed. U.S. Department of Health and Human Resources, NIH Publication No. 84-1691. April 1984, p. 144.

Chapter 13

1. Allan Parachini. Survivorship: A new movement among cancer patients. *Los Angeles Times,* February 3, 1987. (Pat Ganz, M.D., UCLA study is mentioned, p. 37.)

2. Judi Johnson and Linda Klein. *I Can Cope: Staying Healthy with Cancer*. DCI Publishing, Minneapolis, Minnesota, 1988, p. 129.

Chapter 14

1. M. H. Witkin. Psychological concerns in sexual rehabilitation and mastectomy. *Sexuality and Disability* 2:54–59 (1979).
2. Daniel Goleman. Emotional preparation aids surgical recovery. *New York Times*, December 10, 1987.
3. Wendy Schain. Breast cancer surgeries and psychosexual sequelae: Implications for remediation. *Seminars in Oncology Nursing* 1(3):200–205 (August 1985).
4. Maurice D. Steinberg, et al. Psychological outcome of lumpectomy versus mastectomy in the treatment of breast cancer. *American Journal of Psychiatry* 142(1):34–39 (January 1985).
5. National Cancer Institute. National survey on breast cancer: A measure of progress in public understanding. U.S. Department of Health and Human Services. NIH Publication No. 81-2306, November 1980.
6. Laurie Stevens, et al. The psychological impact of immediate reconstruction for women with early stage breast cancer. *Plastic and Reconstructive History* 73-4:619–626 (April 1984).
7. Wendy Schain, et al. The sooner the better: A study of psychological factors in women undergoing immediate versus delayed breast reconstruction. *American Journal of Psychiatry* 142:40–46 (January 1985).
8. Ibid.

Chapter 15

1. National Cancer Institute. National survey on breast cancer: A measure of progress in public understanding. U.S. Department of Health and Human Services. NIH Publication No. 81-2306, November 1980.
2. Wendy Schain. Patients' rights in decision making: The case for personalism versus paternalism in health care. *Cancer* 46:1035–1041 (1980).
3. Edwin Scheidman. Presentation at American Psychological Association, Chicago, 1975.
4. David Shottenfeld and Guy F. Robbins. Quality of survival among patients who have had radical mastectomy. *Cancer* 26:650–655 (1970). Also Lawrence Winick, et al. Physical and psychological readjustment after mastectomy. *Cancer* 39:478–486 (1977).

Chapter 16

1. Susan Sontag. *Illness as Metaphor*. Vintage Books, New York, 1979, p. 21.
2. Ibid., pp. 52–53.
3. Ibid., book jacket, back cover quotation.
4. Interview with Françoise Giraud. *Coronet*, November 1960.

5. Susan Brownmiller. *Femininity*. Fawcett Columbine, New York, 1984, p. 41.
6. Ibid., p. 15.
7. Caroline Bird. *Born Female: The High Cost of Keeping Women Down*. McKay, New York, 1974 (Chapter 11).
8. Eda J. LeShan. *How to Survive Parenthood*. Warner Paperback Library, New York, 1973. (Chapter 8).

Chapter 17

1. Joan Bloom. Psychological response to mastectomy. *Cancer* 59(1):189–196 (January 1987).

About the Author

DEBORAH HOBLER KAHANE, M.S.W., was thirty-one when she was diagnosed with an early stage breast cancer. Active in the field of cancer care for more than sixteen years, she is a writer and health educator who has created numerous breast cancer programs for the American Cancer Society. A seasoned public speaker who has appeared on numerous television and radio programs, she often lectures on the importance of early detection of breast cancer to medical, business, and women's groups. She lives with her husband and two cats in southern California.